The Electronic Classroom

*A Handbook for Education in the
Electronic Environment*

edited by
Erwin Boschmann

Learned Information, Inc.
Medford, NJ
1995

Manufactured in the United States of America

Published by: Learned Information, Inc.
143 Old Marlton Pike
Medford, NJ 08055-8750

Composition: M. Heide Dengler

Cover Design: Jennifer Johansen
Jeanne Wachter

Editor: Kathleen L. Miller

Price: $42.50

ISBN: 0-938734-89-X

The Electronic Classroom

Preface
  Erwin Boschmann, Indiana University Purdue University
    Indianapolis ....**ix**
Introduction
  Stephen C. Ehrmann, The Annenberg/CPB Projects,
    Washington, D.C. ....**xiii**

PART 1
The Vision

In Search of the Electronic Classroom
  William M. Plater, Indiana University Purdue University
    Indianapolis...**3**
Technology and the Inevitability of Educational Transformation
  George P. Connick, and **Jane Russo,** The Education Network
    of Maine, Augusta, ME **14**
Pedagogical Issues
  Ray L. Steele, Ball State University, Muncie, IN **21**
*Implementing the Vision: Electronic Classroom Design
    and Construction*
  Garland Elmore and **Ali Jafari,** Indiana University Purdue
    University Indianapolis..**30**

PART 2
Classroom Applications

*Prototyping the Electronic Library:
  Using the Perseus Database to Teach Greek Culture*
  Gregory Crane, Harvard University, Cambridge, MA **53**
Biology: A Field Trip to a Rocky Intertidal Zone
  Raymond J. Russo, Indiana University Purdue University
    Indianapolis..**63**

iii

Law in Action: Interactive Software for Learning and Doing
Daniel Burnstein, Beacon Expert Systems, Inc.,
Brookline, MA..**71**

Learning Introductory Physics With New Electronic Media
Gregor M. Novak, Indiana University Purdue University
Indianapolis..**84**

Computer-Based Education and Decision Support in Medicine
Robert Greenes, Decision Systems Group, Boston, MA.................**94**

The Alternative Science Laboratory
Stuart W. Bennett, The Open University, England **103**

Doing Chemistry With Technology
Steven Gammon, University of Idaho, Moscow, ID.....................**109**

Teaching Tools in Music
G. David Peters, University of Illinois, Urbana, and
Darrell L. Bailey, Indiana University Purdue University
Indianapolis **119**

Teaching Visual Analysis Using CAV Interactive Videodisk Technology
Suzanne Regan, California State University, Los Angeles, CA **130**

Instructional Technology in the Military,
Dexter Fletcher, Institute for Defense Analyses,
Alexandria, VA **138**

PART 3
Extending the Classroom: Regional Networks

Computer Networking in Distance Education
James D. Lehman, Purdue University, West Lafayette, IN **147**

Teaching and Learning in the Extended Classroom: Nursing Telecourses
Diane Billings, Indiana University Purdue
University Indianapolis **156**

The Tools of Self-Direction: Student Services in the Electronic Classroom
Pamela MacBrayne, University of Maine at Augusta, and
Jane Russo, The Education Network of Maine,
Augusta, ME..**165**

PART 4
Further Extending the Classroom: Global Networks

*Cross-Cultural Team Teaching: Electronic Mail for
Literary Analysis*
Helen Schwartz, Indiana University Purdue
University Indianapolis..**173**

Networked Collaborative Research and Teaching
Armando A. Arias, Jr., California State University, Monterey Bay, and
Beryl Bellman, California State University, Los Angeles........**180**

*Electronic Student Response Systems in Corporate
Distance Education*
Barbara J. Garvin-Kester, Thomas A. Kester, and **Alan G. Chute,**
AT&T, Cincinnati, OH **186**

*BESTNET International: A Case Study in the Evolution from
a Distance Education Experiment to a Virtual
Learning Environment*
George S. Metes, Virtual Learning Systems, Inc., Manchester, NH;
Rodrigo Gutierrez S. and **Vincente Lopez Rocher** of
Centro de Ensenanza Tecnica y Superior, Tijuana, Mexico;
Armando Valdez and **Ricardo Jimenez** of
Instituto Tecnologico de Mexicali, Mexico...............................**195**

PART 5
Monitoring the Electronic Classroom

*Using Formative Evaluation to Increase the Educational
Effectiveness of Technology Products*
Karen J. Hoelscher, Western Washington University,
Bellingham, WA **205**

Working Together with Technology
Linda S. Fowler, AT&T, Cincinnati, OH......................................**215**

The Ethics of Teaching and the Teaching of Ethics
Rushworth M. Kidder, Institute for
Global Ethics, Camden, ME...**222**

The Future of Electronic Education
Robert A. Dierker, Library of Congress, Washington, D.C. **228**

Index...**237**

Preface

Erwin Boschmann

*Erwin Boschmann is Professor of Chemistry
and Associate Dean of the Faculties at Indiana
University Purdue University Indianapolis*

Not even the invention of the printing press has provided the huge opportunities for change in education that new technology has brought. We can now transcend limits of distance and time, teach more persons at a lower cost, in a more personal way, and adapt to individual learning styles. Even more important, we can allow the learner to participate actively in the educating process. Universities of the future may no longer be physical places, but instead act as brokers of syndicated educational services. The consumer, not the provider, will be in control.

At the leading edge will be those who are willing to take risks by not waiting "until the technology is perfected." They will realize that off-campus teaching will affect on-campus teaching—not the reverse. On the other hand, they will retain on the highest pedestal the basic precepts of pedagogy as they welcome technological innovation. Just as the quality of a book is not affected by the kind of truck which delivers it to the bookstore, so the technology media are tools, not ends.

Some years ago, the opportunity literally fell my way to teach in an electronic classroom. I had neither sought the challenge, nor was I expected to take it on. Yet, there I was with a brand new, state-of-the-art electronic classroom with more than 50 pieces of technology at my disposal, allowing me to share with my students the smallest, most intricate detail of an ancient coin, or to replay the explosion of the German aircraft *Hindenburg* on one screen while generating hydrogen gas from sodium and water on a second screen and writing the chemical equation for the process on a third screen. The technology has allowed me to bring to my classroom events from other classrooms or other continents. It allows me to broadcast my class to students who prefer to take chemistry via television. It allows me to communicate with students in ongoing and individual ways. It allows me to graphically show before-and-after conditions of the effects of pollution in the environment and to see on the faces of students the impact it leaves in their minds.

Studies during the last several decades[1,2,3] have proven that with the introduction of just one technology, television, learning proceeds at least as well as it does in the traditional way. Once coupled, through the power of technology, with the element of interactivity, both the amount and the speed of learning go up.

The use of technology in my teaching has taught me several lessons. Initially there is a rather steep learning curve and a very heavy investment of time—even to the point that my teaching has suffered. However, once the medium no longer is the message—just as chalk in my hand never was the focus—then technology becomes powerful. I considered afresh how students learn. I questioned what was of fundamental importance to the course. The experience provided professional renewal. I learned that students like to be active participants, and they volunteer for special projects. I learned that, once introduced, students soon come to assume technology as a matter of fact and expect ever more. Technology has ultimately saved me time, has allowed me to reach more people, and has eased communication. Most importantly, through simulation, it has helped overcome a common learning impediment: the need to visualize the abstract.

The following steps are essential to ensuring successful introduction of technology into the teaching and learning environment. First, there must be high administrative support sustained by faculty endorsement. Next, those in leadership roles must be willing to commit funds, energy, and staff to develop and maintain the venture. Third, there must be an institutional academic reward system in place to encourage faculty creativity. Finally, the institution must be willing to take risks: risks in launching bold new programs, in hiring innovative staff—even if unorthodox, in aggressively seeking funds, and in creating meaningful curricula. The obstacle will not be lack of finances, for money has a way of flowing toward good ideas. Obstacles will be shortage of committed people with ideas and with willingness to sacrifice their time and talent.

In the near future we will see electronic publishing flourish, and technology will become as common a tool as the overhead projector is today. We might see political science students in Moscow discuss with a class in the U.S. such topics as the Cuban missile crisis, nuclear testing, or global warming. Language students might compare the French being spoken in various parts of the world by "tuning in" to Quebec, to Haiti, and to Paris. Faculty on sabbatical leave will be able to present their findings from the field to colleagues at home. High school students will have electronic pen pals around the world, and have a chance of running a model United Nations by teleconferencing. But that future, with all its promises, will convince us once again that technology does not teach. Only teachers do.

As it continues to develop, technology will challenge teachers to have enough vision to exploit its possibilities for education. For about a century, the invention of the printing press did virtually nothing for education, since only a few of society's elite could read and the concept of mass distribution was not understood. Similarly, the overhead projector spent 35 years in bowling alleys before it found its way into classrooms. We were simply slow to see its potential. Even today, television is used almost exclusively for entertainment. Voltaire's dictum of years ago still applies: "If you are doing anything today in the same way you did it a year ago, you are probably doing it wrong." The call to us as educators is to see the opportunities that new technologies hold for our field.

In this book you will find chapters written by the best thinkers and practitioners, who will take you on voyages to the leading edges of technology in the advancement of education.

References

1. Chu, Godwin C., and Wilbur Schramm. *Learning from Television: What the Research Says*. Stanford University, Institute for Communication Research, 1967.

2. Johnston, Jerome. *Electronic Learning: From Audiotape to Videodisc*. Englewood Cliffs, N.J.: Lawrence Erlbaum Associates, 1987.

3. Schramm, Wilbur. *Big Media, Little Media: Tools and Technologies for Instruction*, Sage Publications, 1977.

Introduction

Stephen C. Ehrmann

Stephen Ehrmann is Senior Program Officer for Interactive Technologies, The Annenberg/CPB Projects, Washington, D.C.

Exciting new pieces of software and innovative technology-based practices are packed into these pages like succulent dishes on a smorgasbord. They clamor for your attention. You will have your own ways of selecting your dinner from this groaning board, but I do have a few suggestions: a) don't wear blinkers, b) think about the most serious challenges faced by your institution and department, and c) think about whether the software or teaching idea will be used long enough, and widely enough, to make a difference to those challenges.

1. Don't Wear Blinkers

Don't ignore chapters that are not within your own discipline or not discussing your type of institution. Software and teaching practices in other fields often contain great ideas that can be adapted to other needs.

For example, software and teaching practices used to help students learn to design or compose in one field are often instructive for other disciplines. Ideas to help the student visualize a musical composition may provide analogies to help students visualize a written composition. An essay that talks about how composition faculty deal with dilemmas of assessing student work when students are doing multiple drafts may be helpful for faculty in other disciplines.

2. Institutional Needs: Meeting a Triple Challenge

When I was in college, in the late 1960s, we would assert, "You're either part of the solution, or part of the problem." I suggest, while reading this volume, that for each chapter whose ideas fascinate you, ask "Are you part of the solution to the most serious challenges facing my *program* and *institution*, or part of the problem?"

Why choose software or a new educational practice based on how it affects an entire degree program or university? After all, most of us tend to place highest priority on problems affecting our own jobs, students, or clients, because we can't afford to think any other way.

Institutions of higher education face a "triple challenge":

1. how to live within very limited budgets
2. how to make their academic programs accessible to all students who need them
3. how to help students graduate with the kinds of skills, knowledge, and wisdom that they'll need to make good starts in their worlds of work, politics, and personal life.

Meet each challenge, and your institution is likely to be materially better off. Fail to meet them? Most institutions can't afford that failure; it would mean decay of their support and their academic programs. Improving one course won't help: it's not enough of a change to influence a student's fate, or an institution's.

Challenge #1–Costs per graduate: A father I know is worried. Tuition at his alma mater is now about 20 times what it was when he was an undergraduate 35 years ago. True, that private university has ascended the prestige rankings during that period, but, he asked me, how can middle class people hope to send their children to college with tuition skyrocketing so quickly?

Higher education faces a stark problem. We live in an Information Age that is exploding upon a Shrinking, Multi-cultural Planet: more people all need more and better education. Yet society is not growing richer as quickly as that exploding need for education. Worse (from higher education's point of view), institutions serving other important needs—health, social security, international assistance, defense, service on the national debt—are also struggling for a growing share of that same public money and support.

Thus each college and university is squeezed between society's growing need for higher education and society's straitened ability to pay for higher education. We cannot wish that problem away, or solve it merely through better lobbying or public relations.

Into this unpromising situation comes lean and hungry information technology, itself ravenous for funds: for electronic libraries, computer clusters, rewired dormitories and revamped classroom buildings, video networks, software licenses, satellite dishes, production studios, staff to help faculty develop courseware, staff to operate networks. . . .

What can each chapter's idea do to help your institution and your department deal with this first challenge? Obviously, each use of technology costs money. But will it also help the institution share resources and thus save some money? Will the new technology replace more costly traditional technologies (e.g., enable students to learn in "virtual space" that is less costly to create and maintain than traditional physical campus facilities)? Will it enable the institution to increase the average size of classes by adding enrollment to smaller classes while improving the quality of learning in larger classes? That last item relates to accessibility, so let's turn to the next challenge.

Challenge #2–Accessibility: The second of the three challenges is enrollment (and retention). That challenge is as difficult today as at any time in our history. If education reform in this country has one top priority, it is that *everyone can and must learn.* We can't tolerate an economy, a polity, or a culture that is hobbled by widespread ignorance and incompetence. Here too, if we're not careful, technology may be part of the problem. It can help create a more exclusive kind of education, one open only to those wealthy enough to pay the fees, only to those who can get to campus to use specialized hardware, only to those with the free time to waste in learning needlessly difficult hardware and software, open only to those who are not blind (literally) to a graphical user interface. . . .

Today's pool of potential learners includes virtually all adults, including many who:

- have different schedules from faculty and from one another
- are distant from the appropriate campus
- are physically challenged
- have varying preparation and learning styles

These students are not a minority or "nontraditional" anymore. Only a minority of today's undergraduates enter higher education immediately after high school and study full time until they have earned a degree.[1] Still more adults remain only potential students, finding that the costs of enrollment and education exceed the benefits.

Raw accessibility of the academic program is necessary but not sufficient if your university and department are to meet this second challenge. Your students are more different from one another than ever before. If your program doesn't recognize this, it will either reject many potential new students (as a body can reject an organ transplant) or else pander to the least prepared. Neither alternative is acceptable.

Failure to meet this challenge of accessibility will hurt the institution. It will lose possibilities to educate the most talented adults and perhaps also suffer a loss of enrollment and a deterioration of academic community.

What can the ideas and software in each chapter do to help your department and university deal with this challenge of accessibility? Which are part of the problem, which part of the solution?

Challenge #3–Educating Graduates with Skills for Tomorrow's World:
Here are a few of the things we already know about the third component
of the "triple challenge":

- Graduates already live in a world that is richer in information, and in the tools for using information, than
  most of them can exploit in their working, political, cultural, familial, and personal lives. They are offered the
  power, but they lack the skills and insight to use it
  appropriately, wisely, and ethically. Jobs that require or
  reward such capabilities are growing in number. Such
  information and such technology alter graduates'
  options in political, cultural, and family life as well.
- Graduates today, like those of past decades, must live
  and work through the efforts of other people, yet higher education by and large is still preparing people to
  work in isolation, rather than in formal or informal
  teams or coalitions.
- Graduates will live in a far more diverse world. For
  some people, the term "diversity" conjures up images of
  underprepared students who speak a different language. "Diversity" should suggest new marketplaces,
  teammates of unpredictable backgrounds and commitments, and equally new and unpredictable political
  coalitions. Modern diversity raises new kinds of challenges to workers, to pluralist democracy, and thus to
  education.

If one institution can educate graduates who perform noticeably better in
this new world than do graduates of another institution, and then demonstrate that it has done so, then that first institution may gain in significant,
material ways. If its graduates get an inferior education, eventually the
institution will pay a price.

For the third time, consider each chapter. Which ones are logical pieces
of an effective, modern education? Which might prove a distraction, drain-
ing student attention and institutional resources away from the central
issues of tomorrow's world?

3. Long Life and Pervasiveness

Technology changes so very quickly. It is easy to forget that education,
the object of the hoped-for revolution, is a slow-moving process:

> 1) It takes years—dozens of courses containing thousands
>   of hours of study—to educate a student; unless a strat-
>   egy based on technology affects a substantial number

of those hours, the life of the adult is unlikely to be influenced very much.

2) It takes even more years to change the curriculum. So if a particular application of technology survives only a few years, no curricular change worth mentioning may result.

Thus it will take years, and a coherent effort by many faculty in many courses, to help the institution respond to the "triple challenge." You ought to ask which of the innovations described in this book have that staying power and that potential to be used by large numbers of faculty at many institutions.

There are (at least) three ways in which a technology-based teaching idea or piece of software may have that potential for pervasive, long-lived influence:

1) The idea or single piece of software can be used by many faculty in the department or institution. Some examples are comparatively obvious, such as the use of word processing in many courses, enabling students to rethink their drafts, and learn by rethinking, or the use of spreadsheets as mathematical construction kits in many disciplines.

   Other multi-use pieces of software are perhaps less obvious. For example, research hints that extensive use of computer conferencing as a medium for course dialogue opens the curriculum to students off-campus, and also provides a more level playing field for learners whose native language is not English, so that their grades improve.[2] Computer conferencing also may provide a moderate pace of academic conversation that permits a wider variety of students to learn through such dialogue.

   A constellation of such multi-use technologies (computer conferencing and other technologies for supporting real-time conversation, learning-by-doing, research, and off-campus access to lectures), forms a foundation for an institution that wants to deal with the "triple challenge": offering a cost-effective, engaging education through teaching teams including the world's experts, truly open to a wide range of learners (classes large enough not to be canceled, and offered in "virtual" space).

2) Each course needs a different type of software, but that software is likely to be furnished in an affordable and appropriate form by the world beyond undergraduate instruction. Such software, which some of us have labeled "worldware," ranges from research tools to productivity software (again the spreadsheet) to the Internet.[3] Worldware can play a key role in efforts to emphasize student learning through work on complex, realistic projects. Many authorities have argued that students

become more involved in learning when they work on complex, open-ended projects. Engagement is perhaps the single most important determinant of educational outcomes.[4] Such projects are a key part of acquiring the higher order thinking skills and commitments needed to meet the third of our three challenges: skills for living and working in the 21st century. Projects motivating students to work in groups can also be important as the students learn to work with others from different cultures. Finally, students, if motivated by projects, may be able to take on more of the burden of helping themselves to learn and thus indirectly improve faculty productivity.

3) Each course needs a different type of software, where the cost of developing, maintaining, and upgrading the software is low enough, and the demand and rewards of using it are high enough, that many appropriate versions of such software will be produced and maintained. This last is what we've expected of textbooks, but for a variety of reasons it hasn't produced a flood of appropriate software.

Which of the pieces of software described in this volume will be short-lived Mayflies that are used by only a few faculty? Which ones will prove to be members of a long-lived family of widely used software? Are there clues we can look for? I think there's no substitute for history. Ask whether the software closely resembles other software that has *already* earned the income or new grants that have enabled needed upgrades. Does it resemble other software *already* in wide use in many types of courses?[5]

In a Nutshell

It's time to let you go to the smorgasbord. Summarizing these three pieces of advice:

- First, remove any disciplinary and institutional blinkers you might ordinarily wear. Regardless of whether the software or teaching idea described is in your discipline or from your institution, is it suggestive of ways of meeting problems that are important for you and your institution?
- Second, ask whether the idea and software described in each chapter could help your *department* or *institution* meet the "triple challenge" (control of costs, wider and more equitable access, educating graduates who can excel in tomorrow's world).
- Third, is the software likely to persist *long enough* and be *used widely enough* to be seriously useful in helping your students, program, and institution meet that "triple challenge"?

Notes

1. Pew Higher Education Research Program, "Breaking the Mold," *Policy Perspectives*, II:2, (January 1990).

2. Hiltz, S.R., "Correlates of Learning in a Virtual Classroom," *Research Report CIS-89-22*, Newark: New Jersey Institute of Technology, 1989.

3. Paul Morris et al., *Valuable, Viable Software in Education: Case Studies and Analysis*, New York: Primis Division of McGraw-Hill, 1994.

4. Study Group on the Conditions of Excellence in Higher Education, *Involvement in Learning: Realizing the Potential of American Higher Education*, Washington, D.C.: National Institute of Education, September 1984.

5. Ibid.

PART 1

The Vision

In Search of the Electronic Classroom

William M. Plater

*William Plater is Dean of the Faculties at
Indiana University Purdue University
Indianapolis*

"What the white whale was to Ahab, has been hinted; what, at times, he was to me, as yet remains unsaid."

Thus begins Ishmael's famous discourse on "The Whiteness of the Whale" in Herman Melville's *Moby Dick*, a novel which, in its own way, celebrates one of the last century's most important technologies.

When I think about "the electronic classroom," I am reminded of Ishmael's disquieting need to explain at length what "the whale" was to himself as well as to others, and, more importantly, to make not just the whale but its consuming manifestation as "the white whale" into a symbol of legendary and enduring proportions.

Few people pay much attention to "classrooms," even teachers. But mention "the electronic classroom" and instantly the name conjures forth such a rich array of prospects, both alluring and disquieting, as to make any school's crew uneasy about what lies beyond the horizon or beneath the surface. The idea of "the electronic classroom," at once hidden and near, meaning so many different things to so many people, has become an object of intense pursuit. Concluding his chapter, Ishmael rhetorically asks his readers, "Wonder ye then at the fiery hunt?"

American higher education has encountered few symbols that have so thoroughly captivated the attention of practitioners of every form of education. Across elementary and secondary schools, through corporate offices, into the warrens of governmental bureaucracies, and at last penetrating the lecture halls, labs, and classrooms of postsecondary education, "the electronic classroom" has become a symbol of change, of improvement, of the future itself. Whether taken as a vehicle for mass institutional

3

change as envisioned by the faltering "Edison Project," which proposed to revolutionize American schooling, or as evidence of a single college's commitment to remain abreast of the world-wide information revolution, the "electronic classroom" has become the name we all give to our hopes for an improved, more effective, and more efficient way of learning.

The ease with which we use a term that at once is both concrete and yet completely open to definition by speakers and their audiences belies the importance of the idea, of the symbol. As the chapters of this collection richly illustrate, the concept of the electronic classroom is neither spatially nor temporally limited, as are most familiar classrooms, and the term implies more than the environment where teachers go to teach and students go to learn. As a symbol, the electronic classroom has become a name given to a changed relationship among learners, faculty, their institutions, and the purposes that bring them all together. It is a name that says those who will use the electronic classroom are themselves committed to change and to "the fiery hunt."

Taking the role of a still naive Ishmael, I hope to offer a preface to the hunt for the electronic classroom through the pages of the essays of this volume and into the virtual sea of information beyond, where many early reports from those who have created and used electronic classrooms are now available to those who would give their own definition to the term. There are a few things you should consider before starting the hunt.

By whatever definition, electronic classrooms are expensive. Not only is the new technology that gives the old classroom its distinctive panache costly, but invariably the old space has sufficient defects of heating, cooling, seating, wiring, and safety as to require remodeling that is typically many times more expensive than the electronic equipment itself. Yet these costs are investments, and they will invariably be modest in comparison to the costs involved in preparing faculty (and perhaps students) to use the new environment most efficiently and to understand the fact that the very means of learning have been changed.

Moreover, if the first electronic classroom is successful, then it must be viewed as only the beginning of a process that may well change the entire institution. The physical space designated on architects' plans and room schedulers' charts as "the electronic classroom" is only the point of origin for activity—we assume learning—that occurs more or less continuously in many places, but with a connection to the room that has become a center. From such a center, other forms of the electronic classroom will necessarily diffuse throughout the institution. But cost is only the first indication of a new order.

The nature of change inherent in the pursuit of the electronic classroom may be considered in four broad categories: (1) when, where, and how people learn; (2) what and why they learn; (3) the evolving role of faculty; and (4) the future of the institution itself. The evidence of change and examples of meaningful improvements in learning are the subjects of the essays in this collection. What follows is a context for evaluating whether or not an institution should pursue the electronic classroom—as an actual learning environment and as a commitment to a new order. As electronic classrooms in all their variety of form and purpose are created and used, they may well transform education worldwide. Such is the power of symbols that people enact.

When, Where, and How People Learn

"I shall ere long paint to you as well as one can without canvas, something like the true form of the whale as he actually appears to the eye of the whaleman . . ." (page 260)

Imagine the ideal electronic classroom. If we assume that "the true form" can range, at its simplest, from a single desk with an individual workstation connected electronically to a network, up to a large lecture hall connected electronically to a full range of multimedia devices as well as to a network, then we might ask what the essential and defining characteristics of this special place must be. Understanding that there is no single, widely accepted definition, most of those engaged in the hunt for the true electronic classroom would require some type of connectivity from a computer (an information manager) to information resources that exist independent of the current user. While one might gain access to the information by a variety of means—a video disk, a satellite, a CD-ROM, a videotape, or a database on another host computer—the possibility of contact with information resources stored or activated outside the place where the learner is located appears to be essential. The electronic classroom must be interactive—among electronic components and persons within the room itself and between the classroom and other information sources.

True, there are some very interesting and exciting learning resources, including a few described in this volume, which can be self-contained within the room and which can be used without connectivity beyond a single device and without interaction beyond the student and the teacher, each at opposite ends of the proverbial log circuit. However, these are limited and limiting applications of the potential of an electronic classroom, not yet the true form we seek. Without any disparagement intended, these are pseudo-electronic classrooms—rooms with technology sufficient to emulate both interactivity and communication. As we become more sophisticated in developing learning resources as well as electronic tools, the limitations of such classrooms will become more apparent. Communication with others and connectivity with information beyond the classroom are essential aspects of the electronic classroom worthy of the costly effort to find (or define) it.

The primary reason for insisting on interactive communication outside the physical classroom itself—at least as a possibility—is because of the capacity of electronic technology to create an open information system and a more open, flexible model of student-teacher interaction. Conventional classrooms require all participants to be in the same place at the same time and to use essentially the same, standardized information base—typically a common text, augmented by supplemental readings. Even classrooms which use telephones and television merely to connect distance learners with the classroom do not qualify because they are still part of a closed information system.

Properly used, the electronic classroom permits students and teacher to be in separate locations connected by a shared purpose and a network instead of the same moment in time or the same room on a campus. Moreover, communication with information sources greater than the combined knowledge of the instructor and the students is essential. Not only is the information expansive, but it is dynamic—evolving with the needs of the class and the passage of time. Unfolding world events and iterations of the human genome can become part of a course as iterations of a mode of inquiry rather than as artifacts, just as novels or paintings become examples instead of finite embodiments of genres, styles, and periods, examples which can be explicated, compared and criticized beyond the artificial confines of an assignment. Students become collaborators with their teachers in a shared process of discovery.

While such inquiry has always been possible, the electronic classroom makes access to information integral instead of supplemental. As the point of origin, the electronic classroom begins a process of learning that must be allowed to continue across time and place, drawing on the two principles of expanding information resources and communication outside the classroom.

Whether its full potential is exploited or not, the electronic classroom must be designed and defined to permit the learner to have a direct, perhaps eventually the controlling, role in deciding when and how interaction as a mode of learning occurs. The electronic classroom is thus less a physical landscape than a mode of interaction. Currently, most classrooms are designed to give control to the instructor by restricting the technology, through either physical access or the path of student inquiry. In the future, the sheer capacity of networks will overwhelm the need to restrict learning and, instead, will lead to a transformational use of the electronic classroom to permit learning to occur among a group of individuals at different times, at different paces, and at different places—even when they happen to gather in the same place at the same time.

In the past, the efficiency of the lecture or the group demonstration or the display of an object or the student dialogue obligated the instructor to regulate the mode and frequency of interaction. The capacity of the electronic classroom creates the potential for a three-dimensional space—of time, place, and mode of interaction. We now have to learn how to use this multidimensionality to enhance learning.

What and Why People Learn

"And thus there seems a reason in all things, even in law." (page 401)

As we all recognize, an evolving global economy is restructuring the formal educational systems of countries worldwide. Not only are governments and corporations expressing dissatisfaction with what and why people learn, but many companies—and some governmental agencies—are taking matters into their own hands. Moreover, many students and prospective students concur with these directions. In legal practice, electronic access to information and to the processing of information are leading many law schools to reconceive the way in which students and faculty interact and to imagine new curricular designs; in business and medicine, information technologies have had an even more pronounced impact on curriculum.

The quality improvement movement, for example, has made investment in continuous employee education a cardinal principle; regardless of the particular manifestation of employee education, it is intended both as a palliative to the inadequacies of formal education at all levels and as a means to continuous change within the company or industry; the use of new knowledge is viewed as the best insurance for competitive advantage.

Within government, the demand for assessment of student learning has become the focal point for a national debate on postsecondary education, with states taking individual action but in a loosely concerted and coordinated effort, perhaps preempting or anticipating national standards. Regardless of the examples one might select, there is mounting evidence that decisions about what and why people learn are no longer being left to the faculty and the administrators who support them.

Outside the academy, the idea of the electronic classroom is just as important as a symbol of a new era in education from pre-school to postgraduate continuing education. This convergence of symbolism from three sectors which have traditionally observed distinct boundaries is more than interesting. It reflects a growing sense that technology will provide the vehicle for changes in what and why people learn, as well as how, when and where. Just as the idea of the electronic classrooms frees everyone to imagine a ubiquitous, universal, integrated system of education that is cross-national if not transnational, it also invites speculation about what should be learned and why (thus one important reason for the debate on national standards).

The speculation is healthy, but the initial prospect of implementing new "learning packages" is a matter of some concern. One early characteristic of the external interest in redefining education has been to break down learning objectives into smaller and smaller components—into modules and sessions instead of all courses with the potential loss of coherence that has come with semester or year-long courses. As corporate and government offices are equipped with electronic classrooms that bring university experts to the educational customer, the goals and purposes of learning may shift from faculty-constructed curricula to customer-designed packages.

Already some professional schools have begun to redesign their degree programs to build on modules instead of courses and on student-paced competency instead of fixed semesters or terms. Collaborative learning and group response work have also migrated from corporate and professional practices to academic strategies, and the capacity of electronic systems to permit reformatting the content of courses, curricula, degrees, and lifelong professional development has accelerated a perhaps inevitable shift in what and why people learn.

The most obvious result has been stress on the idea of a "course" with a specified content, a fixed term, and unique outcomes. By specifying competencies and specific outcomes, the means to achieve them are no longer restricted to a single mode; more importantly, the success of the individual learner can be evaluated—or at least valued—by someone other than the instructor. The ability to re-engineer the traditional basic building blocks of education into packages more directly responsive to the needs of employers or to personal advancement is having an as yet unappreciated impact on the very nature and structure of education, at all levels. For obvious reasons, economic development and employment are driving the changes, but the impact has already begun to be felt in subject areas formerly separate from vocational or professional education—in literature, music, mathematics, languages, social sciences, visual arts, and many other disciplines only hinted at in this volume.

As the symbolic and literal potential of the electronic classroom encourages persons outside academe to exert influence on formal learning, the focus shifts from the faculty expert to the inquiring learner. The probable evolution of the electronic classroom will lead increasingly toward a student-centered system because of the ability of the student to address the numbing amount of information that becomes available each year within specializations and across fields of inquiry. Smart systems, Internet gophers, and software that sorts information by individually specified criteria offer still rudimentary tools that will enable students to become highly sophisticated information managers.

Information can be collected and applied in ways that transcend traditional disciplines, forcing practitioners to become personal integrators and, as one of the authors of this volume says, "problem solvers." Necessarily, students will learn their craft of collecting, sorting, integrating, synthesizing, and applying as an inherent aspect of learning in every course that is offered via an electronic classroom. No one can expect to cope with the information resources becoming available except through the capacity of electronic multimedia support systems, and the electronic classroom will be the laboratory in which personal styles, attitudes, and competencies are formed.

The Evolving Role of the Faculty

"Oh! Pythagoras, that in bright Greece, two thousand years ago, did die, so good, so wise, so mild; I sailed with thee along the Peruvian coast last voyage—and foolish as I am, taught thee, a green simple boy, how to splice a rope!" (page 429)

The implications of the electronic classroom for faculty—pre-kindergarten through post-graduate—are enormous. Distracted by the electronic gadgetry of multimedia systems with big screens and satellite links and the dazzling MTV- or George Lucas-quality digital imagery, many faculty—including this one—are naturally daunted by the prospect of mastering the tools now available. Those devices and capacities which are just beyond the horizon—imagined but not yet seen—are even more intimidating; they have capacities beyond our imagination to control, and thus the sense of becoming marginal to a system, no matter how sophisticated, raises fundamental questions of role, now and then. Known for his theorem, his absolute faith in numbers, and his mysticism, Pythagoras may serve as a fair abstraction of faculty today, who stand at the edge of a new era of knowledge based in part on new information and in part on new ways of using rediscovered information.

Many faculty have anticipated the fact that they can learn how to use the electronic classroom from their students. Already wise in the ways of Nintendo, MTV, and Prodigy, young people are learning how to use hypercard stacks, Boolean searches, and electronic mail in first and second grades. Many states are supporting efforts such as the Buddy System project in Indiana or the TENET project in Texas through which young people—and their families—are allocated computers at home, where they combine in-school work with access from homes to information resources which in some cases are worldwide. Freed from time, geographic, spatial, and pedagogic restraints, the emerging learners have vastly different expectations about what they are learning and how.

When asked to demonstrate their competence or mastery of a subject, they may surprise us with results we do not yet know how to evaluate. When an interpretative analysis of a novel is submitted as a multimedia "event" incorporating sound, image, and text, what criteria are applied? In our struggle to understand how students interpret our assignments, we may learn that our own course goals and objectives are not the right ones—for ourselves as we envision courses as the building blocks of degrees, or for our students as we guide them to independence.

We also know that student expectations of us, as faculty, will be different from anything we have encountered before—even those of us who recall the transformation in postsecondary education wrought by experienced, returning veterans of World War II. Classrooms were never the same again, and the shift likely to occur in the next decade will be even more pronounced. The special capacities of the electronic classroom—based on interaction and communication—can change the relationship between student and teacher from hierarchy and control to collaboration and support. Authority may become a shared responsibility.

The role of faculty in the electronic classroom is most likely to evolve toward that of enabling students to discover knowledge for themselves by using information resources in personally meaningful ways to attain course (or assignment) objectives specified by the instructor. The ends of learning may be redefined in the process, shifting away from course grades or even degrees as the ultimate objectives and moving toward the application of knowledge to specific ends as part of a lifelong continuous education. The electronic classroom may accelerate a process already underway to separate learning from schooling and to restore faculty to the role of mentor.

If we imagine ourselves as young and green, we can learn from those still foolish in understanding but wise in technique. Collaboration frees us to accept as well as to give. We can learn to splice the rope which will hold together the knowledge of the past with its use and the creation of new knowledge in the future. The electronic classroom provides one exceptional opportunity for faculty and students to use simultaneously the same tools and information resources for coordinated but different purposes. Students may be more creative and efficient in the use of technology to find, sort, synthesize, and manipulate information, and in the process may teach their teachers. However, the faculty must continue to help students develop the skills of analysis, synthesis, and evaluation. The chapters in this volume offer convincing insights into how faculty are accepting their new roles, and in turn providing leadership for remaking education.

And leadership is the key element in the evolving role of faculty. Most of the debate on the future deployment, management, regulation, application, and financing of technology is occurring with only minimal participation from faculty. Through their lobbyists and expert witnesses, the cable, television, and telephone industries are staking out vast empires of information access. Government and private sector forces are competing for ownership of the network of networks. The entertainment industry and popular presses are deciding the future of intellectual property and copyright. Faculty have yet to play a decisive or even distinctive role in these fundamentally important decisions, except as individuals representing a professional association or serving as an expert witness for one interest group or another. If faculty are to play a role in determining how these technologies will be used within education, they are likely to do so based on their expertise and experience within the electronic classroom.

The Future of the Institution Itself

"Here's the ship's navel, this doubloon here, and they are all on fire to unscrew it. But unscrew your navel, what's the consequence? Then again, if it stays here, that is ugly too, for when aught's nailed to the mast it's a sign that things grow desperate." (page 435)

Ahab's speech for many readers—or viewers, who recall Gregory Peck's powerful performance as Ahab—is the intellectual center of the novel. A reward for the whaleman who spots the elusive prey, the doubloon itself becomes a symbol for the choice the crew must make in deciding to join Ahab's quest for the whale. In richly metaphorical language, Ahab speaks for generations of pilgrims, searching for the true form of whatever preoccupies them.

The case being made for the importance of the electronic classroom in the preceding sections is self-consciously extravagant, but for a purpose. It has become a symbol in the ways suggested, and as such it plays a far more active role in transforming education and its institutions than might be apparent from any one classroom, no matter how lavishly or imaginatively equipped. As a symbol, and thus as a catalyst to action and change, the electronic classroom may play a similar role for faculty and institutions as Ahab's doubloon did for the crew of the *Pequod.* Well, not exactly the same role, because we do not expect to lose the ship or the crew of American higher education in the process. But the electronic classroom poses the same awesome dilemma of acceptance or rejection that Ahab— the great realist—forces his shipmates to confront.

In searching and researching the electronic classroom, administrative officers and faculty should bear in mind Ahab's warning. To embrace the inherent and potential changes of the electronic classroom in all its current and future forms is to undo many of the structures and strictures which now define and confine education. Elements of control and discipline that come with courses and grades, curricula and degrees, are based on an unquestioned authority to certify accomplishment within prescribed and known domains. If we unscrew our navel, what will happen? What are the consequences?

At the same time, to leave the electronic classroom—as a symbol and as a transforming tool of government and business—nailed to the mast of education, ignored but still glittering, would be a reminder indeed of just how desperate we are to avoid change. Unlike computers, digital imaging, telefacsimile, and other specific technologies, the electronic classroom has taken on the role of symbol precisely because it represents the integration and application of technologies that lead to fundamental change and not merely to the use of the technologies themselves.

Recognizing the significance of electronic technology as suggested in this essay, the faculty and administration at IUPUI have embarked on a course Ahab would not have permitted. We have created several advanced electronic classrooms, including one of the most visible in the entire Indiana University system. A lecture hall accommodating about 500 students was renovated and equipped as a showcase of technology and learning. It is described elsewhere in this volume. Other rooms were similarly remodeled and equipped to meet specific educational objectives, including distance learning, networked student interaction, and visual display. Moreover, technologies were adapted to a mobile delivery system, and many "ordinary" rooms can become electronic merely by moving a rather fancy cart full of interactive devices into the room and plugging it in to the campus and world networks.

These doubloons were tacked on to the campus infrastructure to encourage faculty to explore the potential of the technology and to adapt it to their current work with the expectation of their becoming the leaders who would remake the university from the inside out instead of reacting to the external forces noted earlier. The electronic classrooms and the personnel who support faculty in using them were intentionally designed and deployed to serve known faculty needs (and to address complaints of students, more often regarding the physical conditions of the rooms). From a base of comfort and familiarity that comes from experience, faculty have been encouraged to explore and expand, and to introduce new colleagues to the potential of the electronic classrooms. The evidence of success is reflected in several of the essays and in the collection itself. Faculty at IUPUI have been able to chase our figurative whale without unscrewing our navels.

The success of individual faculty in using the potential of these new learning environments has led to several major steps in our self-conscious evolution toward a new model of higher education. One has been the concept of the university as a community learning network, which reflects a commitment to the citizens of the region manifested in a series of connected, interacting learning centers which range from a person's home to corporate and institutional sites throughout the city—all anchored by the central IUPUI campus. The concept also recognizes that learners will draw from many different sources in creating their own meaningful "program," which may not coincide neatly with our curricula or degree requirements.

The second major development has been the design of an whole new University Library to serve as the intellectual and electronic hub of the campus. It will be an information center as well as a repository for materials and a community space for face-to-face interactions. More importantly, it will be the link among classrooms on and off campus as well as the gateway to as rich and diverse external information resources as we can locate worldwide. The importance of the University Library as the symbolic and functional center of the electronic campus cannot be understated.

As Ishmael discovered by surviving his own voyage in search of the whale, it is the community of sailors—or scholars in our case, but broadly conceived to include all those who learn for their own improvement and the good of the whole—that gives the symbol meaning and that makes the passage possible. Universities in particular, but education in general, have an important role to play in reaffirming community as the purposeful and meaningful interaction among individual members. Electronic classrooms provide a means with the potential for positive change that we have never before seen. The search is surely worthy of the effort.

Related Readings

Hayford, Harrison, Hershel Parker, and G. Thomas Tanselle, *The Writings of Herman Melville: Moby Dick or The Whale*, Volume Six, Northwestern University Press and The Newberry Library, Evanston and Chicago, 1988. All quotations are from this volume, with the page numbers indicated in parentheses.

Plater, William M. et al., "The Community Learning Network," a concept paper prepared and distributed by IUPUI; available through an Internet gopher.

Plater, William M., "The Place of the Human-Made World in General Education," in *Cultural Literacy and the Idea of General Education*, Eighty-seventh Yearbook of the National Society for the Study of Education, University of Chicago, Chicago, 1988.

Plater, William M. and Amy Conrad Warner, "Turing's Anteroom: A Metaphor for Student Centered Learning," Proceedings of the East-West Conference on Emerging Computer Technologies in Education, Moscow, Russia, 1992.

Technology and the Inevitability of Educational Transformation

George Connick and Jane Russo

George Connick is President of The Education Network of Maine

Jane Russo is Executive Assistant to the President, The Education Network of Maine

Throughout its history, America has periodically redefined its educational systems to meet the evolving needs of a complex society. The provision of universal, free public elementary and secondary education, the creation of the junior college to expand educational access at the postsecondary level, the crafting of the GI bill after World War II to assist veterans with their re-entry into society, and the development of state and federal financial assistance programs for needy students are notable examples. Indeed, the ability of public policy makers to recognize the need for fundamental curriculum and organizational change at critical periods in history has been a significant strength in American society.

The most recent warning about problems in the schools came in the mid-1980s with Terrel Bell's disturbing report titled, *A Nation at Risk*. In it, Bell cautioned that major problems with America's educational system would have to be addressed soon if this country was to retain its pre-eminent role in world society.

In the intervening years since *A Nation at Risk* appeared, many reports containing similarly alarming messages were published. Their recommendations consistently called for the redesign of the schools' curricula as well as their organizational structure. Yet, the overriding sense of many Americans is that little, if anything, has occurred in the way of significant and substantive change.

There is, in fact, a great deal of change occurring at all levels of education, but it is happening, by and large, sporadically and in relative isolation. Throughout American history, education at the K-12 and postsecondary level has been largely focused locally. School districts, and even colleges, remain fiercely autonomous, seeing their mission and purpose through the eyes of their local, tax-paying constituents. This governance structure was necessary as long as education was labor intensive and limited by the distance students could travel to the local school. In that environment, the aggregation of students, teachers and resources (i.e., library collections) was sensible and productive.

Today, however, telecommunications technologies are challenging the fundamental tenets upon which our entire educational system has been constructed. Modern telecommunications allow us to span distances and cultures instantaneously. The need to aggregate people simply to communicate with them has disappeared. We now have the capability to provide individuals, at locations of their own choosing, with vast, and rapidly expanding, collections of print and visual materials and the means to share limited resources among many educational institutions.

The tools for another major transformation of American education are here today. What is lacking is widespread understanding of the power and meaning of those tools for the revolution underway—a revolution that promises to transform the role of educators by the beginning of the next century.

Seymour Papert uses a striking example in his new book, *The Children's Machine: Rethinking School in the Age of the Computer* (1993), which, in its first chapter, contrasts the rate of change between education and the medical profession:

> Imagine a party of time travelers from an earlier century, among them one group of surgeons and another of schoolteachers, each group eager to see how much things have changed in their profession a hundred or more years into the future. Imagine the bewilderment of the surgeons finding themselves in the operating room of a modern hospital. Although they would know that an operation of some sort was being performed, and might even be able to guess at the target organ, they would in almost all cases be unable to figure out what the surgeon was trying to accomplish or what was the purpose of the many strange devices he and the surgical staff were employing. The rituals of antisepsis and anesthesia, the beeping electronics, and even the bright lights, all so familiar to television audiences, would be utterly unfamiliar to them.
>
> The time-traveling teachers would respond very differ-

ently to amodern elementary school classroom. They might be puzzled by a few strange objects. They might notice that some standard techniques had changed—and would likely disagree among themselves about whether the changes they saw were for the better or the worse—but they would fully see the point of most of what was being attempted and could quite easily take over the class. (pp. 1-2)

Historically, public policy makers and educational leaders have had to address three major educational issues: access, quality, and productivity. These are essentially the same issues we face today, except that each of them has become significantly more complex, assuring that any attempts to address them today will entail disruptive and wrenching change.

Let's look first at access. Recent reports have cited statistics showing the extent to which, in just the 50 years since World War II, the demographics of American society have changed, challenging the ability of the schools to respond. Twenty percent of our students, for example, will be poor, 15 percent will be physically damaged, 60 percent will come from homes where the mother also has a paid, full-time job, 20 percent will come from homes where a language other than English is spoken, and 50 percent will be children of color. Information is so broadly based and the acquisition of knowledge so complex that new ways of teaching and learning are essential if students of such great diversity are to be truly engaged in the learning process.

In the past, quality has been seen as antithetical to providing broad educational access. In other words, real quality was defined by the extent to which institutions were selective and students were sorted on the basis of ability. Today, this concept is outmoded. We can no longer afford to allow our students to fail to learn. To do so is to ensure America's social and economic decay and to risk our collective future.

Because education has been historically labor-intensive with no apparent alternative to that condition, the costs of education continued to rise regardless of how resourcefully schools and colleges responded to the changing needs of society.

Remarkably, it is now possible for us to address all three of these public policy issues using the same tools that have transformed American business, industry and many professions—pervasive telecommunications technologies and enormously powerful computers.

Many institutions are adapting these tools to extend educational access, prepare students for work in an age where these tools are already the tools of almost every trade, and link them to a wider community of learners and new sources of information. Mind Extension University (MEU) offers one such model. An innovator in the delivery of higher education, Mind

Extension University, based in Englewood, Colorado, uses interactive television and other telecommunications technologies to deliver college-credit courses in a range of programs to 36,000 students across the country through institutions such as Penn State and the University of Minnesota. The University of Maryland has recently made a four-year bachelor of arts program available nationwide through MEU.

Maricopa Community College offers computer conferencing in the form of an Electronic Forum, which links 20,000 students to faculty and peers for purposes of communication and as an interactive writing tool for English and other disciplines. Maricopa also uses a computer system to monitor students' academic progress, the results of which are available to both students and instructor. Syllabi, calendar, testing and electronic mail are all readily accessible to students on this comprehensive system.

In response to a mandate by its Board of Trustees, the University of Maine system developed a plan to provide community college access to Maine's growing population of older, commuting students. Maine has no system of community colleges and, at the time, there existed no practicable way to serve students across Maine without resorting to an expensive project of off-campus construction and then hiring instructors to teach in these remote locations.

The solution emerged in the form of a statewide network of existing off-campus locations linked to an interactive television system. Through this extensive network, students at remote sites are taught by a professor who is simultaneously teaching to a classroom of students on campus. An audio talk-back system permits these students to communicate with the instructor and with other distant students. Inaugurated in 1989, the Network began delivering 40 courses to over 30 locations in rural Maine. Today, the Education Network delivers approximately 65 courses to more than 85 locations throughout the state. It also offers students across Maine a full range of academic and student support services, including access to all of the University libraries and the largest state, national, and international libraries directly from desktop terminals.

The Education Network of Maine is one of a growing number of programs that use information technologies to help extend educational resources to a greater number of students while connecting them to an expanded network of information and services. But any investment in expensive technological networks at a time of budget shortfalls and "downsizing" must be solidly predicated on a compelling public policy imperative. In 1985, Maine was 48th among states in high school graduates enrolling in any form of postsecondary education and 50th among states in adults participating in higher education. The use of technologies to expand educational access in Maine was considered only after extensive planning revealed that, when combined with existing facilities and human resources, an interactive television network offered the most accessible, productive means to that end. Without a clear and pressing need, and strong indications that the new technology could effectively extend the University's programs to the state's underserved populations, Maine's significant investment of funds in technology, personnel, and faculty and staff development would only have exacerbated already attenuated budgets, alienated faculty, and inspired the distrust of public policy makers and taxpayers alike.

As important as establishing a compelling reason for the introduction of telecommunications is the strong commitment by the institution's leaders to advancing and articulating that vision. Any plan to significantly alter traditional methods of teaching and learning must first be clearly and convincingly drawn by the institution's leadership; lacking this, the confidence and allegiance of the campus community, vital to the program's sustained development, would be lost. When the Board of Trustees placed responsibility for creating the statewide community college with the University of Maine at Augusta, the University's president, together with his staff and faculty leaders, envisioned a preliminary solution and, as part of an extended process of public information, discussed the plan and its wider community implications at numerous meetings with the campus community, private and public colleges, superintendents, civic groups, legislators, and the state's governor. The creation of a statewide consensus proved crucial to the Network's ability to attract funding, to build institutional, school and corporate partnerships, and, ultimately, to assure its productivity and cost-effectiveness.

The involvement of a visionary and committed leadership is essential, too, if change is to occur expeditiously. Given the demographic and budgetary imperatives faced by higher education at all levels, institutional innovation designed to increase access, quality, and productivity can ill afford to be delayed by endless debate about its inherent worthiness. The role of the institutional leader is, in part, to invest the campus community with a singular purpose, outline the resources and tools available and those needed to accomplish its mission, encourage dialogue and discussion about the plan's development and implementation, then mobilize quick and effective action across campus. Perhaps most importantly, leadership can funnel resources, support, and tools into the hands of those who will effect real change—the institution's faculty. It is the faculty, finally, who will design and manage how technically-mediated instruction will occur, ideally in a way that introduces new power and responsibility to the learner. This is an exciting but unfamiliar role for faculty and students alike, and one that is not without its share of risk.

But risk and excitement are part of the process of educational reform. The introduction of change at one level invariably stimulates additional, higher-level change—sometimes with paradigm-shattering and, for a time, uncomfortable, consequences. Information technologies enlarge our traditional concepts of education as they force institutions to rapidly address barriers of geography, time, distance, student numbers, student preparation, course and degree options, and student services. These institutions find they are serving greater numbers of students with a larger number of course and program options, but may be straining the resources of an already harried staff. The experience of teaching with and through technologies redefines pedagogy as it enlarges its scope. Instructors really must become less the purveyors of knowledge and more the facilitators of the learning process, a role that may make some faculty uneasy. Traditional concepts of educational time and space are forever altered as these tools put the choice of where and when to learn more squarely in the hands of the student. And because teachers are not physically present during instruction, students are encouraged to invest more responsibility in the direction and intensity of their own learning—some may not be ready for the experience.

As they force systems of higher education to tackle the thorny inter-campus issues of course transfer, tuition and fee charges, residency requirements, and testing and assessment, technology-driven programs tend to weaken and blur institutional boundaries. Articulation and other campus agreements born of their implementation slowly reshape and broaden campus transfer policy and, in the process, make it more responsive to the needs of all learners. But it may also ignite long-smoldering battles over turf.

These risks are more than compensated, however, by the introduction to students and faculty of a welcome diversity of learning. From systems which transmit the campus classroom to remote locations, to less place-bound models which support active, independent modes of learning, these programs fill an educational vacuum created by the particular needs of today's disparate population of students. The integration of technologies across the curriculum allows even traditional, campus-based courses and services to better fit individual preferences and needs, from learning style to developmental level. If learning occurs best when the learner is actively engaged in the process, these tool-rich programs promise to improve education by personalizing it, connecting students to a wider pool of teachers and learners, and freeing them from the constraints of a single institution's facilities and schedules. This important shift in the organization of many institutions will become increasingly common as students, particularly adult students, come to expect such flexibility from their educational institutions. The service concept, long a management imperative in business, is relatively new to education, but rapidly finding a warm reception in this increasingly competitive field.

The multi-faceted approach to learning made possible by the new electronic modalities is an important contribution to the academy. But more important, perhaps, has been their liberating influence on the university's traditional conservatism, bringing diversity and new direction to the academy as they shape new programs and add fresh and spacious dimensions to traditional courses. As they promote epistemological experimentation and innovation, technology-rich programs, based on real community need and strong institutional leadership, promise to make American higher education more responsive to a nation sorely in need of its services and, in turn, help to free the University from some of the more debilitating and costly effects of its long tradition of cloister.

Pedagogical Issues

Ray L. Steele

Ray Steele is the Director of the Center for Information and Communication Sciences, Ball State University, Muncie, Indiana

You are here not merely to make a living. You are here to enable the world to live more amply, with greater vision, with a finer spirit of hope and achievement. You are here to enrich the world, and you impoverish yourself if you forget the errand.—Woodrow Wilson

One of the few physical environments in our society today that differs little from the way it was in 1856 is education. It is often just a box with uncomfortable seats and a chalkboard, but the lighting has improved. This is the professional environment in which we are to prepare the next generation of leaders to keep the United States competitive in the information age.

Usually in the field of education we are encouraged to speculate and philosophize on that which our preliminary research indicates may work or which might, at some statistically significant point on a chart, be of sufficient interest to pursue for further study. Due to economics and other circumstances beyond our control, we are rarely able to tackle a major environment or problem area with an applications-oriented outcome as our initial goal. Webster defines pedagogy as the art, science, or profession of teaching. He, too, was not certain as to just what it is we do.

My purpose in this chapter is to discuss those problems related to the art, science, and profession of teaching which I believe can be impacted both positively and negatively by the application of information age technologies.

The Initial "Aggravation"

In 1982, while teaching in the Executive MBA program at the University of Pittsburgh, I became aggravated by the lack of basic support for professionals (teachers) in the education environment. Since this was about the same time that John Naisbitt, in *Megatrends*, reminded us that we were living in the information age, I found it ironic that one of the most information- and communication-intensive environments, the multi-billion dollar education industry, was so far behind in providing its professionals with basic information tools. Let me note that this was not a problem based upon the unwillingness of the staff to be supportive. It was, instead, based upon an approach that simply would not dependably work. It was a poor system, the wrong paradigm.

Thus began the work which led to the first Campus of the Future, a voice, data, video, fiber optic infrastructure and satellite project serving all 45,000 people and the 55 buildings of the University of Pittsburgh campus in 1983. By 1987, we had underway the Teaching Environment Model of the Campus of the Future at Ball State University and the Schools of the 21st Century Project, the first K-12 school district to employ voice, data, video, fiber optic infrastructure, and satellite to its academic environment. We opened the American School 2000 school district project in Westfield, IN, winning an "A+ for Breaking the Mold Schools Award" from then U.S. Secretary of Education, Lamar Alexander. In K-graduate levels, we found that a new system, a paradigm change, was necessary to achieve the results we sought. We have lessened the aggravation.

In each of these projects, we selected pedagogical problems as our targets and applied technologies to help faculty and administrators to improve their teaching and learning environment and cut back barriers to good teaching, research, and service opportunities in academia.

We have shifted from an environment dependent upon moving and managing boxes to an environment in which we move and manage information.

Education in the United States is still admired around the globe, but needs to improve now to keep up with both competition and information age opportunities. In education institutions, it has not been money which has hampered progress, though that is always a concern. Instead, it has been an old approach to a new problem which has slowed real progress.

The Nature of the Problem

Students at most levels are extremely resilient and often they learn and succeed in spite of the environment and those of us charged with teaching. However, there are some aspects of what we present as teachers, which can help to overcome an initial lack of interest and stimulate extended efforts, which usually result in improved learning.

Engagement with subject matter and time on task at most levels from K-undergraduate are two critical issues rarely in dispute anymore, in many cases, perhaps as important as basic intelligence for much of what is being taught at these levels today. Dr. Grace Lazavik and her mentor, Dr. W.J. McKeachie of the University of Michigan, spent significant time and effort in the '60s and '70s looking at what makes a good teacher.[1] Here are some conclusions on good teaching.[2] Generally, someone who is knowledgeable and current in his or her field, organized, employs good communication skills, and cares about students' learning will achieve reasonably good student evaluations, and often peer evaluations will be similar as well. That, to me, is a reasonable set of criteria for good teaching.

While there are lots of specialty areas and varying specific exceptions to the above generalizations, they will operate quite well for a very broad segment of the population noted. I am interested in impacting large numbers within the teaching and learning environment and I am also interested in reversing some bad habits which have been reinforced by old systems which do not support the teaching/learning environment well.

As a teacher, I must keep up with my field, and scholarship will usually result in updated information, some new research interests and, perhaps, some publication in whatever is the accepted format. Note that one serious problem academe is currently facing is a tendency to cling to the printed, refereed journal at a time when we constantly hear the plea for less paper and more electronic information. Electronic journals, or even just databases accessible via Internet or other electronic sources, can today provide adequate space and access worldwide to readers who wish to obtain a given article. The marketplace of ideas can then accept or reject what is written, without benefit of the scrutiny of a very limited group of readers or referees. There is a different paradigm in this and yet we are slow to shift toward it. A different approach may work even better at achieving qualitative review.

If a faculty member keeps up with his or her field of scholarship and then takes the time to organize the content and to develop requisite support materials to help make it understandable, the next serious barrier to success is often getting the information communicated in an environment where the classroom is often ill-equipped and electronic support for the presentation of ideas is either undependable or too costly to use.

Confidence, Cost, and Convenience

One of three scenarios follows in this phase of getting good scholarship communicated to the intended audience.

Typically, some audio-visual or media resources center is asked to provide physical delivery service to a location at a given time. Work-study students cart everything from slide projectors to VCRs to personal computers and monitors to the location, and sometimes they arrive on time, intact and with all bulbs, cables, and other devices working. Sometimes, the teacher even understands completely the operating nuances of each different variety delivered once the support person, who may or may not know how to operate the equipment, leaves. Sometimes, they do not. When this scenario results in things not working dependably and easily, the erosion of confidence in this system follows, and instead of investing the extra time it takes to prepare the resources to help communicate concepts, the yellowed notes, or perhaps the overhead, returns to the forefront as the teaching tools.

The second scenario involves a few of the more fortunate who understand, support, and lug around their own equipment, or are sufficiently well-positioned to have access to a few specially equipped and supported facilities. These facilities are costly to create, require support, and can usually handle only a few users who are experienced in their functionality. Thus, these limited access teaching environments, while often very functional, end up creating a have/have-not distinction between the elites with access and the balance of the faculty and students who may not access them. Cost is the obvious barrier and the have-nots can excuse, with frustration, going back to the yellowed notes and overhead.

The third scenario represents a bit of a paradigm shift. It is a campus-wide system approach which provides for most, if not all, classrooms to have access to networked system resources. The only thing that moves is information. With rare exceptions, the various kinds of support equipment for the teaching and learning environment are managed in a networked central information center.

Faculty do what they are best at—they select and organize information to help them communicate their scholarship. The network provides access to the desired information, no matter what the format. The control and display functions are provided locally in each teaching environment and thus, the faculty member can manage time and resources to achieve the maximum impact on the student audience. Since a telephone is also in each classroom, even the least technically-oriented faculty member can get immediate help if there is a problem. Confidence in the system is enhanced.

Since it is a system serving all, not just an elite group, the elimination of the have/have-not problem is more likely. Because this approach represents a significant change in how equipment is managed and purchased, how staff is managed, and because of its potential for serving much larger numbers of users more often, the cost also becomes more manageable.

Obviously, the third scenario also helps to eliminate barriers which impede the well-prepared from succeeding in the classroom with the communication of the scholarship. Thus, those faculty who care enough to not only do good scholarship, but to organize and support its communication in the classroom, are now reinforced and supported by their environment. There is no reason to retreat to the yellowed notes and the ever-present overhead.

Connecting Problems and Solutions

While improving the teaching and learning environment should be easy to connect with improving the quality of education in this nation, an argument Dewey and other educators have made countless times, it is not automatically accepted by many who are not comforted by change.[3] Resource allocation, management, and control changes are involved and they are not easy to shift.

Solving pedagogical problems should represent the most acceptable reasons for change in an academic environment. Therefore, let us connect some system-related solutions to problems in the academic environment.

The typical mission of any academic environment at the postsecondary level is scholarship and/or research at some level to keep up in one's field, teaching, and some form of service. Billions of dollars in education are expended annually in the pursuit of these activities. A good portion of this mammoth expenditure goes to pay for people, some for the physical environment, and some for the technology to support that environment.

Over the past decade, a significant amount of the technology money has been spent on buying stand-alone boxes, personal computers of whatever level, to serve individual user needs. Some has been dedicated to data networks, a modest amount to satellite systems, and some to improving voice systems. It is very rare to find many examples of integrated technology systems which have been installed.

However, if we look at the pedagogical problems faced by faculty in the complex academic environment, they tend to be as follows.

In **research and scholarship**, timely and easy access to needed information resources becomes the essence of productivity. The political scientist or the biologist each needs convenient and timely access to the information sources which the researcher selects for its appropriateness and completeness. This suggests network access from an office to a campus system or off-campus information resources which may provide voice, data, video, text, or image-based information.

If we do not provide such access, how can we hope to compete for leading research grants and scholarship support opportunities? After all, in research and scholarship, it is the creativity and knowledge of how to select and locate information on the part of the researcher and the time it takes for the gathering and the evolution of conclusions which we pay for through research grants. Those with more productive environments are going to have an edge in the competitive research and grantsmanship areas. Publications, one of the measures of faculty progress, are going to be more likely to come in greater quantity from modern environments than from places tied to the past. Systems and access via systems to networks in the environment are more likely to attract talent to one campus over another.

Turning to **service**, a mixed bag area of the traditional mission in education, we can quickly come to some issues of consequence by looking at the area of training programs. It is common to most educational institutions to be involved in offering training programs and seminars to their constituencies. Two of the most common of the client areas served are business and health care.

Ask yourself whether you would elect to do training and related service courses from a campus supplier with an antiquated learning environment if you had a choice. The information age has proved that some choices do exist and if your environment is steeped in the tradition of the 1856 classroom, and your competition understands how to employ a system with a network which can bring modern resources cost-effectively to the training and service course room, who will get the opportunities? Sacred cows who would chose to do little to shift into the information age are no longer sacred, let alone as successful as in the past.

Finally, let us talk about perhaps the most critical function performed by the postsecondary education environment. **Teaching** is clearly the historic function assigned to academe. It is that mysterious process by which we encourage others to aspire to discover new truths from old wines and it is our opportunity to attract new talents to continue the essential areas upon which our functioning society depends.

As we have come to painfully recognize in many other previously U.S.-dominated industries, in this new global economy, the European Community countries and the Pacific Rim nations are no longer willing to accept our dominance in areas such as automobiles and computer chips. Why must they think any differently about education? If that is true internationally, why should young and aspiring local institutions, often more willing and adept at accepting technology than their complex senior counterparts, think any differently about competing for top students? K-12 institutions, which are adapting system-based information age environments, will wonder how long it will be before these new K-12 graduates will demand as modern an environment from their selected college as they had in their K-12 experience. There are some very specific competitive reasons for institutions to move to information age system improvements.

The teacher has numerous needs in a learning environment or classroom, and admittedly, not all learning will occur from a lecture format. However, for the immediate future, I believe we can count on some classroom needs which can be met best by system-based technology in support of the teacher.

As a teacher, I know that I can have more impact on my students by reinforcing what I say with examples and illustrations which are often visual and sometimes audio-based. I know that one carefully selected minute of tape, CD-I, CD-ROM, or other visual experience will enhance engagement with my topic and it will also add clarity. I know that by using technology-based supportive materials, I must more carefully plan my classroom experience. I also know that by using varied resources, I can get more content into the instructional period as well as be more creative in my approach to making my points.

As a realist, I also understand that it often takes more time up-front, not less, to use technology in my teaching. However, the gains come in student participation and interest at first, and as I adjust and update the technology use in future class sessions, I begin then to realize some time savings. It also helps me to maintain focus and to avoid tangents common to classroom teaching.

In the systems-based environment, I can use voice, data, or video-based resources whenever they are required. Rather than explaining a key concept of the author of a text, for very little cost and minimal time expenditure in class and with a little planning, I can bring the author to the class by audio conference because I have a telephone and a network connection in 300 classrooms which I use. With a simple and inexpensive audio conferencing device, I can get the students in a guided dialogue with the author. This is good engaging instruction and it is very cost-effective. Try paying expenses and an honorarium for a 20-minute session live in-class from the same author. It is hard to cost justify and it doesn't get done. The students lose.

If a video conference makes sense to share with students, I request it, and at the appointed time, I turn it on and the network serves me. If, in the midst of a lecture, I suddenly wish to show a picture, obtain a written definition, or show a computer screen display to make a complex point more understandable, I pick up the telephone if I have not already reserved the resource, and it is delivered remotely. If I need a personal computer for display purposes, I bring an infrared keyboard to the classroom and order up access to a personal computer on the network or I bring in my own laptop and plug into the system with a display for all the class to see.

I do not have to lose the moment of creative opportunity because it is too hard or too undependable to get the equipment to the room in which I teach. Also, because we made a system commitment to support the teaching and learning environment, I have 300 rooms in which I can comfortably teach, not just a few special places where only a few of us can gain access.

If I am not as good as I wish to be in the classroom, there are very few others who I can blame. The resources are available and I can be confident of their delivery. I am accountable for my own success. Isn't that what any professional expects from his or her environment?

A Realistic Look at Connecting Funding Issues to Pedagogical Issues

"Whose budget gets gored?" is the usual response to campus improvement projects. Rarely do you find the discussion focused on academic improvements when major technology projects are involved. Yet, the point of all expenditures in any academic setting should be the ultimate improvement of potential on campus to meeting the institutional mission. Typically, there is little direct connection between overall pedagogical issues and expenditures.

When a campus accepts that a system approach with an infrastructure to create a network on campus makes sense, it favorably changes the basics of the economics involved. When the infrastructure extends from a campus backbone to every building and to all reasonable rooms within buildings, the need for continuous and expensive little wiring projects on campus is minimized. When a system provides voice, data, video and satellite-based information to classrooms, the use of support staff can be shifted to more directly serve users. When the system assures that loose equipment no longer needs to be moved from room to room, long-term equipment replacement costs go down. When the system is dependable in providing a personal computer remotely to the classroom, the need for stand-alone personal computers in classrooms, where they are hard to maintain and secure, goes away. Finally, when the system will dependably deliver the information requested, faculty have greater confidence in it and the likelihood of increased use of equipment is high. This should lead to greater value in the investment and it should also mean that with more faculty using more resources on campus, better learning opportunities exist for students. Thus, the connection between approach to funding and pedagogical issues can be made.

Systems must be supported, and that means re-directing the activities of those who worked under the non-system past, not just changing technology. It also means understanding the difference between "enabling and disabling" economics on a campus. New and emerging technologies, as well as those which we are confident will improve the teaching and learning experience, must be handled within "enabling accounting" systems. In effect, you cannot charge for use for those technologies which you wish to get used. You must make a values-based judgment in support of pedagogical issues and centrally fund such equipment. Disabling economics can be found in any system which charges on a use basis for those teaching tools that are essential to improving teaching and learning.

Pedagogical issues can be impacted by systems-based technology decisions. Then, they must also be supported by values-based decisions of enabling economics and by system support and training for those who will use the system.

Conclusion

Most who teach would prefer to do the best job possible. Often, they retreat to old habits and stop trying because they cannot count upon convenient, dependable, and easy-to-use support systems.

Yet systems-based voice, data, video, text, and image technologies are critical to the information age in which we work and they comprise the basis of support systems essential in the '90s to provide improved teaching and learning environments.

Good research and scholarship, teaching and service are the general mission of education and we spend billions annually in support of this. The approach we take to planning and then expending resources, whether piecemeal or holistic and integrated, leads to the ultimate support or lack of support for pedagogical issues. Our accounting systems, whether enabling or disabling, demonstrate our values and ultimately encourage or defeat faculty in the teaching and learning environment.

We have affordable choices, and we have models which suggest there is, perhaps, another approach to improving the teaching and learning environment that works. These networked, systems-based, integrated solutions alone will not solve our quality of education problems. However, they will help faculty to improve preparation, to organize, to maximize instructional time, to better communicate and reinforce points and, overall, by this effort, to demonstrate their care for learning to those students whom they must motivate.

Why is all of this so important now? It is probably no more important now that we improve education than it was five or 10 years ago. However, we are living in the information age and that is no longer arguable. We are also living in the most globally competitive time in our history. We cannot teach students in the environment of an 1856 classroom and then expect them to go and be successful in an electronic world. Also, we cannot hope to have a society that has the talent to help keep the U.S. competitive if we do not take full advantage of the tools available to us in educating the next generation. If anything, we should have environments for teaching and learning that are so leading-edge as to cause high expectations in our graduates who can then cause their future work environments to improve by their own high expectations.

That is good for education, for people, and for the future.

Notes

1. McKeachie, Wilbert James; Isaacson, R.L.; and Milholland, John E. *Research on the Characteristics of Effective College Teaching*, Project No. O.E 850, January 1960 to December 1963, The University of Michigan, Ann Arbor, Michigan.

2. Unrecorded conversations with G. Lazavik and W.J. McKeachie, 1978-80, Pittsburgh, Pennsylvania.

3. Dewey, John. *Democracy and Education*, MacMillan Co., 1916, pp. 10-11.

Implementing the Vision: Electronic Classroom Design and Construction

Garland C. Elmore and Ali Jafari

Garland C. Elmore is Acting Associate Vice Chancellor for Information Technologies and Associate Professor of Communication at IUPUI

Ali Jafari is Director of Research and Development in the Office of Information Technologies and Assistant Professor of Communication at IUPUI

Interest in multimedia facilities coincides with the growing need to incorporate audio, video, computing, and traditional tools in teaching, and with rapid advances in technology that make integration of several media practical for non-technical users. The potential of technology to improve learning, however, is closely related to the quality of the planning process. Projects are too often initiated without adequately addressing the conceptual and system design issues. The result may be that technologies become underutilized, unreliable, or ineffective. They fail to live up to expectations. Good planning can help developers overcome many of the pitfalls.

People define *electronic classrooms* differently. Think about them in three main categories: presentational environments (lecture halls and seminar rooms), independent learning environments (computer clusters and media centers), and remote environments (distance video classrooms and corporate training sites). This division is convenient because the technologies play different roles in each environment. In the *presentational environment*, technologies serve primarily as teaching tools used by the instructor to better communicate with students. In this environment, the instructor operates the technologies. In the *independent learning environment*, technologies are used directly by students; students operate the technologies. And in the *remote teaching environment*, technologies are used to electronically deliver information (instruction) to students at sites distant from the instructor. In this environment a team of technicians is often required to operate the equipment, although emerging technologies increasingly put control in the hands of the instructor.

This chapter focuses on the presentational or classroom environment, but may be useful to those interested in independent and remote learning facilities. It outlines practical requirements for successfully planning an electronic lecture hall or seminar room. Several suggestions are offered for those considering developing an advanced technology facility for the first time. The focus is on methods of approaching technologies, on needs assessment, and on classroom design issues. The chapter is illustrated with examples drawn from experiences at Indiana University Purdue University Indianapolis (IUPUI).

Electronic Classrooms for the Presentational Environment

There are three basic approaches for providing advanced technologies to support instruction in the presentational environment. These approaches are not always distinct. Indeed, components of each are often combined in any electronic classroom, so it's useful to think about them as solutions along a continuum. At one end of the continuum is a solution based on *permanent classroom equipment installations*. At the other end is a solution based on *electronic distribution of information* to a classroom from equipment located at a remote site. Somewhere in the middle is a solution dependent on *portable technologies* delivered or carried to the classroom. Each approach has certain advantages and disadvantages.

Permanent Installations

An electronic classroom with permanently installed technologies is an enhanced presentational environment in which several media and controls are integrated through a simple-to-use menu so that the full potential of technology may be exploited easily by the instructor. Lecture Hall 101 on the campus of IUPUI, shown in Figure 1, is an example. This auditorium serves faculty and students from many disciplines and was designed to accommodate a wide array of requirements, including diverse teaching styles. A permanent, dedicated technology installation was justified because this is the largest and most often used lecture hall on the campus. The installation includes over 50 video, audio, computing, telecommunication, and supporting electronic devices that are used in various combinations during the semester. The main concern with incorporating this much technology is technical complexity, which is a disincentive for faculty in using its multimedia capability. Human-technology interface design and technology-technology interface design, discussed later in this chapter, are extremely important considerations.

Portable Technologies

Although permanent installations are desirable in many cases, the cost of renovation combined with the problem of limited access to dedicated classrooms makes an alternative solution very attractive. The portable technologies solution is based on the traditional instructional support model in which standard audio-visual and computing equipment is rolled or carried into a standard classroom. Advances in today's technologies, however, make sophisticated multimedia systems possible. Solutions include microcomputer-based multimedia presentation software and more powerful analog-digital systems that take full advantage of traditional and emerging technologies. The Multimedia Instructional Portable System of Information Technologies (MIPSit) developed at IUPUI, shown in Figure 2, is an example of the latter. It is a mobile unit that houses many of the same technologies included in a permanent electronic classroom. It has its own human-technology interface device. It can be used as a stand-alone system to run multimedia applications, microcomputer applications, or separate programs in several media. Alternatively, MIPSit can connect through a single jack to other audio, video, and data sources, as well as to permanently installed or portable monitors and projectors in specially equipped classrooms. MIPSit bridges the gap between permanent installations and those based upon electronic distribution.

Figure 1   *Permanently installed technologies in lecture hall 101*

Electronic Distribution

The logical evolutionary extension of permanent installations and portable technologies is an "electronic campus" in which centrally located audio, video, and data systems support classroom instruction through electronic distribution of information. Electronic distribution may support full motion video programs and recordings, live two-way television conferences, high resolution color graphic displays, text and data displays, audio programs, and voice (telephone). These systems include at least four major components: the classroom workstation or another human-technology interface device along with display and audio reproduction equipment; the distribution network or combination of networks; the source equipment, including audio and video players, optical (slide, film) projectors, and servers; and, centrally located media conversion, storage, and switching equipment.

Advantages and Disadvantages

Each approach to developing and supporting the electronic classroom infrastructure has certain advantages and disadvantages. Some of the major considerations are summarized in Table 1.

Figure 2   MIPSit: An electronic classroom on wheels

Table 1

Approaches to Providing Technologies in the Classroom

Approach	Advantages	Limitations
Permanent Installation	• Technology is instantly available and encourages use • More technology can typically be launched	• High capital investment as a campus-wide solution • Dedicated room and diverse needs may limit access to technology
Portable Technologies	• Cost-effective and practical • Excellent interim solution until more powerful, fully digital notebook systems are developed • Can be made available in any classroom • An easy solution for integrating and customizing specialized multimedia systems	• Transportation, security, and logistical issues must be resolved • Repair and maintenance may be difficult for some systems
Electronic Distribution	• Technologies can be shared among many users • Workstations can access resources from anywhere on campus • Systems can search databases and deliver text, graphics, images, and motion video • Less space is required in classrooms • Less time and money is spent on mechanical chores of delivery	• Central campus planning and funding is essential • Extremely costly initial investment, especially if existing networks are inadequate • Not an overall solution for computer and digital multimedia applications at this time • Copyright issues not resolved for material stored and delivered electronically

Goals and Objectives

Electronic classroom initiatives should be considered in the context of overall academic goals and objectives. With thousands or even millions of dollars at stake, campus planning will undoubtedly reveal unique requirements for technology. Good planning will not only help ensure that the investment in technology actually supports the academic agenda, but will provide the best balance between standardization and individual preferences.

Campus-wide standardization is important to ensure that the technology works effectively with other systems and to help make the technology easy to use. At the same time, however, the technology must accommodate individual preference as, for example, by supporting specific computer platforms to meet the requirements of the faculty in different disciplines.

A tiered planning approach is best, with general goals and broad directions established at the highest organizational levels and specific requirements and solutions determined at lower levels. Indiana University developed its technology plan from this model. With a budget decentralized to campus-level responsibility centers, Indiana was positioned to take advantage of central and regional perspectives in formulating a system-wide technology plan.

Establishing overall goals and providing initiative for electronic classroom development is effective when it becomes a priority of the highest organizational units. For example, the Information Resources Council, established at the beginning of the decade specifically to articulate the technology goals and directions for Indiana University, also assumed responsibility for planning a centrally supported multicampus technology project. This project was clearly one of the institution's highest priorities and, as a result, funding was secured to establish advanced technology auditoriums incorporating permanent technology installations, portable technology classrooms, and interactive (two-way) television classrooms, as well as complete the high-speed data networks, on each of eight campuses. With significant development already underway at the flagship campus in Bloomington (IUB) and the capital campus in Indianapolis (IUPUI), the Council had an opportunity to build on the strengths of each campus and further define the role of technology in supporting teaching, research, service, and administration.

In a multicampus system, the institutional technology plan provides the context for meaningful campus and school planning. It also encourages complementary development and investment in technology. While the campus technology plan falls under the umbrella of the institutional plan, it must be tailored to meet local needs. Most importantly, the campus technology plan must be solidly founded on the campus academic plan. This seems obvious enough, but it is all too easy to short-circuit the process. Without a clear academic agenda it is difficult to develop a technology program to help each of the campus' colleges, schools, and departments meet their objectives. For this reason, academic units should be encouraged to list specific objectives and work with the campus technology support units to develop a realistic timetable for reaching those objectives.

If the academic plan doesn't already exist, developing one is a major undertaking that requires a commitment by the highest level of campus leadership. The academic plan for IUPUI, for example, began with a two-year comprehensive self-study under the direct supervision of the Chancellor and Dean of Faculties and involved the faculty, students, and staff in all schools and divisions. Its value and relevance to the technology planning and decision making process cannot be underestimated. Be prepared for change when the academic agenda comes first!

The campus technology plan elaborates from the campus academic plan and provides the framework through which each college, school, or department can determine its own technology priorities, consistent with its unique objectives. Developing the campus technology plan at IUPUI first required cooperation and coordination among the information service providers to better respond to the academic initiatives. That partnership not only led to a common plan, but eventually to the merger of the computing, telecommunications, and media organizations. Now offering a single point of contact and support across all technologies, the Office of Information Technologies and its service unit, Integrated Technologies, continue to work closely with academic units, each of which is represented on its advisory committee.

The Integrated Technologies Advisory Committee plays an important role in coordinating campus and school technology plans. It also ensures that school technology plans *actually* support the school and campus academic agenda, and helps minimize needless duplication. At the same time, it provides an opportunity for the campus to refine its technology plan to meet the evolving needs of schools.

Active and positive participation in the second and third tier planning process was encouraged, at least in part, by decentralizing the student technology fee income and giving oversight responsibility to the committee. Decentralizing the student technology fee provided approximately $2.5 million in new income to the schools, with the proviso that it be used in direct support of learning. Schools were asked to file an academic and technology plan with the committee and receive endorsement before spending the students' fee funds, thus ensuring overall coordination and review each year.

One of the advantages of a partnership between campus technology support units and schools is that all share involvement in, and commitment to, the electronic infrastructure. The Indiana University School of Business at IUPUI, for example, developed its technology plan to include six advanced electronic classrooms. Two classrooms were renovated each year for three years, with the cost shared by school and campus units. The classroom designs are consistent with campus technology requirements and include the common human-technology interface and technology-technology interface discussed later in this chapter. One of the electronic classrooms is shown in Figure 3.

Needs Assessment

After the goals and objectives have been established, specific needs must be determined. The needs assessment should include interviews with both faculty and students, as well as with others who may use the electronic classroom. Don't assume that faculty and students have the same needs, or that they will be concerned about the same things. Faculty are likely to tell you about the problems they have in sending the message; students concentrate on receiving the message. Faculty will explain how difficult it is to log onto the campus mainframe during a lecture; students will complain that they can't see the computer text from the fourth row! You have to address both concerns.

Don't assume that the faculty and students will be interested in discussing technology. In fact, they may be most interested in discussing problems that appear to be unrelated to your purpose or, at least, for which you have little or no direct responsibility. Whereas your goal may

Figure 3 *A medium-sized electronic classroom*

be to introduce advanced technology into the classroom, the faculty member's goal may be to let you know that the back door squeaks loudly, the presenters platform is too small, and the room is often left in disarray by the previous class. Similarly, the students will tell you that the seats are uncomfortable, the lights are too harsh, and the room is generally too hot or too cold.

The needs assessment will help you understand that technology is only one part of the solution. Understanding that the *total* learning environment must be considered and improved is one of the best lessons to learn, and it has shaped the IUPUI approach more than any other principle. To be effective, technology service providers must work closely with other support units, particularly physical plant personnel, campus architects, and administrative affairs staff, to coordinate priorities and funding to bring a total solution to the problem. Your ability to provide leadership in this arena will be directly related to your long-term success.

Achieving Perspectives

Encourage as much involvement from different groups as early as possible to achieve the proper perspectives. Just as faculty responses differ from those of students, there are differences among groups of faculty and among groups of students. One of the most obvious differences is in approaches taken in teaching (and learning) across disciplines. The Department of Mathematics *really does* want (and need) those three-panel chalk boards on vertical tracks that can be thrown overhead and out of the way as the instructor progressively reveals a complicated formula. Until the service provider understands that the math student is typically a page (chalkboard) behind the instructor in copying the necessary information, he or she may see little reason to include two or even three screens in an electronic classroom.

Understanding different perspectives and teaching styles will help you determine which technologies to include in developing the electronic classroom. In a large, general purpose auditorium a wide variety of options may need to be included, such as DOS, Macintosh, and UNIX workstations, because faculty from many disciplines use different tools. In a smaller, dedicated electronic classroom the technology options may be more formal, tailored specifically to the needs of a relatively homogeneous faculty. In any case, it's best to have a thorough understanding of the requirements before you begin. This will become painfully obvious the first time you realize that screen placement was based on legibility standards that assumed 80-column computer text and you now have an angry (and vocal) faculty member trying to use material developed using 132-column text.

Other important perspectives can be gained from administrative, physical plant, housekeeping, and security personnel. Don't underestimate the value of these perspectives. Representative groups that contribute to the overall support and maintenance of facilities will provide important information that will be perfectly obvious to them, but remote to your thinking. Each of these groups will appreciate being involved in the planning process and may come to your rescue when you find that some aspect under their responsibility was neglected or forgotten during the planning process.

Classroom Design Issues

Designing an electronic classroom can be divided into three major categories. The first category is *environmental design,* closely associated with the project architect. The second category, *technology design,* focuses on integration of audio, video, optical, and computer technologies into one workable system. The third category, *interface design,* deals with ergonomics and human-technology systems.

Environmental Design

The design of an electronic classroom should provide a comfortable learning environment and fully support diverse applications of technology. Each student should be able to easily see and hear the instructor and all media projections, as well as read text on the marker boards and projection screens. Several design elements deserve special consideration.

Comfort Factors. One mistake that could easily jeopardize the entire electronic classroom project is to install advanced technologies in a poorly designed, uncomfortable learning environment. Advanced technology will not remedy a problem caused by inadequate underlying classroom infrastructure, such as poor heating, cooling, or ventilation, unacceptable sight lines, or unattractive wall and floor coverings. As obvious as this point sounds, many developers overlook or underestimate the importance of the environment. This may be because funding for the technologies is often provided by a unit that does not have overall responsibility for the physical plant, and the priorities of the two units are often driven by different compulsions and restraints. As a general rule, establish a design team (discussed later in this chapter) and work closely with others who will need to coordinate their priorities to provide an overall solution to the electronic classroom project. Listen to what the faculty and students say about the environment during the needs assessment, then let the team do its work before deciding on the technologies.

Projection Screens. Projection screen selection and placement in an electronic classroom are difficult and critical aspects of the design. The screen decision should be based on the assumption that computer text will be projected and each student must be able to see the entire image (i.e., read every character) from any seat in the classroom. If the design permits, two projection screens are recommended. This provides support for two simultaneous media, such as computer and video, computer and film or slide, or local and remote displays during a video conference. The second screen also provides redundancy in case one projector fails and provides additional space for display text.

Writing Boards. A dry marker board is strongly recommended for the electronic classroom. Dry marker boards, as opposed to chalkboards, provide a dust free environment that reduces cleanup and may extend the life of the electronic technologies in the classroom. Although there are many high-technology solutions for writing, do not assume that an overhead camera or electronic writing surface will totally replace the traditional wall-mounted writing board. Remember that the writing board has it own unique advantages and remains the most popular medium for many classroom presentations. The design of the classroom should support the simultaneous use of writing board and projection images.

Lighting Systems. A full-range lighting system that can be dimmed by zones is necessary to support projections of video and computer images. The system should provide sufficient intensity in the presentation area to adequately illuminate the writing boards and the instructor, but light should not spill onto the projection screens. Remember that a lightly colored floor covering in the presentation area will reflect light onto the screens and wash out a projected image. A medium flat tile or carpet is a better choice. The lighting system in the seating area should provide enough intensity for each student to take notes and read without eye strain. Manual lighting controls should be placed in front of the classroom and at entry doors, but all lighting controls must be capable of automation through the human-technology interface system described in the next section.

Acoustics and Audio Systems. Depending on room size and acoustic properties, sound reinforcement may be required for the instructor. The system selected may be distributed, with loudspeakers placed throughout the classroom or auditorium ceiling, or it may be point source, with one or two speakers located behind the presentation area. There are advantages and disadvantages to each solution. An audio or acoustics specialist will be able to evaluate the specific situation and discuss the best solutions with the design team. In addition to sound reinforcement for the instructor, the presentation media, such as video, film, CD, and computer audio, will require a point source sound reproduction system, preferably with high-fidelity, properly rated stereophonic speakers on either side of (or behind) the projection screens.

Ergonomics. The classroom environment should be ergonomically designed for comfortable teaching and learning. The physical characteristics of chairs and tables should be carefully considered. The location and height of the lectern, the height of the keyboard drawer and the writing tablet should be carefully specified. The Information Technologies Laboratory at IUPUI designed and developed lecterns for use in electronic classrooms, such as the one shown in Figure 4. All designs incorporated a multisync video/computer monitor, automated keyboard drawer(s), and a touch-screen control panel. The newest version includes a document camera on an automated robotic arm.

ADA Compliance. The electronic classroom design should meet or exceed the requirements of the Americans with Disabilities Act. Most requirements are easily met during the design phase, but may be costly to retrofit later.

Technology Design

The design and integration of technology in an electronic classroom should provide a flexible, reliable, and powerful system for a variety of instructional applications. Faculty members can provide valuable information about their requirements. This information will translate into the specifications and design for the electronic classroom. Don't forget to talk with the students! Students can provide some of the best advice and will accurately describe technology problems (and solutions) related to the room being considered for renovation. After considering end-user input, try to design the classroom technology with the following features and characteristics in mind.

Multimedia. The system design should support simultaneous (side-by-side or windowed) displays of computer, video, and traditional optical

Figure 4 *A functional lectern with monitor, camera, and control panel*

images, as well as sequential displays. That is, the design should accommodate several media used at the same time or following each other so the instructor can choreograph the presentation in various ways to most effectively reinforce major points.

User-operated. The instructor should be able to operate the technology without assistance from a technician. The human-technology interface must be extremely easy to use, with simple menus displaying few options and programmed with carefully considered default settings.

Expandability. The design of the system should easily support technology expansion. Adding a second computer or a second video source should not require the replacement of the video switch or other supporting elements.

Reliability. The design should be highly reliable. Weak, unpredictable, or untested components which may eventually fail should be identified as part of the system analysis and eliminated from consideration during the design phase. Base hardware selections on campus experiences with certain brands of technology rather than on vendor recommendations. If in doubt, call colleagues at other institutions who will most surely offer advice. Learn from the experience of others.

Upgradability. The design should permit easy replacement of hardware and software to improve the system. For instance, replacing a computer with one of a higher video resolution or one of another platform should not require the replacement of the video projector, video switch, or related supporting elements.

Multiplatform. The design should not be based on or dependent on a single computer platform. Unless the campus has standardized on a single platform, make certain the technology design will accommodate easy integration of Intel-based, Macintosh, and UNIX computers. Make sure the design will accommodate many video output devices and can control traditional classroom technologies, such as 16mm film and slide projectors.

Maintenance. The design of the technology system should support effective and efficient maintenance. Off-the-shelf devices and components from reliable sources should be used to help ensure easy replacement of parts. Try not to modify equipment around your system design since that will make equipment more difficult to repair or replace. Make sure the vendor furnishes complete detailed drawings of the system and labels all the wiring and connectors. If possible, make sure your campus electronic maintenance department can make repairs to the equipment you specify. If not, make sure the vendor can quickly respond to your maintenance call. Check your vendors' records for support by talking with references.

Security. Security is a major concern in some institutions. An electronic classroom is a showcase for expensive equipment which may attract thieves. It is advisable to physically and electronically secure equipment.

Interface Issues

Good design of interfaces is critical for any successful electronic classroom project. A poor interface design will result in frustration and anxiety which discourages the use of technology. Interface issues are addressed from two perspectives, Human-Technology Interface Issues and Technology-Technology Interface Issues.

Human-Technology Interface Issues

Using technologies in an electronic classroom requires interaction and operation of many technologies. In a complex system, even a seemingly simple task such as showing a videotape or a computer image will require control of several types of equipment, each with tens of switches and knobs. A Human-Technology Interface (HTI) system is used to automate and simplify operation of technologies in an electronic classroom. The HTI system is a medium through which the instructor exercises control over a variety of multimedia equipment. Depending on the technologies installed, the HTI system could be as simple as an AB switch or as sophisticated as a computerized touch-screen control panel located on the instructor's lectern.

The technology architect of an electronic classroom should assume that instructors do not have experience in operating electronic equipment. Indeed, many are not familiar with audio mixers, video switchers, video projectors, laser disk players, or emerging technologies. Therefore, the HTI system should be designed to automate and simplify operation as

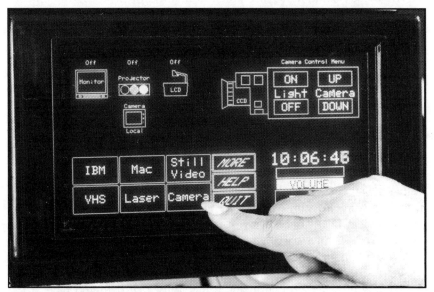

Figure 5   The Technology Access Governor (TAG) system

much as possible.

In evaluating the HTI, assume that faculty members have only a few minutes to learn to operate the technologies. Operation may be simplified by providing automated default values for all equipment settings. For instance, touching the play button on the HTI touch screen should automatically turn on the VCR, sound system and video projector while dimming the classroom lights and switching the video projection to the VCR input. All this should be done instantly and in the background.

The Information Technologies Laboratory at IUPUI, which specialized in the engineering and design of several HTI systems, developed the Technology Access Governor or Touch and Go (TAG) system shown in Figure 5. Several versions of the TAG systems have been developed for various types of electronic classrooms and portable technology systems. The most recent development of TAG, the TAG+ system, provides fully automated control capability of multimedia classroom technologies through the use of a flat touch screen, or a windowed menu on a Macintosh or DOS workstation.

Expert Help System

Assume that there will always be a chance of technology failure or other complication in the electronic classroom. Even with easy-to-use human-interface systems, there is the chance of user error. Once there is a problem, the instructor should be able to get help from a technology expert or consultant quickly and conveniently.

The most cost-effective and practical method of providing emergency help in the classroom is through a telephone. A telephone installed in the classroom should be programmed to dial the appropriate expert. This simple solution works well during regular staff hours. However, it does not work when the consultant is on vacation, on break, or is using the phone. An expert help system is necessary in these situations to create a reliable communication link between the instructor and the best available consultant.

An example of an expert system is the On-Line Expert Help designed and developed at IUPUI. This is a computer hardware and software system which adds features to TAG. A computer circuit board plugs into TAG and interfaces with a telephone line or a cellular phone system. It is equipped with a digital voice module and telephone encoding and decoding circuits. Database software stores telephone numbers of several individuals. The expert system keeps track of work schedules, phone/pager numbers, and the level of consultant expertise. The system is fully automated and user friendly. When an instructor experiences difficulty, he or she touches "call for help" on the touch screen panel. The online help system automatically dials the most expert consultant available for that date and time. If the consultant does not respond, the system automatically dials and uses a speech synthesis module to ask for the next best available consultant, all in the background. Once the consultant is found, TAG sounds an attention signal and advises the instructor to pick up the phone to speak to the consultant. This system is especially useful during evening and weekend classes when there may not be many consultants on duty.

Technology-Technology Interface Issues

Recent developments in microelectronics have resulted in productions of smaller and less expensive computers and multimedia technologies. Powerful portable technologies are often as small as textbooks. Faculty members may carry these portable technologies, including notebook computers and small Compact Disc-Interactive (CD-I) players, along with textbooks and paper materials into classrooms to support their teaching. By connecting a notebook computer to a video projector or an LCD panel, students can benefit from multimedia interactive presentations developed by the instructor.

Miniaturization is complemented by rapid development in LCD, video projector, and related technologies. The continued improvement in display technology, with overall reduction in price, will provide opportunities for campuses to equip more classrooms with permanent video installations. The availability of video projection systems in classrooms will encourage more faculty to use electronic media.

Interfacing portable technology (i.e. notebook computer, CD-I) to per-

Figure 6 *The Multimedia Communication Outlet (MCO)*

manently installed technologies (such as video projector and networks) is not always easy. Unfortunately, some proprietary equipment is designed without regard to a compatible interface or protocol. Interfacing a video projector with Macintosh computer is different from interfacing DOS, UNIX, NTSC, SVHS, and other equipment, for example. The electronic classroom should be designed to accommodate various computer platforms and video sources that will likely be connected to the video projectors, sound system and networks.

The best method of solving these technology-to-technology issues is through the use of a "universal" interface system. The Information Technology Laboratory developed such a device, the Multimedia Communication Outlet (MCO), shown in Figure 6. This interface system supports connection of all video sources and computer platforms to projection equipment, sound systems, and networks. The MCO concept provides a "smart" connector that also automatically switches many devices easily and reliably. By placing the MCO outlet in several electronic classrooms on campus, faculty members will be able to move freely with portable technology from one MCO equipped facility to another.

Classroom Design Model

Classroom renovation projects are often designed and supervised by campus or consulting architects who provide leadership for the overall effort and bring essential expertise to the project. Architects will probably not be very knowledgeable about advanced classroom technologies, however, unless they have specialized in this area. Their reputation will preceed them if that is the case. Otherwise, assume that they will use standard classroom or auditorium guidelines that are inadequate for an advanced technology facility. Recent changes in technology require careful re-evaluation of architectural guidelines. Start by examining the solution the architect proposes to meet your specifications for supporting projected images from 80-column or 132-column computer text, for example. Make sure that the architect will guarantee that the design will meet performance expectations. Define performance expectations precisely.

Design of an electronic classroom should proceed on a reciprocal basis, with interaction among technology experts and full participation from representative members of the faculty. Figure 7 illustrates an alternative to traditional architect-centered models. It emphasizes a dynamic reciprocal relationship between the technology users (instructors), the architects, and the media or technology service providers or consultants.

In the electronic classroom design model, faculty members provide information concerning their teaching styles and use of technology in the classroom. When combined with input from students, such information provides the foundation for architectural design, ergonomic design, and user interface design. In this approach the media technologist consultant team plays a major role. It advises the architect concerning requirements and specifications, and will determine the technology to be incorporated in the design. The team will evaluate the advantages and limitations of technologies and architectural solutions according to requirements established by the needs assessment.

Technologists and consultants will be familiar with some types of technology and less familiar with others. Consequently, biases may cause under-specification or over-specification of certain technologies used in the classroom. For example, a consultant in acoustic and audio engineering may over-emphasize the use of audio systems and room acoustic treatment while ignoring or under-estimating the importance of computer equipment and video projection quality. Another consultant may have a video production background and promote the use of expensive broadcast quality equipment which may not be needed in electronic classroom applications or which may be too complicated to operate. These biases can creep into campus technology units as well as outside consulting firms. Be sure to assemble a well-balanced technology team.

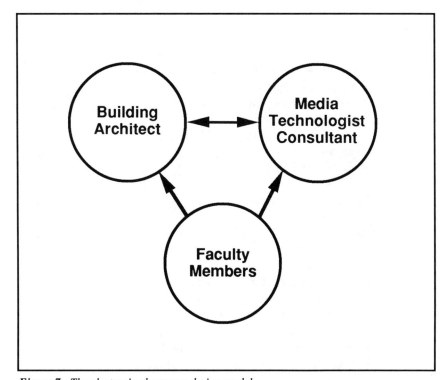

Figure 7   *The electronic classroom design model*

Conclusion

This chapter has considered some of the design and construction issues inherent in implementing the vision for electronic classrooms. It has focused on the presentational environment and has described some of the advantages and limitations of permanent installations of technology, portable technologies, and electronic distribution of multimedia. The planning process is most important, and must precede environmental design, technological design, and interface design. Several suggestions have been offered in each area.

The case studies that are described in the remaining chapters of this book represent the wide range of experience individuals have in using electronic classrooms. Each scenario will help illustrate the potential of advanced learning technology and will hopefully encourage some faculty to try methods used successfully by others. In anticipation that you will soon be involved or are already involved in implementing the vision for an electronic classroom on your campus, we conclude by summarizing some "do's" and "don'ts" that have evolved from experience at Indiana University Purdue University Indianapolis:

Do. . .

- Study the campus academic plan and list the specific goals and objectives of the schools and departments.
- Develop a strategic technology plan to respond to the academic agenda and clearly articulate the role of advanced learning technologies.
- Consult with faculty members and determine their technological needs.
- Listen to what students have to say about the learning environment.
- Visit other institutions and learn from their good and bad experiences.
- Draw the big picture before beginning the design.
- Assemble a well-balanced team to develop the conceptual and system design.
- Design technology for immediate use but make sure it can be upgraded to support emerging technologies.
- Concentrate on the functionality and usability of technology, rather than on commercial hype.
- Make sure that an experienced technologist reviews and approves the entire design and all drawings before they go out for bid.

- Train local technical staff to repair and troubleshoot technology.
- Require a complete design drawing and schematics from the architect or vendor for future maintenance and upgrades.
- Develop faculty support to go hand in hand with infrastructure development.

Don't. . .

- Let a technology vendor or salesperson design or influence the design of the classroom.
- Introduce advanced technology into a poor learning environment.
- Eliminate the marker board (chalkboard) from the electronic classroom.
- Forget that technology is constantly changing and improving.
- Order equipment prematurely.

References

Elmore, Garland C., "Campus-Wide Technology Planning to Support the Academic Agenda." Association for Educational Communications and Technology, Washington, D.C., 1992.

Elmore, Garland C., "Facility Design as a Component in Academic and Technology Planning." Computer Services Management Symposium, Association for Computing Machinery, St. Louis, MO, March 1992.

Elmore, Garland C., "Integrated Technologies: An Approach to Establishing Multimedia Applications for Learning." *EDUCOM Review,* January-February 1992, pp. 20-26.

Elmore, Garland C., "Planning and Developing a Multimedia Learning Environment." *T.H.E. Journal,* February 1991. pp. 20-26.

Jafari, Ali, "Designing and Engineering a Teacher-Friendly High-Tech Classroom." *Ohio Media Spectrum,* Vol. 42, No. 4, 1990, pp. 22-26.

Jafari, Ali, "Issues in Multimedia." *Technology and Teacher Education Annual,* March, 1992, pp. 289-294.

Jafari, Ali, "Putting Together a Multimedia Electronic Classroom. Society for Technology and Teacher Education STATE." March 1993.

"MIPSit Multimedia Instructional Portable System Fact Sheet." Office of Integrated Technologies, Indiana University Purdue University Indianapolis, February 6, 1991.

"Multimedia Communication Outlet for Today's Classrooms Fact Sheet." Office of Integrated Technologies, Indiana University Purdue University Indianapolis, Spring 1993.

"Multimedia Project Fact Sheet." Office of Integrated Technologies, Indiana University Purdue University Indianapolis, Spring 1990.

"TAG2, A Research and Development Project at the Learning Technologies Laboratory Fact Sheet." Office of Integrated Technologies, Indiana University Purdue University Indianapolis, 1990.

Classroom Applications

Prototyping the Electronic Library: Using the Perseus Database to Teach Greek Culture

Gregory Crane

Gregory Crane is project director and editor in chief of The Perseus Project at Harvard University

*P*erseus 2.0: *Interactive Sources and Studies on Ancient Greek Culture* is a large, heterogeneous database on ancient Greek culture. It includes 30,000 color images of art objects and archaeological sites, 40 megabytes of Greek texts in English translation with accompanying Greek original (two-thirds of all literary texts that survive from 800-300 BCE), an atlas with more than 2,000 maps of the Greek world, a 35,000-word Greek-English lexicon, a growing set of essays and many other tools. Planning started in mid-1985 and, with major support from the Annenberg/CPB Project, we began work on the database itself in 1987. A collaborative project involving many institutions, Perseus had its headquarters at Harvard University until the fall of 1993, when it moved to nearby Tufts University.

While Perseus is in many ways complex—it is not so much a single database as a network of individual databases—our initial goals were fairly straightforward. Classicists had already in the late 1970s begun to work with a massive database of Greek texts, the Thesaurus Linguae Graecae (TLG), which has now grown to more than 400 megabytes of text available on CD-ROM.[1] Intrigued by what we could do with one category of material—the core Greek texts—we wondered what would happen if students of Greek culture had at their disposal not just texts, but all major source materials for ancient Greek culture. Where the TLG collected all Greek

53

texts over more than 1,000 years, we limited our scope to 800-300 BCE, a period that not only is the most often studied but (conveniently from a logistical perspective) that also embraces a relatively small portion of surviving Greek materials. It was possible for us to create a database that could not only grow with time but that was already from the start fairly comprehensive.

Making the Information Available

In the humanities and the social sciences alike, access to massive amounts of information—whether in electronic form or stored as books and journal articles—is often critical. In developing and testing our hypotheses, we need access to work through a large amount of data, searching for patterns, sorting through piles of irrelevant information in search of those items relevant to our topic. The practice is not all that different from that of researchers in many other fields. It seemed clear to us that mechanical logistical barriers set artificial limits on the questions that we could ask and that, in this regard, the professor at a major research university faced the same general problems as the undergraduates in their introductory courses—and even the curious students in K-12 who found the subject interesting and wished to explore it. Beginners and the most advanced researchers both adjust their work so that they pursue those questions which the tools at their disposal—their library, perhaps specialized archival collections or museum holdings—facilitate. All of us, whether consciously or not, balance our interests against what is feasible. We found that researchers who most successfully transcended traditional intellectual boundaries—e.g., literary critics who wished to place literature in the context of art and archaeology, historians who sought through anthropological theory and ethnographic studies to gain new insights into classical Greece, philosophers trying to grasp 2,000 years of intellectual development attempting to master enough Greek to confront Plato and Aristotle in their own language—were often acutely sensitive to the mechanical problems of access that set limits on their work.

For students, on the other hand, access was often an insurmountable problem. Where experts could effortlessly put their hands on concordances, indices, bibliographies, major essays and other tools, students rely primarily on the books which they buy, the handouts they receive, and the notes that they take. Undergraduates researching "women in Homer" normally concentrate on those passages in the text which they can remember—often the most striking and thus least typical pieces of evidence. By contrast, no scholars would depend solely upon their memory for such a task, but would turn to whatever pre-existing tools they had. A classicist might, for example, get started not only by reading secondary sources but also by using a concordance to skim through the 263 passages in which forms of the standard Greek word for "woman" appear. We wanted to create a database which would allow students regular access to tools similar in kind to those of their professors and which would allow students to pursue more ambitious and intellectually rigorous topics than had previously been practical.

In talking with other teachers of classics and of similar disciplines (professors of Shakespeare, archaeologists specializing in Mesopotamia, historians of China), a number of negative reactions are common.

First, many experts are actually afraid that, if students have access to more powerful tools and can ask more penetrating questions, instructors will lose their authority. In fact, we have found that as students can put their hands on more information and their research projects become more challenging, their respect for and interest in the expertise of their instructors increases. Students who can put their hands on 263 passages in Homer that discuss women virtually never think that they know everything, but grow much more sensitive to the limits of their actual knowledge. Instructors need to spend time encouraging students to pursue their own

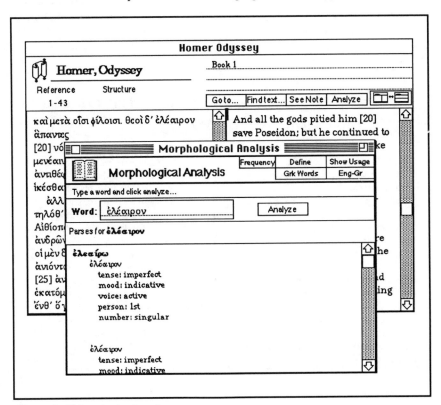

Figure 1   Using the Analyze feature

ideas, to develop their own hypotheses, and to take intellectual risks. The goal is not to produce a "perfect" research paper, but to create a thoughtful synthesis that carefully exploits its evidence while remaining sensitive to factors that it has not yet encountered.

Similarly, new technology—videodisks and especially high-quality digital images—have forced us to rethink our standards for various categories of evidence. The representation of art and archaeology has undergone striking changes in the past several years. A printed book (like the convenient and affordable *World Art Library* series published by Thames and Hudson) might have 500 images, but these will largely be small, black-and-white pictures. A standard videodisk, by contrast, can store 54,000 videoframes while a single CD-ROM can store 10,000 "screen-sized" images that are superior in quality and resolution to any videoscreen and equivalent to full-page pictures in affordable print publications. The production costs of videodisk and CD-ROM vary but are, if anything, cheaper than a printed book (the CD-ROM itself usually costs less than the plastic jewel case and two page paper liner that accompanies it). The simple quantitative jump changes the way in which students can interact with published representations of art. Hundreds of thousands of painted Greek vases survive from antiquity and these include often detailed pictures of mythology or daily life. Where a standard print book might include four or five gen-

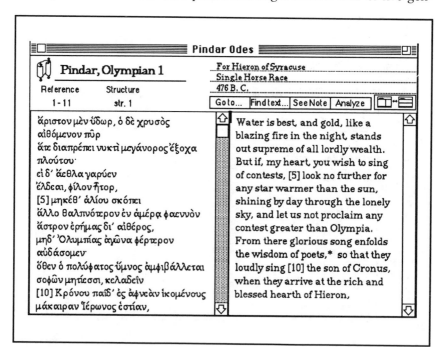

Figure 2 Primary text display

eral views of a Greek vase, we were able to include an average of 20 views per object. In the case of complex vases with many scenes and figures, we could include more than 100 views and details—a level of coverage heretofore possible only in very expensive and narrowly distributed scholarly monographs. Now, students can examine these art works at a new level of detail, and the questions which they can now pose can be correspondingly more demanding.

The digital coverage can, however, be so good that some museum curators expressed concern that no one would want to see the objects themselves. Just as some instructors feared that the ability to get more information would diminish student respect for genuine expertise, some curators feared that very high-quality representations might distract from the objects.

In fact, we found that the better the visual documentation, the more interested students became in seeing the original objects. We mounted a teaching exhibition at the Harvard Art Museums in the spring of 1992 (Crane 1991b, 1992). Our students had access to digital images of the objects both in central computer labs and in the gallery itself. We found that the students used the database to familiarize themselves with objects, to identify interesting features, and to see how our particular objects relat-

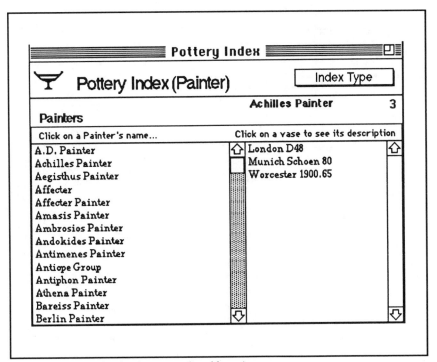

Figure 3 Detailed index for pottery listed by painter

ed to Greek vases as a whole. The more such knowledge they acquired, the more interesting and vital they generally found the art objects themselves to be. The database educated the students so that they knew ahead of time what to look for and developed a new set of questions that they could only get from direct access to the objects—the ability to move around them, to see figures at their true scale, to watch the play of light across the surface of the vase.

Second, many teachers have seen the Perseus database in presentations and private visits to various Perseus development sites around the country. The idea of instantaneous access to information may seem to make study too easy. Students do not have to work as hard to gather as much material. The database "dumbs down" the work.

Most instructors rapidly discard this initial attitude. While Perseus is a flexible tool—closer to a small library than a specific curriculum—and can be used in many different ways, Perseus does not so much make hard problems easy as render impossible tasks feasible. With more information at their fingertips, students can spend more time analyzing and thinking about their tasks. Rather than writing the conventional research paper from a fairly limited set of secondary and primary materials, students can work much more extensively with primary materials, posing hypotheses,

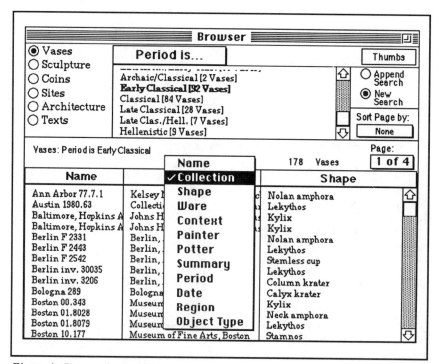

Figure 4 *Browser for art objects*

checking them against the evidence, revising their ideas, and checking more evidence.

The Power to Learn

Not all students, however, respond immediately to such open-ended and independent research tasks. A number of instructors have used Perseus to develop basic skills and knowledge. "Paths," guided tours through the database, can familiarize students with its contents, draw attention to key aspects of vase painting, the composition of Greek epic, or the formal structure of panhellenic Greek sanctuaries. Straightforward exercises can direct students' attention to particular details and can train them in the practice of careful note-taking and observation. The development of basic skills can lead into progressively more sophisticated work and can gradually make it possible for more students to exploit skills and to develop interests which they otherwise might not have suspected that they possessed.

Teaching with a large, heterogeneous database such as Perseus is extremely challenging. Many instructors begin by looking at the database as a kind of interactive work book, an adjunct tool designed to reinforce the traditional course. While Perseus can, in fact, be used in this fashion, the database, with its wealth of material and its space, invites decentralized teaching. Even if all the students work on the same topic (e.g., "what constitutes wealth in the archaic Greek period and what does this tell us about Greek society?"), the database is usually large enough to support many different approaches: some students will concentrate more on art and archaeological materials; others may focus on the historian Herodotus, while still others will concentrate on the poet Pindar or the tragic playwright Aeschylus. In such a class, lectures become less an end in themselves and more than a means to facilitate the learning which students do on their own. Professors do not simply give students information; they brief them in the background and in the skills that they will need to do work on their own. In a productive model, instructors spend the first month of class providing an overview of the course and then examine the students on their proficiency in this material. During the rest of the semester, the students drive the course. Topics may be provided, but only as a starting point. The professor becomes a facilitator who helps the students pursue their own work and interact more effectively with one another. In the end, the final examination may be based on materials which the students themselves uncovered and discussed, or the instructor may have no final exam at all and assign a term project instead. In courses with 15 or 20 students, this format works very well, but even in larger classes, it is possible to break students up into smaller groups and then to have these groups lead general class discussion. In the second part of the course, the students might meet once for a lecture, once in small groups to discuss what they found in the database, and once more as an entire class.

Addressing the Mechanical Issues

For all the promise of these new databases, simple mechanical issues remain. The database may lower logistical barriers, but students (and faculty) need access to functional computers in preparations, in discussion sections, and in lectures. We were able to design a version of Perseus that runs on an entry-level Macintosh with CD ROM. We used Apple's HyperCard software as a publication medium because it provided reasonable performance at a low cost. We concentrated on the Macintosh platform because it alone could, when we were developing Perseus, support this database. Newer versions of Windows and software such as ToolBook would make the PC a suitable platform for Perseus or Perseus-like databases. Perseus 1.0 is currently available from Yale University Press for $150. An entire new Macintosh computer system that can run Perseus costs, in early fall 1993, less than $2,000. By the standards with which we began work in 1987, these are very good prices. (We had hoped to put Perseus out on a machine that cost less than $3,000, and have thus exceeded this goal.)

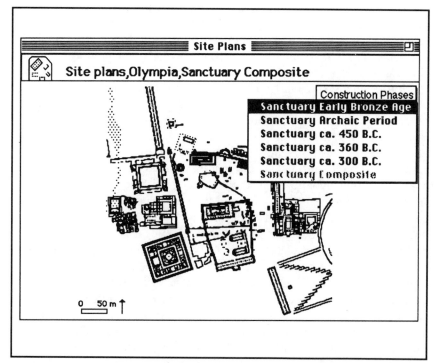

Figure 5   *Composite site plan for sanctuary in Olympia*

Nevertheless, $2,000 is still a substantial sum. Even $150 is more than individual students can realistically pay. If students need to walk 10 minutes each way, perhaps wait for a machine, and then wrestle with the vagaries of a noisy, general computing lab (where file servers get turned off, system software changes mysteriously and other unpredictable things happen), it only makes sense to use the database when they plan to spend an hour or so. In the long run, databases such as Perseus will only have their full effect when students can own their own copies and can work with them casually on their personal machines. During a two- or three-hour study session, a student should turn to the database half a dozen times for queries that last between 30 seconds and 30 minutes (just as their instructors will pull individual books off the shelf while working). Prices should continue to go down and the numbers of students who can afford such a tool will increase, but this process takes time. In the meantime, even allowing a class of 30 students to use the database may not be feasible at many sites, where the database runs on only one or two machines. The images in Perseus can be used in lecture and these images (unlike slides) can be made available to students who have access to the database (without worrying about fingerprints or dirt getting on slides). But displaying a clear computer image still requires at least $5,000 in extra hardware and, ideally, $10,000 for very good image quality.

Nevertheless, the rewards for using a database such as Perseus (or developing a similar tool for some other discipline) are great. We have found that we can dramatically change the practice of teaching and learning, allow students to pursue their own interests at their own pace, and even demonstrate that a very traditional discipline can integrate modern research tools and techniques into their courses. Students who write papers with Perseus are much better prepared for the kinds of research that they will do in subsequent work than if they work with traditional printed publications alone. We are still at an early stage of development and have only just begun to understand how best to use Perseus and tools like it, but the preliminary results are exciting, the intellectual challenges fascinating, and the long-term prospects open-ended.

Notes

1.The TLG distributes its own CD-ROM and those interested in acquiring a copy should write to Professor Theodore Brunner at the Department of Classics, University of California, Irvine. On the impact which this database has had, see Raymond (1989), and Watkins (1991).

References

Crane, Gregory, 1988. "Redefining the Book: Some Preliminary Problems." *Academic Computing* 2:5, Feb.

Crane, Gregory and Elli Mylonas, 1990. "Ancient Materials, Modern Media: Shaping the Study of Classics with Hypermedia." In George Landow and Paul Delaney (eds.), *Hypermedia and Literary Studies*. MIT Press.

Crane, Gregory, 1991a. "Composing Culture: The Authority of an Electronic Text." *Current Anthropology* 32, June 1991, pp. 293-311.

Crane, Gregory, 1991b. "Hypermedia and the Study of Ancient Culture." *IEEE: Computer Graphics and Application* 11, pp. 45-51.

Crane, Gregory, 1991c. "Aristotle's Library: Memex as Vision and Hypertext as Reality." In James Nyce and Paul Kahn (eds.), *From Memorex to Hypertext: Vannevar Bush and the Mind's Machine*, pp. 339-352. Academic Press.

Crane, Gregory, 1992. "Making New Connections: Greek Art, the Perseus Project, and the Museums as Classroom." *Harvard University Art Museums Review* I (2), Summer 1992, pp. 1-3.

Edmunds, Lowell 1993, "Computers and Classics: The Third Phase." Forthcoming in *Arion*.

Marchionini, Gary, 1992a. "Evaluating Hypermedia-Based Learning." In D. Jonassen and H. Mandl (eds.), *Designing Hypermedia for Learning*. Berlin: Springer-Verlag, pp. 353-373.

Marchionini, Gary, 1992b. "Self-Directed Learning through Hypermedia: Assessing the Process." In P. Carlson (ed.), *Tools that Teach: Hypertext and the New Technologies of Knowledge*. MIT Press, in review.

Marchionini, Gary and Gregory Crane, 1992. "Evaluating Complex Systems and Processes: Methods and Results from the Perseus Project." *ACM Transactions on Information Systems* 12 (1994) 5-34.

Mylonas, Elli, "Universes to Control: Classics, Computers and Education." In [Phyllis Culham and Lowell Edmunds], *Classics: A Profession in Crisis*. University Press of America, 1990.

Mylonas, Elli. 1992. "An Interface to Classical Greek Civilization." *JASIS* 43:2, March, 1992.

Raymond, Chris 1989. "Humanities researchers experience a 'sea change' in the use of computers in their disciplines." *Chronicle of Higher Education* 35, no. 44, A6.

Watkins, Beverly 1991. "A database of Ancient Greek literature revolutionizes research in the classics." *Chronicle of Higher Education* 38, no. 4, A24.

Biology: A Field Trip to a Rocky Intertidal Zone

Raymond Russo

*Raymond Russo is Professor of Biology
at Indiana University
Purdue University Indianapolis*

Computer simulations have become quite common in the sciences. They allow students to study phenomena difficult or impossible to view in reality. However, most of these simulations have a severely limited user interface. It is often only possible to interact with the computer by entering numbers or words into a simulation and receiving graphs or tables as output. These restrictions have limited the reality of the simulation and reduced the opportunity for the student to learn methods of experimental design and data analysis. One of the first simulations for personal computers to step into virtual reality was Flight Simulator. With the development of computer-controlled devices, such as videodisc, CD-ROM, head-mounted video goggles, and the data glove, other modalities have become available to developers to create a more realistic user interface. But these advances are of little consequence if they are not merged with pedagogical goals teaching higher cognitive skills (Crow, 1989).

In the 1960s and '70s, a series of seminal investigations was published explaining the interactions among predators and prey that determine community structure. Connell compared the intertidal zones of the Pacific Northwest with those of Scotland (1961a, 1961b, 1970). His conclusions were that while competition for space limited the distribution of barnacles in Scotland, predation by certain species of snails played a far greater role in limiting their distribution in the Pacific Northwest. Dayton (1971) extended Connell's study along an exposure/desiccation gradient from the protected shorelines within Puget Sound, through the Strait of Juan de Fuca, to the outer Washington coast. Dayton's study documented the importance of disturbance by abiotic factors on the underlying process of competition for space. Finally, Paine (1969) elaborated on the interaction among predators and their effects upon community structure. These publications form the basis of the following computer simulation.

Multimedia Simulation of the Intertidal Zone

This chapter describes the current state of development of a multimedia simulation about the rocky intertidal zone of the Pacific Northwest. The simulation is designed to allow students to accomplish two primary goals: first, to visit a site which is exotic and unlikely to have been visited before, and second, to teach students how to design and analyze experiments through successive trials making incremental improvements in each resolution. The simulation allows investigations on organisms living within the intertidal zone at Friday Harbor Labs, the marine laboratory for the University of Washington. Very few undergraduates have had the opportunity to study at a field station, and most are attracted to the beauty and uniqueness of the Pacific Northwest. Among the cognitive skills promoted by the simulation are experimental design and data analysis. However, experimental design disconnected from the biological phenomena is uninteresting. The simulation teaches proper experimental design by beginning with simple experiments, moving the student toward experiments which manipulate several independent variables simultaneously with the appropriate number of replicates and multiple controls.

There are several ways the instructor may use this simulation. By following the Scenario, students are exposed to the complete set of problems and experiments. They receive a grant from a research foundation and must navigate first to Seattle and then to the marine labs located on the San Juan Islands in Puget Sound. Along the way, there are many opportunities to explore the area around Seattle and the San Juan Archipelago. Eventually, the student arrives at Friday Harbor Laboratories where an explicit map of the grounds of Friday Harbor Labs allows entry into any building by clicking on the proper spot. The instruction in experimental design begins with a simple request by the director of the laboratory to identify the organisms living in each band of the intertidal region, the zone between the high and low tide marks. The simulation builds through a series of problems of increasing difficulty and culminates by conducting experiments on the factors affecting the distribution of the important species in the intertidal zone.

The instructor may limit the assignment to a single experiment appropriate to the student's level. In this case, the student uses only a part of the simulation and avoids much of the general information provided in the other approach. A student could complete a single experiment in one or two 45-minute sessions.

Features of the Simulation

To increase the information content and reality of the simulation, we have developed a series of features giving students control over content and rate of exploration.

The first feature is a series of **information-rich maps** (Figure 1) used by the student to navigate to a specific location and explore the area. We created a set of maps which increase in scale, allowing students to explore the Puget Sound area, the San Juan Islands, the village of Friday Harbor, and the Friday Harbor Laboratories grounds. The student explores these areas by rolling the mouse over the map. As the browse tool (the hand with pointed finger) passes over each attraction, a short description appears in a text box in the corner of the screen.

Locations marked by an arrowhead or diamond enclosed in a white circle activate a view from that point. The arrowhead denotes a single still image looking in the direction the arrow is pointing. A diamond enclosed in a white circle denotes a **navigable scene**. By clicking on the white circle, a navigable scene is shown in a window superimposed upon the map. Above the picture is a set of controls that allow the viewer to pan left or right. Most navigable scenes allow the student to pan a full 360 degrees, just as if they would turn around to view their complete surroundings. When the student has looked around, the window is closed, returning the

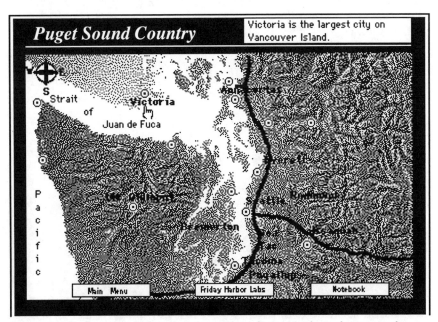

Figure 1   *The Puget Sound Country information-rich map. As the student moves the browse tool (pointing finger) over the map, descriptions of each locality in the info box*

student to the map to explore other locations. With a click the student may explore the next map. There are some 20 navigable scenes on each map. A hierarchy of three maps allows the student to gradually converge on the Friday Harbor Marine Laboratories.

A third feature of the rocky intertidal zone simulation allows the student to actively become involved in doing the experiments. From the collection of organisms to the collection of data via complicated experiments, the student continually interacts with the computer. We have paid particular attention to the design of the user interface for these activities. The student works with familiar tools. As a student undertakes a task, the object under study is visible. As the task progresses, the student uses the mouse to guide the pointer that has been changed to look like the real-world tool that would accomplish the task. For example, after arriving at Friday Harbor Laboratories the student is given the assignment of collecting as many different organisms as can be found in the intertidal zone at Cattle Point. The low tide will occur at 10:14 a.m. Cattle Point is the southernmost point on San Juan Island. The collection task opens with a panoramic view of Cattle Point extending from high tide to the lowest tide level (Figure 2).

The pointer is an open hand which "grasps" when the mouse button is depressed. If an organism exists at the location of the grasping hand, the pointer changes into a miniature image of the organism. The student drags the organism to the collecting bucket and releases the button allowing the organism to drop into the bucket. Different organisms are collected from different zones.

Figure 2   *Cattle Point Collection Site. Students collect organisms by placing the open hand where they want to collect, then dragging and dropping the organism into the bucket*

After collecting several organisms, the student returns to the laboratory where collected specimens are kept alive in salt water aquariums. In the laboratory the student finds tools such as an observation aquarium, a dissection microscope, refrigerators, and an equipment storage room which are available by simply dragging the organism to the tool. For example, an organism may be viewed in an observation aquarium by dragging it from the holding aquarium to the observation aquarium. For close inspection of any organism, the specimen is dragged from the holding aquarium to the dissecting microscope. The organism may be manipulated under the scope by rolling it in any direction giving a view of another side of the organism. The storage room contains a variety of equipment which may be used to exclude predators or competitors from the substrate in experiments in the field. Thus the student has a virtual marine in which laboratory to interact with the simulated environment.

The identification of the organisms can be accomplished in a variety of ways. The student may go to a library and check out an identification key or picture book about fauna of the San Juan Archipelago. The library contains three full hypermedia texts with color pictures, explanations of intertidal organisms, and descriptions of their ecology. The library also has a reserve shelf with a set of 10 original articles by authors who conducted experiments in the rocky intertidal zone. If a student prefers verbal interaction with established investigators to identify the organisms, 15 senior scientists are available to help the student identify and learn about the organisms collected.

Experimentation

The primary pedagogical purpose of the simulation is to teach experimental design, which we do by means of three typical studies. The simplest of these is descriptive in nature, allowing the investigator to determine the type of organisms living in the habitat. The students are given several ways to identify the organisms. They are encouraged to use morphological characteristics in their task and use either an identification key or a synopsis of intertidal invertebrates from the library. They may also request the help of investigators at the laboratories. The summarizing activity for this problem asks the student to correctly classify 16-20 organisms found in the intertidal zone.

The second study describes the pattern of distribution of the organisms of interest and determines their density. This is begun by pointing out that there seems to be distinct bands within the intertidal zone. This becomes obvious from the general coloration of the intertidal zone. The bands are parallel to the water line and are created by the organisms living within each zone. The student identifies the composition of each zone by more careful collection of organisms using rectangular plots. Four transects are available to sample, each of which is composed of 8 to 18 one-square-meter, high-resolution photographs. The density of each species within each band can be determined by counting the organisms appearing in a high-resolution photograph of the plot. Note that the student must "do" the actual work of counting. The act of counting organisms is more than just counting, since counting involves repeatedly identifying each organism. Because we supply the data in picture form, the student must perform the same activity an investigator would have to. This analogy between reality and simulation increases data collection and analysis skills. The summarizing activity is a report on the density and range within the intertidal zone of four dominant sessile organisms. In order to reduce the work, the students may collaborate with other individuals and report information for other species.

The third study manipulates one or more factors suspected of limiting the distribution of one of the dominant organisms. The question is posed: "What factor(s) limits the upper and lower boundary for a particular species?" The student must now design an experiment to provide an answer (Figure 3). The design of experiments is not a trivial task since it includes the synthesis of habitat-specific information drawn from previous knowledge of biology, thus leading to the suspected cause of phenomenon. Our intention is to help the student recognize the most likely factors which limit the distribution of organisms. Some of the factors the student investigates may have little or no effect upon the distribution of most species, but will be important to one species or guild.

These experiments usually begin with the investigator creating or modifying a substrate to create one combination of the independent variable(s) of the experiment. For example, if the student wanted to determine the density of *Balanus glandula,* an acorn barnacle, at mean tidal level in the absence of *Balanus cariosis,* he/she would select a plot of substrate at some tidal level and remove all of the *Balanus cariosis,* leaving only *Balanua glandula.* The student creates this experimental treatment by using a chisel tool to remove *B. cariosis.* The student also must create other treatment combinations of the independent variable(s) which form the experiment, including a control treatment. In this case the control is to leave both species of barnacles on the rock. When the initial treatments are set up, the student uses a time machine to select a time in the future when the experimental substrates would be seen.

The approach taken is to provide the greatest flexibility in allowing the student to study any factor of choice and to build a bottom-up model of the dominant organisms living within the intertidal zone. Artificial life or automaton (bottom-up) modeling has emerged recently as an effective tool for creating complex systems by developing a relatively simple set of rules describing how an individual of one species interacts with individuals of any other species and the conditions of its immediate environment. If we have correctly described each rule for all of the species, the non-linear interactions of organisms create a system which will exhibit community level phenomena, like zonation.

The experimental result of a particular treatment combination is a picture, actually a collage, composed of images of individual organisms located in the pattern found on the substrate. The student collects data from this experiment by examining the substrate subjected to each treatment and will have to decide how to quantify the data by counting or measuring something in the picture. The purpose of data in this raw form is to allow the student to decide how quantification should be done. Students must compare several dependent variables and select the one method best suited for their needs. Counts and measurements tell a story of each species.

Our automata model will allow students to investigate the effects of at least six different factors on any of the dominant organisms living within the intertidal zone. Specifically, students can investigate the effect of: temperature-desiccation, log damage, the density of the large predator guild (two starfish species), the small predator guild (predatory whelks), the density of a competitor guild (any of three species of barnacles and one mussel), and of the disrupter guild (limpets and chitons).

Students will find that both biotic and abiotic factors affect the density of these dominant species: barnacles (*Chthamalus stellatus, Balanus glan-*

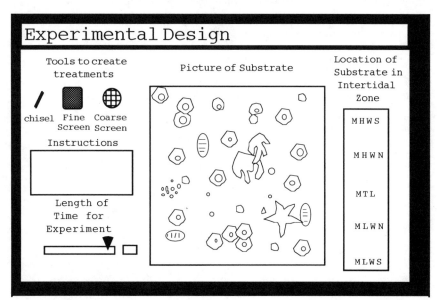

Figure 3 The Experimental Design Screen allows the student to apply a particular treatment to a substrate for a specific time

dula, Balanus cariosis), some types of algae (*Endocladia Fucus, Hedophylum, Laminaria,* and *Ulva*), a mussel (*Mytilus edulis*), and the limpets (*Tectura scutum, Lottia pelta, Collisella digitlis, Acemea mitra*).

As a summary exercise students identify the factor limiting the distribution of the dominant organisms in the intertidal zone and must support the culpability of a specific factor with the support of experimental evidence. The learner's peers evaluate the reasoning and evidence presented in the summary activity.

Acknowledgments

I owe the greatest of thanks to the investigators at Friday Harbor Laboratories for their help and support of this computer simulation. The Rocky Intertidal Zone simulation was developed under a grant (USE-9150764) from the National Science Foundation.

References

Connell, J. H. 1961a. "Effects of competition, predation by Thias lapillus and other factors on natural populations of the barnacle *Balanus balanoides.*" *Ecological Monographs.* 31:61-104.

Connell, J. H. 1961b. "The influence of interspecific competition and other factors on the distribution of *Chthamalus stellatus.*" *Ecology* 42: 710-723.

Connell, J. H. 1970. "A predator-prey system in the marine intertidal region. I. *Balanus glandula* and several predatory species of *Thias.*" *Ecological Monographs* 40:49-78.

Crow, L. W., 1989, "The Why, What, How, When and Who of Critical Thinking and Other Higher Order Thinking Skills," in *Enhancing Critical Thinking in the Sciences*, Ed. Linda Crow, Second Edition, Society of College Science Teachers.

Dayton, P. K. 1970. "Competition, Disturbance, and Community Organization: The provision and subsequent utilization of space in a rocky intertidal community." *Ecological Monographs* 41: 351-398.

Paine, R. T. 1970. "The Pisaster-Tegula interaction: Prey patches, predator food preference, and intertidal community structure." *Ecology* 50:950-961.

Law In Action:
Interactive Software
for Learning and Doing

Daniel Burnstein

*Daniel Burnstein, a former courtroom lawyer,
is now president of Beacon Expert Systems, Inc.,
Brookline, Massachusetts, where he designs
and produces instructional software on law
and negotiation*

This chapter will focus on the use of interactive software at Harvard Law School and hypertext software for lawyers and businesspeople to learn negotiation theory and prepare for bargaining sessions. The adjective "interactive" refers to the capacity of the software and hardware to give the user the opportunity to make choices and process that input to create an individualized path through software. The term "hypertext" means linked text. Hypertext is usually shown on the screen with a reverse video or in a different color. When the user clicks on the work or phrase, the computer displays the linked text that explains that term. Within the definition there is usually one or more hypertexted words which give the user the ability to take a hypertext voyage among these electronic footnotes.

Interactive software, both videodisk and hypertext with expert system features, have garnered enthusiasm from a small cadre of "true believers" over the last 20 years. The software has a unique ability to involve and stimulate the user (Bork, Flagg, Gery). Videodisk enthusiasts commonly cite research statistics that emerged in a number of Department of Defense studies that videodisk users learn one-third more in one-third less time than they would using traditional seminar/book modes of learning. Hypertext enthusiasts point to research on the learning advantages of allowing users to pursue their own paths through the hypertext. To achieve

71

high quality it is critical to do formative evaluation of the program's *accessibility, responsiveness, flexibility,* and *retention* by the user of his or her path through the program (Flagg). Many of the Harvard Law videodisks were greatly improved by the formative evaluations conducted by Professor Flagg's educational technology students from the Education School.

For the student, interactivity (or program responsiveness) creates a personalized learning experience that is useful as a stand-alone learning experience; for the faculty member, it provides another channel for learning and skills building that combines some of the best features of the lecture and clinical approaches to learning. Prof. Donald Trautman of Harvard Law School and co-founder of the Center for Computer-Assisted Legal Instruction (CALI), based at the University of Minnesota and Chicago-Kent School of Law, has observed that interactive software provides a means for "raising the level of discourse in the classroom." CALI is an active consortium of some 120 law schools which pay dues to receive the approximately 75 lessons, games, and related materials distributed to the members. Law schools are reluctant, in varying degrees, to adopt educational technology. Briefly stated, the obstacles to the creation and use of this exciting technology include: time and expense to create the programs, fear of new technology, unwillingness of tenure committees to credit the technology as original scholarship, and a deeper fear of replacing faculty with machines.

As interest grows in the technology, faculty will come to appreciate the ability of the software to (1) cover introductory material in an interesting manner without taking away from valuable class time; (2) have quality control over out-of-class learning; (3) give the faculty members feedback on whether the classroom learning is actually being absorbed; and (4) provide mastery learning to a wide range of student learning styles and capabilities.

The history of educational media is akin to the search for the Holy Grail. Each new development is welcomed with open arms, and great expectations. Slide-tape programs that went "beep" in darkened classrooms to synchronize each new slide were considered to be "high tech" at one time and initially viewed with the hope of curing many of education's ills. It didn't happen. The "halo effect" fades quickly. Educational technology should instead be seen as technology that is actually helpful in furthering traditional educational objectives and not be driven by the latest products. John Henry Martin, a pioneer in developing computerized literacy programs with support from IBM, once remarked that he had trouble figuring how to use 16 colors and, before he knew it, the hardware people were pushing him to purchase and use monitors displaying 256 colors.

Most serious developers of educational technology realize that there should be close attention to what the educational goals are of any given lesson. The best designers start out with a series of objectives. Less talented developers depend on the glitz of the medium to dazzle. (See Bloom) Mary Alice White, Professor of Psychology and Director of the Electronic Learning Laboratory at Teachers College, Columbia University, has lectured many times on the need to educate each new generation to be wise in the ways they utilize new technology—to see through the lies and hype contained in each new wave of communication media. She wonders if we are adequately teaching students to critically assess the evening news, and all other programming on television. Clearly, she means for us to help students be skeptical of videodisk and hypertext, as well as video games.

For 98 percent of our human existence on the earth, during the prehistory time, the primary source of educational experience was the tribal story teller. Everything that uses technology should be measured by its ability to capture the spirit of the story teller and enrich the experience of the audience. The purpose of educational technology is to tell an engaging story harnessing the power of appropriate tools. This chapter will describe the creation, learning paradigms, and benefits to faculty and students of two different types of educational software: (1) the *Interactive Videodisc Library* from Harvard Law School, and (2) *Negotiator Pro* hypertext software from Beacon Expert Systems.

Interactive Videodisk: What are the Harvard Videodisk Lessons?

Founded in 1983, the Harvard Law Videodisc Project (now Educational Technology Department) sought to utilize the videodisk technology to provide practice skills to law students and lawyers. Rather than practice on one's clients, the interactive lessons are intended to force users to make decisions, often in real time, that are similar to the demands of actual legal practice. Stanford Law School has produced a similar series of videodisk lessons that were also created by Tim Hallahan. Typically, the user of the some 22 Harvard videodisk lessons is a law student or practicing lawyer who seeks to hone his or her skills in a variety of areas including: court room evidentiary objections, pre-trial motions and depositions, ethics, negotiations, search and seizure law, landlord tenant law, expert witness evidence, and so forth. The average videodisk lesson takes about an hour to "play." Approximately 25 states have approved the Harvard (and Stanford) lessons for continuing legal education credits.

What, physically, is an interactive videodisk lesson? It is software that controls a videodisk, and the videodisk can hold up to an hour or two of moving video or as many as 54,000 slides or other graphics on each side of the disk. The Harvard law lessons are *level three* disks that use the computer to control the videodisk player, and tend to be very interactive in the sense that they give the user more choices and respond to the input of the user. To date, and for the first eight or so years, the Harvard videodisks

have been delivered on 12-inch analog videodisks. In the future most interactive media will probably arrive on the smaller digital compact disks.
However, as of 1995, compact digital disks cannot yet provide up to 30
minutes of 30 frames-per-second, full-screen moving video required by the
Harvard lessons. The project has recently spent a fair amount of programming resources to have the option of delivering the lessons in a one-screen
format instead of only the previous two-screen format (one screen for the
computer text and one monitor for the video). This gives users more
options and helps pave the way when CD-ROM players will become the
standard for delivering interactive media.

What Type of Team is Needed to Develop Interactive Videodisks?

Creating an interactive videodisk is a team effort that requires the skills
of many individuals over a period of a year or two. To give recognition of
the complex teamwork needed, I have described the cast of characters and
the skills they brought to the table in creating some 22 videodisks over
some eight years. The Harvard project was initially successful because of
the special skills of Tim Hallahan (founding director, creative visionary,
detail-oriented, highly organized, content expert, with good writing and
video editing skills).

Ellen Miller was an early supporter and later overall administrator with
superb editing skills, extensive video knowledge, and a unique ability to
protect and grow the project amidst weak support from the Law School's
academic deans. David Williams was a skilled audio-visual professional,
excellent video editor, very detail oriented, yet with creative sense of the
overall direction of the videodisk, possessing the people skills to coordinate large numbers of actors, production assistants, sound people, camera
people, lighting people, and basically to act as the producer on a number
of the video shoots as well as disk designer of the highest capabilities.

John DeGolyer was a first-rate technologist and computer systems person. He could supervise the most difficult and brilliant student programmers while keeping track of the evolving computer hardware and software
standards, and could persuasively argue to keep the project in the *middle*
of the mainstream, *off-the-shelf* technology that was affordable, and he did
the job when all around him were losing their heads and becoming driven
by the latest high-tech toys. The Harvard Videodisc Project received many
grants and student assistance, and it put its code for handling the videodisk
and hypertext into the public domain on the Borland Turbo Pascal bulletin
board; this practice has been continued by the current Education
Technology Department.

Scott Glanzman, the current director, is a talented programmer and
lawyer. Jeremy Seeger, current systems administrator, is a creative educa-

tional technologist and programmer.

This list must also include the best actors and actresses in the Boston area, including Dennis Achacoso, Gerri Librandi, Ron Salley, as well as the camera, lighting, sound, edit room experts, and dedicated student programmers.

How Has the Educational Technology Project at Harvard Evolved?

This project started as an underground, completely unfunded effort, and during the first 2 to 3 years, the focus was on showing the viability of an "experimental" medium. The tone and attitudes of the project were generally that of a research and development shop. The next four years were spent developing a set of lessons with dependable tools. The last two years under the direction of Scott Glanzman and Jeremy Seeger have been centered on quality control, providing extensive written materials to support the lessons, shoring up a user base to assure financial stability, and bringing the distribution in-house from a commercial publisher with selected regional resellers. Glanzman is excited about a new initiative with a core curriculum professor to transfer a course to the medium of interactive video. If this effort is successful, the user will see one of the best Harvard lecturers doing a Socratic style class with interruptions for quizzes, feedback, remediation, and supplemental materials.

What Educational Support is Provided to Faculty?

Faculty or law firms who lease the lessons now receive the (1) Guide to Installation and Troubleshooting, (2) Guide to Training with Interactive Videodisks in Legal Education, and (3) Lesson Guides for each of the videodisks. The training guide provides "methods of integrating the interactive video lessons into legal education and training programs, such as evidence, clinical fieldwork, trial advocacy, and negotiation." The Lesson Guide gives faculty:

1) A lesson overview with an index of issues presented, a summary of the general purpose of the lesson, fact pattern, intended audience, and role of the student when taking the lesson. There are also suggestions for how to use the videodisk lessons within the curriculum.

2) An annotated script that contains the specific content of the lesson with the script, questions and answers, interrupt points (choice points), legal references and teaching notes

3) An appendix with copies of documents, if any, used in the lessons.

The Guide to Training with Interactive Videodisks has sections describing the advantages of videodisks, learning objectives, and how to use videodisks to teach: evidence, trial advocacy, in clinical fieldwork programs, and negotiation courses.

Who Uses the Videodisk Lessons at Harvard Law and Elsewhere?

There are currently a number of clinically oriented courses using the videodisk lessons and almost half of the students are exposed to the technology during their stay. Outside of Harvard Law School, where there is less focus on policy and analysis and a greater emphasis on practice, the videodisks are more widely utilized. There are currently about 1,000 lessons total being leased by about 80 law schools and 20 law firms. The average lease price ranges from $200-$400/year depending on the number of lessons and other factors. There is special pricing that permits the key legal services and backup offices to have the programs available for their training needs.

An experimental lesson, *Boyd v. Deaver*, has generated the most interest amongst the non-clinical professors because it allows the students to learn how a case is developed. It had an experimental design because evidence, documents, and witnesses were made available through 25,000 still images (Hoelscher, Burnstein). The richness of user choices came from having several orders of magnitude more choices for the students than the typical videodisk using a limited number of moving video segments that eat up the disk quickly. Its lead designer was John Ciampa of R.I.T., where the disk was produced. The faculty were intrigued by the process by which the students were able to view evidence, decide which witnesses to interview and how long to spend with the witness, and what memos of law to read. The lesson gives students the opportunity to build a theory of the case, and actually construct a law suit. Since this lesson was based on an actual civil rights case that generated detailed District Court and First Circuit opinions, students can view these opinions to see how the case "came out." This disk was the subject of a doctoral thesis (Hoelscher).

Other than with the handful of clinical courses at Harvard Law School that are currently assigning interactive software for their classes, the lessons have yet to be incorporated into the core curriculum. Glanzman is pleased that the clinical and trial advocacy students are coming back on their own before exams to take additional videodisk lessons, and he observes, "I feel the satisfaction of a host when dinner guests eagerly return for seconds and thirds."

The slow rate of acceptance into the so-called core curriculum is understandable. The lessons are seen as adjunct to the clinical experience. The responsibility for the project is given over to a non-academic dean. The support of this dean over time has been critical to the survival and growth of the project, because for one, before this dean's involvement there was never an expectation the project would be renewed longer than year to year.

The next step in this process would be to expand the supervision of the project to include an academic dean, who should consider (1) how educational technology should generally be integrated into the core academic curricula, (2) which lessons are appropriate for which courses, and (3) meeting with faculty and working with them to find out how they can best be supported in the use of the lessons. Even with this sort of support, change will come slowly. Harvard is obviously a traditional school, with faculty who are busy with their research, writing, teaching, and consulting. Yet, all law schools are under pressure from the profession to better integrate real-world practice issues into the law school experience, and it is very possible the faculty will come to see the videodisks as providing a useful complement to their research. With some carefully planned demonstrations at the faculty senate, and encouragement from the academic deans, these lessons will no doubt be better integrated into the curriculum at Harvard and other traditional law schools.

Videodisks: Early Designs, and Use of Multiple Endings and Pathways

Some of the earlier educational technologies used computers to give the user choices (Mitre's *TICCIT* system, and Control Data Corporation's *Plato* system). The earliest pilot examples included a simulated card game (you could win or lose the game) and a California driving test (if you chose the wrong answers you wouldn't pass and get a license). David Hon invented creative ways to utilize mechanical input devices. One early project had the user giving CPR to a mannequin and using the *CPR Disk* meant the life-sized doll either "lived" or "died." On a later project, David Hon used a real welding gun refitted with lights controlled by the oxygen and hydrogen controls, that when aimed at a light sensitive screen, permitted aviation welders to learn the correct distance and mixture of gases, and be certified in a much shorter time than the traditional lecture, lab practice, and testing by observation.

What these interactive videodisks had in common with the Harvard law disks were, depending on the choices of the user, there would be different pathways through and/or endings to the videodisk. In the *Search and Seizure* videodisk the user could choose to be either a senior police official or a member of the District Attorney's Office accompanying police officers obtaining and serving a search warrant. The user is required to protect the constitutional guarantees of the Fourth Amendment so that evidence seized would stand up in court. Dependent on their competence, the District Attorney in charge of this operation gives feedback to students ranging from critical advice to "hit the books," to praise and an invitation to take part in more search-and-seizure operations. Just as the users' efforts are noticed and scored in the Search disk, different scores result in the trial videodisk lessons. There the user plays an attorney in court who must "object" by hitting any key, and then give the basis of the objection. The lessons score how well you do at keeping objectionable evidence out, and the judge gives you feedback based on the merits of your input.

The ideal design of having an infinite amount of pathways through a lesson depending on the student responses is limited by the disk capacity, budget, time, and resources of the funders and distributors. We would typically have no more than three different pathways at each of the 30-50 major decision points. There would be between 80 and 180 points where the lesson could be interrupted, including questions and feedback screens. In the more sophisticated designs, there are many points at which the user had a choice either of being pro-active and "stopping the action" to make a decision and change the flow of events, or of sitting back and inevitably getting in trouble by being passive.

Videodisks: They Require Good Production Values

A realistic hurdle to get over with interactive videodisks is the comparison to commercial television; and if you fall too far from the mark, the user will fault you for being "low budget." Therefore, one needs to use a capable camera person, excellent writing, lighting, sound, and editing to create a believable scenario.

The typical 2-3 hours preparation for a classroom hour of instruction becomes about 100 hours for a computer-based lesson (text only) and about 400 hours for an hour of interactive video instruction. This is not to say that amateurs cannot go it alone and create wonderful, inexpensive videodisks. Examples of very low budget disks that are fantastic include: *How to Get Out and Stay Out; The Story of Cathy,* which was made by two mental health professionals for $5,000 (Rosenberg), as well as the effective English as a Second Language (ESL) lessons created at the University of Massachusetts, Boston University and Harvard. The first interactive Harvard lesson was an interactive videotape created by Tim Hallahan, David Williams, and Ellen Miller for $25 worth of tape and much volunteer effort.

It might seem odd to use mediocre behavior as the defining paradigm for teaching. The creative insight of Tim Hallahan, however, was that people would not learn as much from truly terrible role models or fantastic role models. One would repel and the other would be viewed as a distant but ultimately irrelevant model for "the rest of us." Therefore, Tim uses lawyers with variously right and wrong behaviors to sharpen the eye and mind of the user in the approximately 10 trial videodisks he has authored. In them, the student watches a civil, criminal, or family law trial and then makes objections to evidence being introduced by the other side. The judge then calls on the user to defend his or her objection and state the basis for the objection. Tim used this paradigm, even in live seminars, to get the students and newer practitioners trained to use "in real time" their book-learned knowledge of evidence objections and other court-related procedures.

Another paradigm utilized in the law disks was a fairly difficult level of questions. This would typically result in students missing some 50 percent of the questions as they "played" the lesson. The net effect of such design was that the users were never able to relax and get into a comfortable groove. In fact, the users typically sit on the edge of their seats, and when taking the lesson with 1-3 other people, engage in vigorous debate about what is, in fact, the right answer. Of course, you would not use this design with students who are not as confident as the average law student.

Negotiator Pro is a program that is designed around the paradigm of a business or legal checklist. There are up to 35 question-and-answer spaces available to the user to create essay responses or to use brief checklists that are printed out to create a negotiation briefing book before actually going into a negotiation. The main value of the program is its relatively unique combination of a just-in-time learning environment with a brainstorming tool for everyday business and legal problems. There is an extensive knowledge-base of information that sits underneath the customizable checklists. There are hundreds and hundreds of mini-tutorials on a wide variety of negotiation topics that are interconnected electronic footnotes. The program doesn't think for the user, but helps the student/professional come up with the best solutions.

Unlike a traditional book, the hypertext allows the user to browse through the information and instantly move from text to footnote and then onto other cross-linked footnotes to pursue whatever topics each individual wishes. In this sense the software is endlessly interactive and individualized, unlike a book which essentially follows a single linear path selected by the author to satisfy the needs of all learners. (Conklin, Kussell). Creating hypertext software for the PC or Mac requires much smaller teams of people than a videodisk production.

Hypertext: The Early Design Issues

The inventor of hypertext and its tireless promoter is the brilliant and witty Theodore (Ted) Nelson. Early on Ted believed you should link text in multiple ways to allow connections that existed in nature, as it were, to be replicated in a learning and doing environment. Nelson visualized that the links would not just be words, but also pictures, video, charts, graphs, sounds, and more would be at the end, and the beginning, of these links. Nelson also visualized that there would have to be a "meter in the sky" to keep track of copyright usage and payments.

Ironically, the early vision I had of *Negotiator Pro* was to simply provide users with a list of important issues to consider being set out in a word processor file as a series of questions that the user would answer for a particular negotiation. This was no less or more than the proverbial "checklist" that lawyers, CPAs, and businesspeople have come to use and love. Then, George Wood, Ph.D., consultant to the Harvard educational technology projects, artificial intelligence guru, brilliant programmer, and all-around savant, suggested that the program really needed hypertext and an expert system with "if-then" rules imbedded. Three years and a small fortune in programming later, these features are implemented in a modest way in the DOS, Windows, and Mac versions of *Negotiator Pro.*

The first try at programming the expert system profiling method was attempted by the author as the lab assignment of the Harvard Law School course, *Artificial Intelligence and Legal Reasoning.* Somehow, the course title always provoked mirth in those hearing its name for the first time. The class was informed that only domains with definite rules commonly recognized by experts in the given field were appropriate for an expert system. That wisdom was cast aside, and the author set about creating a rich environment, consisting of some 400+ mini-tutorials on negotiation theory and 200+ bibliographic references. It gave the user the ability to create their own set of questions and hints that permitted them to model any type of negotiation from anti-trust to zoning. Programmers created nice screens, the capacity to go backward as well as forward, and the ability to easily enter and leave and keep track of outcomes.

The beauty of hypertext is that the user is able to pick any number of different points of entry into the subject matter. Any topic can be read and since each topic usually has cross-references, the user can strike off in any direction to learn what s/he feels is appropriate or desirable. The weakness is that it is possible for the user to miss important concepts or lose track of the "big picture." Thus, the special role of the teacher working with these computer materials is still to (1) provide the big picture, (2) motivate and inspire the students, and (3) provide special insights beyond the computer material.

Good hypertext design can attempt to provide a weak imitation of the teacher's special role, e.g., there can always be introductory, summary, or even inspirational hypertext placed at strategic positions in the program to give the user some motivation, an overview, or context, or even subtext, for the information. The other useful screen in the Windows and Mac versions gives one a "history" of the hypertext that has been examined so that users can wander back along the familiar path, or at a minimum get a perspective of where they have come from and/or where they seem to be going.

Professor Robert Greenes (see chapter later in this book) had to deal with the navigation issue because he has created a marvelously rich learn-

ing environment that has been adopted into the core medical school curricula. The learning environment became so complex that his group
designed a powerful bookmarking system to allow the user to leave and
come back later to find the complete context (path) where he or she had
electronically visited still intact. This impressive system includes: hypertext,
medical zoom images, algorithms, decision modules for quality assurance
and what-if reviews, electronic books and quizzes, semantic browsers, concept matching, indexing of materials, skill building and graphic-based tutorials, image interpretation for radiologists, simulations in cardiology, EKG,
lung, and neurology, and tools specific to accessing patient data, calculators, formulas, and online databases.

What is the overall benefit of having a program that is largely hypertext?
The usefulness of *Negotiator Pro* comes from having a user answering the
important questions related to his or her upcoming negotiation. The process
is useful for its own value. We are trying to create a new benchmark for
negotiation preparation. Roy Lewicki, Professor at the Business College of
Ohio State University and negotiation textbook author, states, "Most nego-
tiators, even experienced ones, fly by the seat of their pants. Planning is
tedious, yet critical to setting and achieving your goals. *Negotiator Pro* offers
a comprehensive software system for planning negotiation and learning
about negotiation at the same time." The negotiation program has generated a surprising amount of press coverage, including articles in the *New York
Times, Wall Street Journal, ABA Journal, Education Law Reporter,* and 40 or
so other publications.

Over the last three years since its first publication *Negotiator Pro* software has been adopted as part of the curriculum or particular classes at a
wide range of graduate schools, including MIT's Sloan School of
Management, Northeastern University Law School, Rutgers Law School,
Suffolk University School of Law, University of Calgary, and the University
of Denver College of Business. Professors have contributed their insights
to a teachers' manual on ways to integrate the software into courses on
management styles, negotiation, labor, international law, alternative dispute resolution, marketing, and sales courses.

A number of users think the software does not "do enough for the
user—that it doesn't give them an answer" after they put in some information. Perhaps this was in part prompted by the expert systems *name* of
the company, which leads to an expectation that the software will *solve*
their problem. As Dr. Michael Kuperstein, formerly of MIT and a pioneer
in applying powerful neural net technology to processing forms, observes,
"I want a piece of software to do something for me. I can look through a
number of books and possibly not get anywhere closer to a solution, but
a good piece of software will always give me a solution—whether it is
totally right or not, at least I have a solution. An example being tax soft-

ware. After using it I have a tax return, at least in draft form, to print out—that is my product for the effort of learning to use the program." In response to these suggestions, the software is being redesigned to move from an open interface to one that results in a product. Perhaps this desire for a more defined process and product comes from the need of users to feel they have both a compass in this new electronic wilderness as well as a "parent" to act as a benign force to push the user to a product that gives closure to the experience.

Conclusion: The Coming Revolution

Currently there are relatively few interactive videodisk and hypertext programs. Yet *BusinessWeek* of August 9, 1993, reports Bill Gates is buying up images from leading art museums, and the leading sources of electronics and sports and entertainment images (CBS, Sony, Time-Warner, AT&T, Apple, MCA, Columbia Pictures) are arranging deals with the advertising world and cable TV companies to bring interactive media into the home. The somewhat ironic refrain in interactive circles has been repeated for 15 years that "this is the year of multimedia." As business rushes to embrace interactive entertainment and sports, the academic world will feel the pressure to upgrade from the blackboard filled with professors' chalk notes to colorful interactive electronic slide shows replete with fades, dissolves, three-dimensional graphs, sound, and even moving video.

The impact of television and multimedia is being felt in the classroom. With the soon-to-arrive plethora of images and data from the Internet, CompuServe, and elsewhere, the question will be not when, but how and why, is interactive educational technology being used. What are our educational objectives and what is the appropriate technology to get there? Are we developing educational technology that puts the learner at the center of the design process (Steinberg)? Consistent with the predictions of the gradually pervasive impact of technology on education and all thinking (Perkins), I predict that one small part of this process will find Lotus Freelance, MicroSoft PowerPoint, Aldus Persuasion, and similar electronic presentation programs becoming part of the standard professor's toolkit over the next two years, and interactive video and hypertext will make similarly timed moves into the university computer lab and home multimedia computer system as more people acquire a multimedia CD-ROM player. University interactive software productions will also increase in numbers and effectiveness, but for this to happen, there will need to be (1) support from deans and administration figures, (2) involvement of younger faculty who have been granted tenure with traditional research products, (3) an entrepreneurial educational technology department that can devise ways to raise the initial funds, and (4) a carefully thought-out distribution plan.

References

Bork, Alfred, "Preparing student-computer dialogues: Advice to teachers," in R.P. Taylor (Ed.), *The computer in the school: Tutor, tool, tutee*, New York, Teachers College Press, 1980.

Bork, Alfred, *Computer and information technology as a learning aid*, Irvine, CA, University of California, 1983.

Bloom, B. (Ed.), *Taxonomy of educational objectives: The classification of educational objectives*. Handbook I: Cognitive domain, New York, David McKay, 1956.

Burnstein, Daniel, "Boyd v. Deaver—Litigation Strategies Videodisc": *An Opportunity to Improve Curriculum and Prototype Expert Systems*, The Second International Conference on Artificial Intelligence and Law, Proceedings of the Conference, ACM, 1989.

Conklin, Jeff, "A Survey of Hypertext," *IEEE Computer*, September 1987.

Flagg, Barbara N., *Formative Evaluation for Educational Technologies*, Lawrence Earlbaum, 1990.

Gery, Gloria, *Making CBT Happen*, Weingarten, Boston, 1987.

Hoelscher, Karen, Doctoral Thesis, Harvard Graduate School of Education, Cambridge, MA, 1989.

Kussell, Peter B., *Navigating the Hypermedia Sea*, The Training Institute of the Foxboro Company, Foxboro MA, 1989.

Nelson, Theodore, *Computer Lib/Dream Machines*, Microsoft Press, 1987.

Perkins, D. N., "The Fingertip Effect: How Information-Processing Technology Shapes Thinking," *Educational Researcher*, August/September 1985.

Rosenberg, B. A., Hagan, B. J., *How to Get Out and Stay Out: The Story of Cathy*, presentation at the Nebraska Videodisc Symposium, 1987.

Steinberg, Esther R., "The Centrality of Learner Characteristics In Computer Assisted Instruction," *Journal of Computing in Higher Education*, Paideia, Ashfield, MA, Vol I, Number 2, 1990.

Learning Introductory Physics With New Electronic Media

Gregor M. Novak

Gregor Novak is Professor of physics at Indiana University Purdue University Indianapolis

Most students who do not intend to major in the subject find taking an introductory physics class a daunting challenge. Physics deals with natural phenomena in terms of abstract concepts which, to the students, appear quite unrelated to everyday experience. A typical student's reaction is either utter frustration or a resignation to a mechanical learning process in which rote memorization of examples is the primary mode of learning.

Physics teachers have always been aware of this problem. They have devised a variety of pedagogical tools to deal with it. Traditional physics instruction proceeds along three separate, loosely connected tracks. Students attend lecture, recitation, and laboratory sessions. To bridge the gap between abstract theoretical constructs and the real world, the physics lecture often includes demonstrations.

A lecture demonstration attempts to bring the real physical world into the classroom. The demonstrated phenomenon, however, has to be simple enough to fit into the small physical space of a classroom, it has to take place in a short time interval, and it has to be manageable by the skillfulness of the average physics teacher. These constraints exclude a large set of phenomena, such as sporting events, that might illustrate the concepts of mechanics, weather events, airplanes, and sailboats that could help students grasp hydrodynamics, crystal growing, atomic microscopy, medical imaging, etc.

In the recitation session the students are taught the art of problem analysis. In a properly run recitation session the entire class gets involved in applying the theoretical principles to the analysis of real-world situations. It is very difficult, however, to keep the attention focused on the relation between the phenomenon at hand and the theoretical principles without sacrificing the quantitative rigor. So the emphasis often shifts to calculators, the intricacies of hand graphing, and other calculational drudgeries. In an introductory physics course the laboratory is supposed to be the place where the abstract ideas which the students have encountered in the lecture and in the textbook become real. In the laboratory, real balls roll down real inclines.

Until the advent of the new electronic media most introductory physics laboratories were subject to the same time and space constraints that plague the lecture demonstrations. A typical indoor physics laboratory experience has to fit on a two-square-meter table and be completed in a two-hour time interval. The actual observation time is much less than that because the data analysis part is the time-consuming component of the laboratory exercise. It is not unusual for a student to spend more than half of the laboratory time setting up and graphing the data. In an introductory class, however, the main purpose of the laboratory experience is to build a bridge between the observed world and the abstract theory. Pedagogical tools are needed that promote observation, critical thinking about relations between observations, and that minimize the drudgery of number crunching and other forms of data analysis. Many new approaches are being developed by imaginative teachers. In Priscilla Laws' Workshop Physics class at Dickinson College in Pennsylvania, there are no lectures. In microcomputer-equipped laboratories students use modern number crunching tools such as spreadsheets to look for relationships that eventually grow into physical principles. In the laboratory students ride around in specially constructed carts to experience forces and accelerations.

The New Media as Pedagogical Tools

The use of visual media to illustrate verbal narrative is probably as old as mankind. Pictures and diagrams have always been important pedagogical tools. Many students are visual learners. For such students diversity of presentation facilitates learning (Stice, 1987).

The introduction of powerful desktop computing tools has made possible many new and innovative approaches to organizing and presenting illustrative materials. Real-time video sequence with sound can be presented in non-linear fashion, edited, and manipulated on the fly. Recently introduced multimedia resources such as Physics: Cinema Classics, Physics Teacher's CD-ROM Toolkit, and the Video Encyclopedia of Physics Demonstrations, can provide motivating introductions to physics concepts.

The merging of the computer and video technologies offers the possibility of a radical expansion of the undergraduate physics courses, including the laboratories. The ability to perform quantitative measurements on video recordings of real-world phenomena that cannot be reproduced in the laboratory in real time can provide a dose of relevance and motivation not otherwise available in the traditional physics course. The multimedia should not replace the traditional tools. Rather, they should be used to enhance the standard tools by speeding up the processing of the information, thereby expanding the range and complexity of the phenomena investigated. The new video technologies can transform the physics laboratory by extending the spectrum of phenomena to investigate quantitatively. We can now include such things as athletic events, rifle bullet motion in expanded time, and crystal growth in contracted time, and perform meaningful measurements of real physical events on captured video frames.

Quite often a short video can convey an abstract idea much better than the best verbal description. As an example consider a two-minute video clip taken from the Physics: Cinema Classics videodisk chapter on the Flare and the Snowmobile. The students would view a full-motion video of a flare being launched vertically upward from a moving snowmobile. They would then be presented with two different still views showing the landing of the flare. In the first case the flare lands ahead of the snowmobile, in the second it lands behind it. After they present a possible explanation for each case, they are allowed to view the full-motion videos of the two events. In the first case, the snowmobile stopped after launch, in the second case it sped up.

The Snowmobile video is an example of a real-life physics event that cannot be duplicated in the laboratory. It is with this kind of enhancement and extension of the laboratory experience that interactive video can significantly extend the content of the physics we teach.

The Launch: A flare is launched vertically from a moving snowmobile. Where do you expect it to land ? Explain your answer:

Figure 1   *Flare Launch. Still from Physics: Cinema Classics*

Case 1. How do you explain what you see ?

Figure 2   *First Flare Landing. Still from Physics: Cinema Classics*

Case 2. How do you explain what you see ?

Figure 3   *Second Flare Landing. Still from Physics: Cinema Classics*

Enhancing the Lecture

Figure 4 is a page from the author's lecture notes, or rather, a card from a hypercard stack.

The window in the upper left corner of the page can display video from a live source or digitally compressed video using QuickTime. The image shown in the window is taken from Physics: Cinema Classics laserdisk. It shows the breaking of the image of a pencil when submerged in optics. This can be shown in live demonstration but it is hard to see until the students know what to look for. I find this interaction between video and live demonstrations particularly useful. The controller under the video window performs the standard video controller functions. The text window on the right contains lecture notes. It contains "hot spots." Clicking on the numbers in the text will bring up the corresponding frame on the laserdisk. The six number buttons under the video window trigger pre-program video sequences. The four buttons on the bottom right bring up simulated ray diagrams.

Livening Up the Independent Study

Desktop multimedia resources provide a refreshing supplement to traditional textbooks. The computer screen can mix text graphics, simulation and video (Figure 5). The instructor's lecture notes as above can easily be edited into a resource the students can explore on their own in an interactive independent study environment.

At IUPUI the Introductory Physics students use a multimedia-based review set which is available from the campus file server. The review material is organized around a set of 850 multiple choice questions.

Students can attempt to answer the question, look up the answer, ask for formulas, or ask for a detailed explanation. From many questions the students can branch to animated simulations such as interactive projectile motion simulation, interactive ray diagrams in optics, etc. We are incorporating QuickTime video clips where appropriate.

Extending the Laboratory Experience

Multimedia will become a part of the hands-on experience of the undergraduate physics laboratories. Multimedia tools empower students to collect data from experiments that could otherwise not be performed since they require high-speed cameras and strobe photography. Video compres-

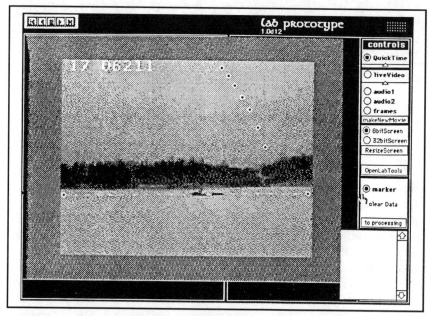

Figure 4   A page from multimedia-based lecture notes

sion tools such as QuickTime and Video For Windows are just the beginning of the new era of integration of information technologies.

Interactive Video Lab, a collaborative project between IUPUI, University of Nebraska—Lincoln, New Hampshire Technical College at Berlin, and North Park College in Chicago, is an example of digitized video use in a laboratory setting. Interactive Video Lab is a desktop computer-based environment in which a student can perform quantitative analyses of real-world events which would be very difficult (if not impossible) to reproduce in the laboratory. In the example below we analyze a digitized version of the snowmobile video clip mentioned earlier.

The laboratory shell has four parts.

1. The Video part, where a student can view a video from a live source or a video from a compressed file and perform some rough measurements.
2. The Data Processing part, where fairly accurate measurements are performed on the data taken from the video screen.
3. The Analysis part, where data can be manipulated numerically and graphically.
4. The Movie Making part, where a QuickTime movie can be made from a video source.

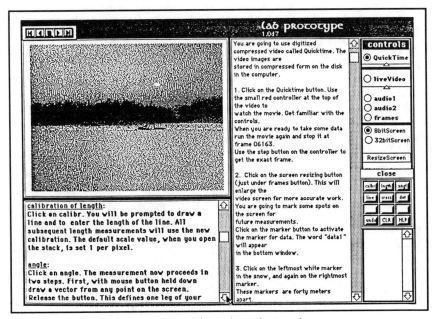

Figure 5 *A page from a review set for independent study*

1. The Video Screen

In a window on the screen students can view full-motion video from a live video source such as a live camera, a VCR, a laserdisk player, or a remote feed (Figure 6). They can also view compressed video using QuickTime. On-the-screen controllers give the student complete freedom to browse through the video. The instructor can insert instructions directly into the video screen. The instructions can be composed on a word processor and inserted with a mouse click. No programming is required.

A set of measuring tools is available. A student can superpose a coordinate system, calibrate the system to reflect the dimensions of the scene, and perform on-the-screen measurements of distances and angles. In the first phase of an experiment students are asked to observe the scene and to use measuring tools to get a rough set of data. They then use this set of data for a quick comparison with theory. In the above case they get a rough estimate of the value for the acceleration due to gravity. In another example they might perform a rough check of a conservation law.

Next, a student would enlarge the video window and accurately mark the relevant data points.

In the snowmobile experiment the student would first click on the markers in the snow. This information would later be used to calibrate the distance measuring tool. The student would then step through the frames of the video clip and mark the positions of the flare. These marks would

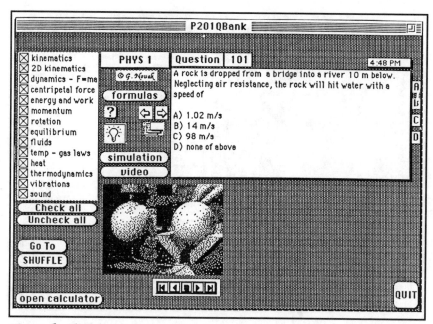

Figure 6   *The lab video screen*

then be used to determine the heights reached by the flare at time intervals determined from the frame numbers.

The Data Processing Screen

The student's data from the video screen are reproduced on a clean background. Fairly accurate length and angle measurement can be made with calibrated tools. The student has to decide how to organize the measured data for future processing. In the snowmobile experiment there are only two data sets: the heights reached by the flare and the corresponding times. In another experiment the data set might be incidence and refraction angle pairs for light rays passing through a block of glass.

The Analysis Screen

The raw data from the Data Processing Screen are imported to this part. The student is encouraged to think of data sets as objects to be manipulated. For example, the heights attained by the flare during consecutive time intervals is a data object from which one can derive displacements of the flare by taking pairwise differences of the heights. From the displacements the student can derive the velocities by dividing each element of the displacements object by the time interval. All the number crunching is done instantly by the computer, as is the graphing. The student can explore the many different relationships between the data. The instructor can provide very detailed, step-by-step instructions that lead to a definite

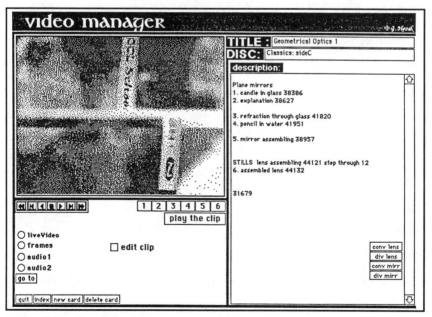

Figure 7 *Expanded video screen*

conclusion, or a student can be given a loosely structured road map with hints along the way and be allowed to devise his or her own way, maybe discovering relations the instructor did not anticipate. It is quite easy to put this lab on a server and set up a collaborative or even distance learning environment.

CD-ROM

The new microcomputer models are now available with built-in CD-ROM drives. The emerging optical technology on the desktop will greatly expand the amount of information available at each workstation. The first large CD-ROM title for physics instruction is currently being prepared by Prof. Robert Fuller at University of Nebraska—Lincoln, and Prof. Dean Zollman at Kansas. The Physics InfoMall CD-ROM disk will be an encyclopedic reference for physics teachers and students. It includes an encyclopedia of physics concepts, a dictionary of mathematics equations, a data handbook, books from publishers and professional associations, catalogs from scientific equipment companies, documents of historical and biographical significance, compilations of labs and demonstrations, and more.

Bibliography

Articles
Hansen, E. "The Role of Interactive Video Technology in Higher Education, Case Study and a Proposed Framework," *Educational Technology*, 30(9), 133, 1990.

Pavlonis, T. "Interactive Video—A Spellbinding Approach to Solid Learning," *Media and Methods*, 24(5), 21-22, 1988.

Stice, J. (1987). "Using Kolb's Learning Cycle to Improve Student Learning," *Engineering Education*.

Rosenthal, S. "It's Show Time," *New Media*, March 1993, 36-39.

Anderson, C., and M. Veljkov (1990). *Creating Interactive Multimedia: A Practical Guide*. Glenview, IL: Scott, Foresman and Co.

Magazines
Multimedia: Getting Started, Apple Computer

New Media, Hypermedia Communications

Syllabus, Syllabus Press

T.H.E Journal

Multimedia Resources
Physics: Cinema Classics, AAPT Instructional Materials Center, Dr. Robert G. Fuller, editor, available from Ztek Co., P.O.Box 1055, Louisville, KY 40201-1055, (800) 247-1603.

The Video Encyclopedia of Physics Demonstrations, The Education Group, Inc.,

1235 Sunset Plaza Drive, Los Angeles, CA 90069, (310) 659-8842.

The InfoMall CD-ROM, AAPT Instructional Materials Center, Dr. Robert G. Fuller, editor, 109 Ferguson Hall, University of Nebraska—Lincoln, Lincoln, NE 68588-0109, (800) 332-0265.

Computer-Based Education and Decision Support in Medicine

Robert A. Greenes

Robert Greenes has appointments at Harvard Medical School and Massachusetts Institute of Technology. He is Director of the Decision Systems Group at the Brigham and Women's Hospital

Medical practice shares certain characteristics with professional work in many fields. A primary feature of professional work is that the practitioner (whether a physician, manager, or professor) tends to function in large measure as a *problem solver*. The problem may be that of organizing and composing a clinical note (or a lecture), evaluating a patient (or a student), carrying out a particular procedure (or experiment), analyzing or interpreting a patient result (or experimental outcome), or determining what next step would be most effective in management of the patient (or in confirming the experimental results or exploring an alternative hypothesis).

In the conduct of professional work, an individual may need to deal with a variety of problems, each of which may involve a set of separate tasks. Each of the involved tasks may in turn require access to specific information resources, and utilize specific skills and methods for manipulating these resources. We have characterized the information technology environment best suited to the needs of the professional as being "horizontal" and "integrative".[1] This is in contrast to the "vertical" orientation of software such as word processing, spreadsheets, expert systems, and database systems designed to support individuals doing more focused work, or individual tasks in isolation. It should, of course, be noted, that most other software currently available is also of the vertical type, including the many applications for personal computers developed for education, decision support, and a variety of other purposes. However, considerable activity is occurring in developing new generations of software engineering environments and toolkits to enable creation of horizontal, integrative applications that take advantage of advances in workstations and in network software and hardware technologies.

Students share many of the same information needs as professionals, in that they are learning the nature of the fields, the kinds of problems with which they deal, the methods for analyzing and solving them, and the kinds of skills and information resources that are required for these tasks. For this reason, problem-based curricula have been widely adopted in professional education in business and law. Problem-based learning has always been the primary mode for students of *clinical* medicine, which is largely taught through an apprenticeship system. More recently this philosophy has been extended to the *preclinical* curriculum as well,[2] particularly at a few schools such as McMaster and Harvard; based on the successful experience at these places, it is being adopted elsewhere as well.

The rationale for preclinical knowledge being taught in a problem-based fashion is based on the following tenets:

a) The traditional emphasis in medical education on factual learning and memorization is no longer sustainable, given the rapid advances in medical science, the concomitant expansion of knowledge, and the limitations of human memory.

b) The relevance of basic science to clinical medicine is best demonstrated through application to realistic and practical problems.

c) Skills in accessing and interpreting information are important elements of later practice, as a result of which the approach provides continuity between preclinical and clinical learning.

d) Lastly, later problem-based access to decision support and educational resources as a primary form of continuing education will rely on the same skills and capabilities.

Information Technology Requirements

A key element of success in problem-based practice is ready access to information resources that can provide the necessary data or knowledge required for particular problem-solving, interpretation, analysis, and decision-making tasks. Furthermore, these information resources need to be manipulated, presented, and incorporated, as appropriate for the particular problem context to which they pertain. Thus, analysis, manipulation, and presentation tools for these information resources are also required.

We have, in the foregoing discussion, defined the requirement for an information technology environment to support professional work as being one that provides horizontal, integrative capability. In this section and the next, we elaborate on the nature of such an environment and describe a software architecture that has been under development in the author's laboratory, which serves as a basis for much of our current work to support physicians and students in the future. Our preceding discussion of the nature of professional work underscores our belief that the benefits to be gained by the approach described herein are not unique to medicine. In fact, from the point of view of this book, we believe it characterizes a robust approach to supporting the academic teaching, learning, and investigative environment of a university.

A Scenario

We outline an example of this requirement, as it might arise in a clinical practice setting in which a physician has ordered a chest X-ray for a middle-aged male patient who has been coughing for several weeks. He has a smoking history, and no signs of infection. The physician reviews the radiology report, which describes the finding on the X-ray of a smooth-margined, 3 cm solitary, non-calcified mass in the right upper lobe of the lung. The physician may wish, in addition to reading the report, to review the X-ray itself. Also, the physician may want to consult an expert (human or computer-based) for a differential diagnosis (ranking of disease possibilities) given the clinical history, symptoms, and X-ray findings. Its rationale may also be requested. Subsequently, the physician needs to decide the next steps in patient management, e.g., whether to carry out a subsequent X-ray procedure such as a computed tomography (CT) scan, or a needle-directed biopsy for further diagnostic evaluation. Increasing recognition of the need for cost-effectiveness in medical care dictates that the physician determine what the appropriate recommended guidelines are for this circumstance. Flow charts or computer models may be consulted to determine whether this clinical circumstance is precisely delineated (or if not, what exceptions may apply), what the recommendation is, and the rationale for it, including appropriate references. A computer-based "what if" model may even be used to predict the chance that the recommended next test, if done, will lead to sufficient increase in certainty of diagnosis to justify treatment. Finally, the procedure is ordered, and the process begins again when the result is available.

The above illustration typifies the wide variety of data and knowledge, including human and computer-based expertise, communication, and synthesis of information that may be required in carrying out the professional work of medical practice.

Medical Information Resources

The above process relies on various kinds of patient data, including clinical assessments, quantitative data, images, and their interpretations. The problem-solving process may benefit from being able to utilize a wide spectrum of knowledge resources,[3] including bibliographic databases, electronic textbook materials, 3-D models and atlases, heuristic or probabilistic inference tools, libraries of archived images with known diagnoses, question/answer databanks, and clinical practice guidelines or protocols for specific problems. They represent a diverse collection of media, formats, and methodologies, including both "passive" information resources (text, tables, charts, images, motion sequences, etc.), and "adaptive" resources (such as simulations, analytic tools, and expert systems).

Paradigms for Information Access

Computer applications that are useful for carrying out the above task encompass a variety of *paradigms* or formats for presenting and interacting with this information, including database query, expert systems, models, and image display. Other supporting applications may be tutorials, self-assessment/testing, electronic textbooks, case libraries. A single application may use a number of types of resources. Different applications may, furthermore, have need for the same resources but utilize them in distinct ways—"repurposing" them.

A "Component-Based" Architecture—DeSyGNER

The development of applications is facilitated if an authoring system exists which supports the construction of such paradigms as the above, and the incorporation of external information resources. If that is the case, then the authoring process can be separated into two kinds of tasks: 1) collecting the information content, and 2) assembling the content according to the paradigm desired. Information content can then be developed independently by content experts. Authoring tools that take advantage of high-speed networking can facilitate integration of disparate information resources into useful applications. Furthermore, by this approach the same information content can be repurposed into different applications, as a result of which sharing and cooperative development are encouraged. DeSyGNER, an authoring environment developed in the author's laboratory, illustrates these principles.

As an example of a "component-based architecture," DeSyGNER (Decision Systems Group Nucleus of Extensible Resources),[4,5,6] produced in our laboratory, is an application construction toolkit used for a number of education and decision support applications projects in which we are involved. This approach is in contrast to the current prevalent mode of independent application development, with its tendency to "reinvent the wheel"; maintain its own content in unique, externally inaccessible formats; and perpetuate inconsistency and isolation.

The DeSyGNER Architecture

The current DeSyGNER project has evolved from a series of experiments in building tools to integrate various educational resources and decision aids on a personal computer,[7],[8] and developing or incorporating knowledge bases that utilize these tools.[9],[10] Tools included text, graphic, list management, book browsing, image manipulation, dynamic flow chart display, simulation, and other functions.[11],[12],[13] DeSyGNER attempts to generalize our experience from these earlier experiments, to provide high-level application construction capabilities for non-programmer authors. The main purpose is to make it easier to build applications by providing "composition methods" or organizational paradigms for constructing certain classes of applications.

DeSyGNER applications are composed from a set of modular information resources, termed *entities*. For each of the application paradigms, specific visual and organizational metaphors, or *composition methods,* are supported. DeSyGNER implements the above concepts by providing a set of kernel services that allows entity types to be defined, implemented, and shared. This is described in more detail elsewhere.[4],[5],[6]

(a) Modular building blocks: Entities

The definition of *entity* is somewhat arbitrary, in that it reflects the level of granularity at which a developer wishes to partition the information tasks of a potential application. An entity tends to be an information resource with a self-contained set of actions that it performs, which do not depend on other entities. Entities are a generalization of *objects,* in the methodology of Object Oriented Programming (OOP),[14] and are invoked and communicate with other entities by means of messages. Entities are responsible for functions such as retrieval, display, update, e.g., in response to user interaction events pertaining to them, response to links coming into them, provision of links exiting from them, and support for associated overlays and index terms.

An instance of an entity is responsible for providing a particular view of its data, that is, the processing, abstraction, or rendering of the data required by context (i.e., the composition or link in which the instance of the entity occurs, as described below). For example, an image is displayed by an invoked image entity with a specific cropping, magnification, brightness and contrast, and overlays associated with a link. From another link, this same image might have a very different appearance.

(b) Application composition methods

Applications are constructed by interrelating various entities, according to particular paradigms that determine how they are organized and by the protocols through which control is transferred from one information resource to another. For example, electronic "book browsing" can be supported by a paradigm in which entities are organized into a hierarchical framework. Page layout is a paradigm that allows entities to be organized spatially. Hyperlinking allows selection by a user of designated regions of an information resource to cause other information resources to be activated. A tutorial can be constructed by including the ability to perform conditional evaluations with hyperlinking. An algorithm visual metaphor can be used to organize information resources, e.g., for portrayal of guidelines with explanations, or for visualizing the structure of a tutorial. Query can be supported by organizing information resources according to index terms, which may be selected by the user.

Composition methods create complex entities out of simpler entities.[15] Hierarchical book layout, spatial page layout, and algorithmic flow control compositions are examples of such complex entities. These may be incorporated recursively as participants in other compositions. These various paradigms can be combined; for example, the entities contained in a hierarchic book layout or a page layout may perform hyperlinking, and they may be retrieved by query. A *link* is a particular form of composition in which an action or event (user-initiated or system-initiated) that occurs in the context of one entity generates a message causing directional or temporal progression to another entity's context.

(c) Extensibility, adaptation, and evolution of standards

Both individual entity types and methods of composition can be extended and adapted to changing requirements. If a new entity type or composition method is needed, it is separately implemented. Entities form a class hierarchy which provides methods for its various capabilities, which can be specifically over-ridden or modified to reflect the new behavior.

Through evolution of entities and their communication needs, we develop standardized protocols for communication between them. The OOP approach allows each object to implement its own internal data storage and access methods, and only requires that objects communicate with each other in agreed upon ways. We do not impose requirements on the internal structure of an entity nor require that it conform to standards for databases, image formats, etc. Thus we are able to begin without standards, unless they already exist; however, in the process of evolution, we can expect convergence on standards.

DeSyGNER is intended to take advantage of evolving network capabilities and incorporation of externally developed information resources, adapting the view into those resources according to the needs of applications. This is depicted schematically in Figure 1.

Future Goals and Directions

A primary long-range goal we seek is a single environment in which both clinical and non-clinical applications can be supported in a consistent fashion. The components of which applications are constructed are seen as potentially being distributed across a network, accessible by any workstation rather than requiring an external host information system in order to gain access to them. Thus, the workstation, not a host information system, is responsible for flow control. Broadband networks are expected to approach gigabit-per-second speeds over the next several years, stimulated by private initiatives of the telecommunications industry,[16] and by the High Speed Computing Initiative.[17,18]

The next-generation implementation of DeSyGNER, now underway, is based on an approach that utilizes *agents* as the means for accessing information resources, processing them, and rendering views as needed by specific entities. Agents are independent processes rather than statically linked objects. Agents may have separate components for data access, processing, and rendering, which may ultimately execute on different computers across

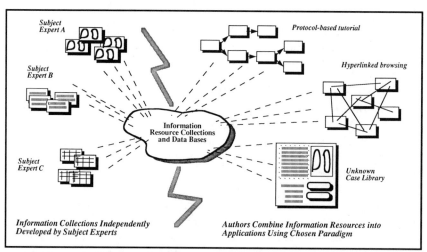

Figure 1 *The software architecture for supporting professional work divides the application development process into two parts: (1) information resource development and update, and (2) incorporation of resources into user interaction paradigms suited for particular purposes. Subject content experts develop databases, tools, and other information resources, and distribute them electronically via the network or other media. Application developers integrate these resources by using authoring tools that facilitate their incorporation and adaptation for the purposes intended.*

network, communicating with each other through client-server protocols. For example, information needed by an entity may be extracted from a relational database by an agent through SQL queries; processed to abstract or summarize it in a particular way, or even combine it with information from other databases; and rendered for display on a particular kind of computer. This architecture enables diverse platforms to be used as sources of information resources, and others for processing. It also facilitates portability of the end user application, since customization of the rendering portion is all that is required for different user workstation platforms.

Acknowledgment

This work was supported in part by grants LM 04572, LM 07037, and LM 07092 from the National Library of Medicine, and grant CA 45574 from the National Cancer Institute. The contributions to the work described here by other present and former members of the Decision Systems Group are gratefully acknowledged.

Notes

1. Greenes, R.A.; Shortliffe, E.H. "Medical informatics: An emerging academic discipline and institutional priority." *JAMA* 1990; 263: 1114-1120.

2. Tosteson, D.C. "New pathways in general medical education." *N Engl J Med.* 1990; 322(4): 234-238.

3. Greenes, R.A. "Desktop knowledge: A new focus for medical education and decision support." *Meth. Inf. Med.* 1989; 28(4): 332-339.

4. Greenes, R.A; Deibel, S.R.A. "The DeSyGNER knowledge management architecture: A building block approach based on an extensible kernel." *Artif. Intell. in Med.* 1991; 3(2):95-111.

5. Deibel, S.R.A.; Greenes, R.A., Snydr-Michal, J.T. "DeSyGNER: A building block architecture fostering independent cooperative development of multimedia knowledge management applications." *Proc. Fourteenth Annual Symposium on Computer Applications in Medical Care (SCAMC)*, Washington, D.C., November. New York: IEEE Computer Society Press. 1990; 445-449.

6. Greenes, R.A. "A 'building block' approach to application development for education and decision support in radiology: Implications for integrated clinical information systems environments." *J Digital Imaging* 1991; 4(4): 213-225.

7. Greenes, R.A. "Knowledge management as an aid to medical decision making and education: The Explorer-1 system." *Proc. MEDINFO 86*, Washington D.C., October. Amsterdam: Elsevier Science Publishers. 1986; 95-899.

8. Greenes, R.A.; Tarabar, D.B.; Slosser, E.T. Explorer-2: "A multi-modal knowledge management framework for medical education and decision support." *Proc. Thirteenth Annual Symposium on Computer Applications in Medical Care*

(SCAMC), Washington, D.C., November. New York: IEEE Computer Society Press. 1989; 1024-1025

9. Greenes, R.A.; Tarabar, D.B.; Krauss, M.; Anderson, G; Wolnik, W.J.; Cope, L.; Slosser, E.; Hersh, W. "Knowledge management as a decision support method: A diagnostic workup strategy application." *Comput. Biomed. Res.* 1989; 22: 113-135.

10. Miller, R.A.; McNeil, M.A.; Challinor, S.M.; Masarie, F.E.; Myers, J.D. "The INTERNIST-1/QUICK MEDICAL REFERENCE project—Status Report." *Western J Med.* 145: 816-822 (1986). Adaptation in this laboratory through generous cooperation of R. Miller and colleagues, and the University of Pittsburgh.

11. Pollack, M.A.; Greenes, R.A. "A pictorial simulation construction kit for enhancing knowledge-based learning." *Proc. MEDINFO 86*, Washington D.C., October. Amsterdam: Elsevier Science Publishers. 1986; 887-890.

12. Stein, L.D.; Snydr-Michal, J.T.; Greenes, R.A. "Realistic viewing and manipulation of radiographic images on a personal computer—a digital interface for educational and other applications." *J. Digital Imaging* 1991; 4(3): 169-176.

13. Abendroth, T.W.; Greenes, R.A. "Computer presentation of clinical algorithms." *MD Comput.* 1989; 6(5): 295-299.

14. Cox, B. *Object-Oriented Programming: An Evolutionary Approach.* Reading MA: Addison-Wesley, 1986.

15. Greenes, R.A. "Approaches to sharing and collaboration through modular systems design: A focus on knowledge management." (Keynote paper.) In *Software Engineering in Medicine: Proc IMIA Working Conf.* (Timmers T, Blum BI, eds). Amsterdam: North-Holland. 1991; 409-428.

16. McGarty, T.P. "Multimedia communications technology in diagnostic imaging." Invest *Radiol* 1991; 26(4): 377-381.

17. Kleinrock, L. "Technology issues in the design of the NREN." Presentation in: *Information Infrastructures for the 1990's, Workshop/Symposium VIII*, John F. Kennedy School of Government, Harvard University, November 29-December 1, 1990.

18. Comm. on Physical, Mathematical, and Engineering Sciences. *Grand Challenges: High Performance Computing and Communications. The FY 1992 U.S. Research and Development Program.* Office of Science and Technology Policy, U.S. Government Report, 1991.

The Alternative Science Laboratory

Stuart W. Bennett

*Stuart Bennett is Director of
Teaching, Faculty of Science at the
Open University, Milton Keynes, UK*

In schools, colleges, and universities, the problem of providing the science student with a good, or even adequate, laboratory experience is becoming ever more severe. The cost of building and equipping laboratories, together with the cost of technical support, is rising at a rate in excess of funding with the result that laboratory availability is at a premium, especially in schools. However, a factor that has probably been just as influential in limiting laboratory work is the increasing regulation, particularly that related to chemical and biological safety and to ethics. No longer is it acceptable to carry out some experiments on the open laboratory bench, to dispose of chemicals down the sink or to experiment on animals (dead or alive) on the scale of even 10 years ago.

The tenet that science is a pursuit based on experiment and active (often laboratory-based) experimentation is an essential part of the education of a scientist and has been held without real question for decades. It is perhaps significant that only now, prompted by financial and regulatory factors, educators are beginning to question this view. So, what is it that the student gains from a laboratory experience, and, can the skills and content be only developed in a laboratory environment? (For biology and earth sciences, the idea of the laboratory should be extended to include field work.)

Perhaps the major skills to be developed are: manipulation, observation, recording, analysis, presentation, experiment design, and evaluation of information. A feel for the laboratory environment or ambience should not be ignored although this quality is difficult to quantify. Additionally, experimentation should be linked to other aspects of the course of study.

Sadly, for many students, the experience of laboratory work does not meet these criteria.

Over the last 25 years, there has been a move to increase the efficiency of student and staff time in the laboratory. Not surprisingly, this has paralleled the availability and development of technology. What has not happened to a significant extent until the last few years, and then only in a limited number of institutions, is a rethink of why students of science are often required to spend more than 10 hours per week in the laboratory.

To date, it is the video recorder and the availability of cheap, high-quality video cameras the have been most exploited in the context of the science laboratory. Early developments were focused on laboratory techniques: the preparation of a chemical sample for infrared spectroscopy or an agar plate for mould growth, for example. Viewing equipment was available in or close by the laboratory and could be accessed by the student at the appropriate time during the experiment. The advantage of such an approach was to free supervisors from repetitive student instruction as well as allowing the student a degree of operational independence.

It was soon realized that video could do much more than simply act as a laboratory reinforcement aid. The high cost and limited availability, plus the skills and training for safe and effective operation, put the use of some equipment (such as the high field nuclear magnetic resonance spectrometer or the electron microscope) outside the realm of many college or university undergraduate students. Nevertheless, such techniques represent essential facets of contemporary science education. Other problems occur with hazardous chemicals, pathogenic bacterial risks, time necessary to complete an experiment, and the need for extensive field work in earth science and biological studies. Through the 1970s, a number of institutions produced excellent video material which widened the scope of experimental and other practical work. Nevertheless, there was the problem that video was designed and perceived to be an essentially passive activity because of its association with broadcast television, a medium usually associated with home entertainment.

The Open University in the United Kingdom began operations in 1970 with the remit to provide distance degree-level education across all disciplines (including science) to students who were not required to have formal university entry requirements. Either one of these two conditions represented a significant challenge but the two together necessitated a major assessment of teaching methods. In science subjects, a critical analysis of what went on in practical classes was needed and it was questioned whether, indeed, it was possible to teach science at a distance. The analysis of conventional university laboratory work at that time yielded some surprising results. Perhaps the most significant was that the time that students spent in the laboratory (up to three-quarters of their total contact time in some cases) was used rather inefficiently. Little attention was paid to the progressive development of skills and the focus of much of the time was centered on "recipe" type experiments which often represented a programme which had, at best, tenuous links to the students' parallel lecture courses. The outcome of this work did much to dampen the opposition of conventional universities to the distance teaching of science. The approach that was adopted by the Open University was directed on three fronts: broadcast television (and subsequently, video), the home experiment kit, and residential schools. By focusing on a set of behavioural objectives, it was possible to design a coherent experimental programme that achieved much of what was possible in the (often inefficiently used) conventional laboratory. Respectability and acceptance were formally attributed by the Royal Society of Chemistry and other learned societies which recognized Open University degrees in science alongside those of conventional universities.

Apart from a period through the 1970s when practical work was the subject of some imaginative thinking (a period which paralleled a burgeoning of distance teaching institutions worldwide), there was a period of retrenchment through the '80s. The rapid development of computer technology in recent years has resulted in major improvements in instrumentation and data handling in the undergraduate laboratory but there has been little change in the general ethos of laboratory work itself. An extensive survey of practical work in first-year classes of British universities shows that the nature and operation of experiments shows little change from the experience of students of 10 to 20 years ago.[1] Certainly, the detail of the experiments had changed but the general approach was the same. Students were often following a "recipe" approach and made few links between their activities in the laboratory and the work they undertook in lectures and tutorials. Whilst each experiment made demands of the students' development of skills, there did not appear to be a progressive development of skills from one experiment to another. It has been estimated that, during the course of the 300 hours that the average chemistry student spends in the laboratory in the first university year, over 100 individual titrations are performed. By any reckoning, it does not take 100 sessions with a burette to become proficient and one can legitimately ask whether the gaining of proficiency at such a technique is an appropriate aim in the 1990s. It is in institutions where resources for practical work are under pressure that the valuable questions are being asked and, in many cases, answered. There are two basic questions. Can laboratory time be used more efficiently by better design of experiments? And, can multimedia developments be used to teach outside the laboratory some of the skills that are normally acquired within the laboratory? The question that we ask here goes further: is it possible to learn experimental science entirely outside the laboratory?

We need to go back to the attributes and skills that have been identified as being essential outcomes of laboratory experience: manipulation, observation, recording, analysis, presentation, experiment design, and evaluation of information. If the total laboratory experience is to be gained outside the laboratory, then a system of technology and supervision is required that will address all these aspects. Translated into technological requirements, we are looking for the system to have the capability of providing the following features: interactive ability, responsiveness to student input, multi-route capability, flexible entry, manipulation, data generation, decision making, data analysis, analysis reporting, experiment design, and ambience.

This is a tall order, but there is convincing evidence that we are moving toward such a technology with progression through videocassette, video disk, personal computer and CD-ROM. Perhaps the best way to illustrate progress is to take as an example some recent development work focused on a chemistry experiment.[2] The experiment embodies a number of advanced laboratory techniques such as handling materials in an inert atmosphere, and involves the student in the preparation, purification, and analysis of a range of compounds of nickel. The route is summarized as follows.

Aim

To explore the effect of the ligand on the geometry of 4-coordinate nickel(II) complexes $[NiX_2(PR_3)_2]$ where X = Cl^-, Br^-, I^-, NCS^-, and PR_3 = PCy_3, PCy_2Ph, $PCyPh_2$, PPh_3

Reagents

PCy_3 is air sensitive and $Ni(NCS)_2$ is not obtainable pure, choice of reagents, quantities, handling

Design of apparatus

Inert atmosphere (degassing solvent, addition and reflux under nitrogen, operation of Schlenk line etc.), product isolation and purification, design details

Operations

Consequences can be followed through and seen, for example, if oxygen is not excluded, phosphine oxide can act as a ligand and this would show up in the analytical data, and colour of the complex

Analytical and spectroscopic data

Elemental analysis, magnetic moment in solid and solution by nmr, infrared

---

CD-ROM technology was chosen because it was the technology that was currently available at reasonable cost that satisfied many of our requirements, particularly that of providing good quality moving pictures (admittedly over just part of the screen) and a database.

The student is given a general method for the synthesis of a series of nickel(II) four-coordinate complexes and asked to prepare two. This involves the student in a choice of appropriate reagents, calculation of quantities, and design of the equipment to be used. At each stage there are in-built help routines. Operation of the equipment is critical and the student has to perform a number of specific operations to ensure that the ingress of air to the experiment is prevented. Should the incorrect tap on the nitrogen line be turned and air admitted, the complex produced will be one with a phosphine oxide ligand and not the phosphine ligand required. This "error" will become apparent when the student comes to interpret the analytical and other spectroscopic information (held on an internal database) that is offered as a result of the experimental procedure adopted.

The critical aspect is that the system is truly interactive being highly responsive to student response. The system can be customised for each student and has an in-built assessment programme. The work can be done by the student at a time that is convenient and, unlike the corresponding laboratory experiment, can be broken off and continued at a later time. The basic programme can be adapted to accommodate a range of different experiments in chemistry and in other discipline areas.

There are two difficulties with this approach. The first concerns the availability of equipment. Today, there are personal computers on the market with built-in CD-ROM drives selling for less than U.S. $1,500. For the institutionally based student, this probably does not represent a problem, but it may be some years before one can assume that this equipment will be available to the distance learner. The major difficulty lies in the software development. The time required to develop a series of experimental simulations is huge and can probably only be achieved through inter-institutional consortia. However, there are currently several groups worldwide making significant advances in the development of science practical work through alternative media.

To return to the original list of requirements of the technology, all criteria can be achieved by this CD-ROM laboratory except for the development of manipulative skills and ambience. A perhaps surprising outcome is that so much of what is worthwhile in practical work can be achieved and in an environment which is relatively inexpensive and safe.

The move from the laboratory may well never be complete and there are, perhaps, good reasons why it should not be. However, there will be a developing transition from the laboratory, particularly in high school and the early college years, as technology develops. Much use has been made already of the videocassette. It does not have to be a passive medium and much can be made by supplying the student with accompanying data to work on. However, it does represent a linear medium which is not friendly for multi-access. The video disk overcomes the videocassette weakness in the access context but cannot be described as a truly interactive medium. The computer's main weakness is the generally poor quality of the visual display and the imagination leap that is necessary to translate to the laboratory experience. These points are summarized as follows.

	video	computer	videodisk	CD-ROM
Quality Pictures	✓✓✓	✓	✓✓✓	✓✓✓
Interactive	✓	✓✓✓	✓	✓✓✓
Multi-route	X	✓✓✓	✓✓	✓✓✓
Technology Generally Available in Home	✓✓✓	✓	X	X
Safety	✓✓✓	✓✓✓	✓✓✓	✓✓✓

The move from the laboratory is not entirely dependent on a high level of technology. The development of experiments that can be carried out in the students' home or non-laboratory environment has done much to improve access to science for the distance learner. The use of micro-scale has enabled experiments to be done that would be outlawed by safety regulations if normal laboratory quantities were used. The videocassette and computer simulations have added a new dimension to extra-laboratory work.

The emphasis should be on experimental design and observation interpretation. Regardless of where the work is carried out, there is no argument to support the "recipe" approach. The focus that new technology has put on the role of experimental work in science is resulting in an approach that should produce better thinking experimentalists irrespective of whether most of the training has been within or without the laboratory.

References

1. M. A. M. Meester and R. Maskill, *First year practical classes*, Royal Society of Chemistry (London), 1993.

2. S. W. Bennett, *Proceedings of the 12th International Conference on Chemical Education*, Bangkok, 1992, and S. W. Bennett, *Chemistry in Australia*, 1993, 60, 80

Doing Chemistry With Technology

Steven D. Gammon

*Steven Gammon teaches chemistry at the
University of Idaho, Moscow, ID*

Chemistry, a blend of mathematics, writing, and visualization, is one of the most suited disciplines for using computers as an instructional tool. As a result, chemistry instruction via computers has been around almost as long as the computer. Since the early 1960s pioneers in the field of Computer Assisted Instruction (CAI), Joe Lagowski at the University of Texas and Stan Smith at the University of Illinois, have been actively involved in the research and development of computers as an instructional tool.[1,2] In 1966, Lagowski submitted an abstract for an American Chemical Society meeting, which read in part, "Generally, the modern high speed computer is considered to be an instrument used primarily in the solution of complex numerical problems or for the processing of large quantities of data in standard ways. However, systems have been developed which permit computers to be used as extremely sophisticated and never tiring tutors." This early vision has characterized the development of computer assisted instruction in the field of chemistry and over the past 25 years has led to the development of some of the finest instructional software available.

The teaching of chemistry using computers has had an impact in many areas of chemistry instruction. This chapter will discuss some of the most important types of software:

1) tutorial software/lecture aids
2) laboratory simulation
3) laboratory data acquisition/analysis
4) modeling and data manipulation
5) instrument simulation/instruction
6) computer/videodisk database

Discussions will focus on the best current examples in each category. All software referenced in this paper has been tested and is available for public use. Software that is not widely available and has not been thoroughly reviewed will not be discussed.

Tutorial Software/Lecture Aids

The majority of instructional software produced for chemistry instruction has been tutorial software. It ranges in approach from simple drill and practice to that which uses the interactive videodisk and CD-ROM technologies.

Currently, the most effective use of the computer as a tutorial tool for the introductory chemistry student is a videodisk/CD-ROM-based package produced by Stanley Smith and Loretta Jones.[3] This award-winning package covers the majority of topics that are covered in both high school and first-year college chemistry courses. The software is designed to run on PC systems that are equipped either with a videodisk player and graphics overlay board *or* a system equipped with a CD-ROM player. Both the videodisk and CD-ROM versions of the software incorporate motion and still video images; the videodisk-based lessons, however, have a much higher hardware cost associated with their delivery with a resultant return of somewhat improved video quality. In addition to the large number of lessons that contain video, the package also contains an excellent set of non-video lessons that cover many of the fundamentals of a sophomore organic chemistry course and freshman chemistry. Some of the topics covered in the organic lessons include reactions, reaction mechanisms, nomenclature, and IR and NMR spectral interpretation. Additionally, this package contains a classroom management system which allows instructors to structure lesson delivery and automate student record keeping. The management system is not restricted to just the authors' lessons, it will also control the delivery of any other DOS-based instructional materials.[4]

The appeal of this software is that it effectively combines both video and still images into a highly interactive learning environment. This software allows the student to move beyond the limitations of presenting chemistry with words and simple figures. For example, students can witness bromine reacting with sodium and the results of mixing silver nitrate with ammonium phosphate. Additionally, many of the video sequences contain information and experiences that can *only* be presented using the computer coupled with video. An example of this is the ability to watch an explosion one frame at a time in 1/30 second intervals. Student response to these lessons has been quite positive.[5] As a result of this response, approximately half of the time spent in the wet laboratory at the University of Illinois-Urbana has been turned over to students running this interactive videodisk package.

Another superior example of an instructional package has been produced by Orville Chapman and Arlene Russell.[6] This package, *FT-NMR Problems*, is a videodisk-based tutorial on the theory, practice, and interpretation of modern FT-NMR. This software requires a PC equipped with a videodisk player and video overlay card. The instructional method is that based on a discovery approach. The videodisk contains close to 12,000 spectra that range from 2-D carbon, ^{19}F, ^{15}N, NOESY, and a variety of DEPT and others. Not only can one interactively learn about most modern FT-NMR techniques and spectra, one can "use" a 500 MHz, 200 MHz, or 60 MHz instrument. This product has been used at UCLA and elsewhere to provide comprehensive instruction on modern FT-NMR to both undergraduates and graduate students.

Recently, there have been some attempts to employ expert systems for chemistry instruction.[7] The PC-based product, *CHEMPROF*, utilizes a "tutor," a teaching knowledge base, and expert systems to provide individualized instruction on nomenclature and oxidation states.[8] What makes this software noteworthy is that it truly is an expert system that continually adjusts to the instructional needs of the student while the instruction is taking place. This allows the students to concentrate on tasks that need practice while spending little time on those that are mastered or learned quickly. Another expert system of note is the PC-based *PIRExS*, which allows one to explore various inorganic reactions and so doing, develop a set of rules that govern these reactions.[9] It has been used extensively as a learning cycle approach to teaching descriptive chemistry to predict the products of reactions and then in the laboratory to test predictions.

Another program of interest is *Lake Study* for Windows,[10,11] which is an interactive package where students are presented with an ecological disaster (dead fish in a lake) and are supposed to apply the scientific method as a means to investigate why the fish are belly-up. The student plays the part of a chemistry detective using the software as a guide. The package incorporates video stills and high-quality graphics. This software provides an excellent example of how a computer program can incorporate active/interactive learning to allow students to explore a "real world" type of problem using a scientific approach.

Finally, an example of software designed specifically as a lecture aid is *Spectral Interpretation* (MS-DOS only). This software has both the IR and NMR spectra of 18 compounds that represent the major functional groups encountered in organic chemistry. The software is structured to allow the instructor to display the spectra and bring up coupling constants, integration curves, splitting trees, and highlight and zoom areas of interest in the spectra. This software is a much-needed improvement over the traditional method of overhead transparencies for teaching spectral interpretation.

There are far too many programs that fall into the category of tutorial software to discuss here. When seeking software, be aware that the quality is quite variable; there are still numerous products that do far more damage than instruction. Keep in mind that all software needs to be tested by both the instructor and students before full-scale adoption.

Laboratory Simulation

One of the most exciting developments in this area is the PC-based program titled *Inorganic Qualitative Analysis.*[12] This program allows students to carry out a comprehensive qualitative analysis laboratory experiment with seven cations and four anions. Just like the "real" laboratory, once the student has completed the analysis of the known ions, the software has the capacity to select unknowns from 1,000 possibilities. During the course of ion analysis, students can add reagents, run the centrifuge, filter, decant, and heat. During each step of the experiment, the students are shown full-color video stills of the results of their chemistry. This program is extremely well laid out and designed. Important features include available online help and the built-in flexibility to allow students to proceed by their own route to the answers. Students are free to run the experiments as many times as they need. This experiment truly is a full-scale substitute for a wet chemistry experiment and clearly establishes what one should expect from laboratory simulation software.

Worthy of mention in this category, once again, is the interactive software of Smith and Jones.[3] Some of the lessons interactively work students through actual experiments. Highlights include: discovering solubility rules by mixing the reagents, performing kinetics experiments with a temperature-controlled water bath, taking spectroscopic measurements with a spectrometer, and collecting and analyzing NO_2 samples. In all cases, the laboratory simulations are strongly tied to content and directed instruction. These lessons are somewhat linear in nature in that the number of options that students may choose are intentionally limited by the software. This has the advantage of ensuring that the students collect meaningful data; however, it also means that these lessons avoid some of the pitfalls and misconceptions that students often encounter in the laboratory. Several universities and colleges throughout the United States have used this product to replace some or all of their wet laboratory experiments.

Laboratory Data Acquisition/Analysis

Until recently, software and the associated hardware for laboratory data acquisition and instruction were restricted to those who could perform most of the development, construction, and programming work themselves. This meant that use of interfaced computers was limited to computer/electronics experts. Fortunately, the "experts" in the area have produced some fine products available for general consumption. The packages described below consist of both the hardware (minus the computer) and software to get up and running with a minimum of effort by the instructor. The hardware associated with each of the packages consists of an interface box that plugs into the computer (game or serial port) and various sensors. The probes with the greatest appeal to chemists—light, temperature, pH, voltage, and pressure—are all available. Potentially, these systems and others like them should spark a revolution in how science is conducted in instructional chemistry laboratories.

Three of the top players in the current market are the IBM Personal Science Lab Vernier Software,[13] (PSL),[14] LabWorks.[15] All currently support the sensors listed above with the exception being the absence of a pressure probe for the PSL. Also, all of the systems have software that is capable of collecting, saving, and displaying data collected by the various probes. The PSL and LabWorks systems are designed to run solely on the PC platform, while the Vernier system is supported on the PC as well as all of the Apple systems. All of the systems are quite adequate for data collection in high school and undergraduate laboratories. In all instances, data can be saved and loaded into a spreadsheet for extensive analysis.

The major differences between the systems described above are in the software and the level of support of ready-to-run experiments. Vernier has designed its acquisition software to be dedicated to the various probes producing graphs and data tables. The data is in a format which can readily be exported to its own analysis package, *Graphical Analysis*, or to a commercial spreadsheet. A big plus for Vernier is that it currently has a laboratory manual including students handouts, 20 student experiments, and 11 teacher demonstrations. These experiments are targeted at the high school and first-year college classroom. Only the Apple II unit allows one to directly program the probes for custom experiment development.

The major strength of the PSL is that the data acquisition software is quite powerful and flexible. A few experiments have been developed for chemistry by IBM and a high school laboratory manual.[16] This product probably has the greatest flexibility for setting up experiments and performing sophisticated experiments that utilize several probes at the same time. Built-in software features, such as the ability to zoom on the graphs, and to have simultaneous data collection from a number of sources, are also a plus. This unit is also well set up to be programmed for those who would like to write their own software and develop custom experiments. It is also configured to have the user develop hardware to drive external devices and build probes; plug-in circuit boards and wiring diagrams of the unit are available from IBM at a nominal cost. Also, there is the potential for the ambitious developer to use the PSL on the Macintosh platform as well. This unit might be the best choice for upper-level courses since the sophisticated interface box is configured to be programmed to run stepper motors and other external equipment.

Like the Vernier system, the LabWorks unit has a number of pre-done experiments for introductory chemistry, and a series of handouts is in the works. The major strength of this unit is that it is designed to be programmed by the student.[17] If one is willing to have the students learn the high-level language associated with the unit, the student can then develop any experiment desired. This feature makes this unit the one with the greatest flexibility for use in a wide range of classroom instructional settings. The only drawback is the time to stray from the pre-packaged selection of experiments.

A build-it-yourself system that is worth noting in this category is that of Ed Vitz at Kutztown University. He has developed extensive methods of having various sensors import their data directly into Lotus 1-2-3 spreadsheets.[18] The advantages are, at least for computer-literate students, that the data are deposited where one ultimately wants them to be for analyses, and equipment is relatively low-cost. Vitz has described his approach and equipment in a *Journal of Chemical Education* paper.[19] Additionally, the *Journal of Chemical Education: Software* has published several complete experiments which are of the build-it-yourself variety and work on the Apple II and PC platforms.[20],[21]

It should be noted that all these systems are also ideally suited for instruction in the lecture hall. The author has had great success in performing "live" titrations, calorimetry, and kinetics experiments for hundreds of students at a time. The use of hardware in this fashion is another way in which technology can make chemistry more "real" for the students.

Modeling and Data Manipulation

Spreadsheets have been the workhorse in this category for a number of years. Books have been published on the topic and papers are continually being published which utilize spreadsheets in new and creative ways for instruction in all disciplines of chemistry.[22],[23],[24],[25] Templates are commercially available for teaching many physical chemistry topics.[26] Since a spreadsheet is a commercial tool, evaluation of various options is beyond the scope of this work, however, if one is teaching chemistry using computers, spreadsheets should not be overlooked regardless of the level of instruction. The above references should prove helpful as a source on how spreadsheets are used in both the laboratory and lecture settings.

Beyond the "simple" spreadsheet, chemists have started to utilize symbolic processors such as MathCAD[27] for chemistry instruction at many levels. Flick Coleman, in a *Journal of Chemical Education* paper, summarizes the compelling reasons for utilizing symbolic processor: ". . .[symbolic processors have the] ability to perform more sophisticated, often iterative, calculations and to mix text, calculations, and graphics in the same document to produce high-quality, easily read, lab reports and problem sets."[28]

Symbolic processors are particularly useful for students to change experimental conditions/equations and see what results these changes have on a graph or computer-generated model.

Another class of software in this category is that designed to help students visualize chemical events normally unobservable by the human eye. *Molvib* for the Macintosh is a good example of such a program.[29] It allows one to display a vibrating molecule (waggles, bends, stretches, etc.) and perform isotopic substitutions and watch the new results. One can view the various vibrational frequencies of the molecules and print eigenvalues and eigenvectors for specific vibrational problems. The program is ideally suited as both a lecture aid and as a chance for students to "play around" with vibrating molecules.

Instrument Simulation/Instruction

Instrument simulators are just what the name implies, computer programs that are designed to simulate the operation of a particular instrument. In many cases the particular idiosyncrasies of an instrument are built into the software. The reasons for using instrument simulators are threefold: 1) to provide training to students on a particular instrument so the students are familiar with the operation of that instrument before they use the actual equipment; 2) to allow students to gain exposure to an instrument that ordinarily would not be available; 3) to allow students to concentrate on interpreting the information that the instruments produce as opposed to having to learn the actual hands-on manipulations.

Two simulators which have become mainstays in the chemistry market are *IR Simulator* and *NMR Simulator*.[30] These two PC-based products are designed to run like a Perkin-Elmer 1310 IR spectrometer and a Varian EM360 NMR simulator, respectively. Students actually "record" their own data from the instruments. The spectra students obtain are of an extremely high quality and are suitable for reference work. The simulators each come with 27 spectra and there are an additional 300 spectra available from the publisher for each.

Three PC-based instrument simulators are available through the *Journal of Chemical Education: Software*. The *Mass Spec Simulator* is designed to simulate a mass spectrometer.[31] The user of the package can collect sample data on a variety of both solid and liquid samples. If the user so chooses, the simulator will make actual noises of the instrument! Another package of note is the *Spec20* simulator which is a "working" Bausch and Lomb Spectronic 20 spectrophotometer.[32] Students can use the instrument to collect data on several samples commonly used in teaching laboratories. If desired, students measure the absorbance of a solution of unknown concentration. Absorbance versus wavelength plots are available as well as online help on how to use the instrument and Beer's Law basics. The third instrument simulator from this source is the *HPLC-An Instrument Simulator*.[33] It simulates a modern binary gradient HPLC system and models reversed-phase column behavior.

Interactive Computer/Videodisk Database

There are a wide variety of important computer programs that fall into this category. One of the most important for introductory chemistry instruction is *KC-Discoverer*.[34] Versions of this package run on both Apple and PC products. The PC product has the option of being able to run using a TV for the video or a video overlay card for mixed video and computer output. This program is both a computer and videodisk database. The focus of this package is the periodic table. There is a tremendous amount of information available with extensive information on every element, ranging from abundance in the earth's crust to the third ionization energy. Where appropriate, graphics are used to show structures of the elements. A powerful database manipulation program is included which allows one to sort and graph the elements to extract information on trends on periods and groups in the periodic table. The videodisk contains reactions of many of the elements with "air," acids, bases, and water; how the element appears in its elemental state; and common uses of the elements. Additionally, there is an artificial intelligence engine that can be used to build "sets" of data which students can then explore and manipulate. As a testimony to this product, once students become familiar with the operation of this software, it has been observed that they will spend extra time exploring the periodic table and its elements on their own. In addition to this product, there are many other similar products on the market that utilize both a computer database and this videodisk.

A winner of the Distinguished Natural Sciences Software (Chemistry) EDUCOM/NCRIPTAL Higher Education Software Awards is *SpectraBook I & II* and *SpectraDeck I & II* for both the PC and Macintosh market respectively.[35] This software contains the IR, MNR, CMR, MS, and physical information for a total of 100 organic compounds and associated functional groups commonly encountered in teaching organic chemistry. The software allows one to sort the compound database a variety of ways: melting points, formulas, major functional groups, and CAS registry index numbers, to name a few. Instructors can use the software as an aid to spectral interpretation by using the interpretive engine built into the software. One feature allows one to highlight areas of the spectra and then be presented with a picture of the structural features responsible. This product, with its teaching components, could easily be classified as tutorial software.

A related program is *The Schatz Index* which is a database of 400 organic compounds (100 added each year). There are no aids to interpretation with this product. The spectral database is limited to NMR and IR, however, it contains a huge amount of information including melting points, formulas, major functional groups, CAS registry index numbers, refractive indices, etc., and importantly, safety data. This package is an excellent resource for finding out specific information on a huge number of organic compounds.

Conclusion

It is impossible to develop a complete listing of all the programs and program types available to the chemistry instructor. As mentioned in the introduction, the software listed here is some of the best of its type and is designed to serve as a guide to get started. The best software available forms the basis from which to compare. Keep in mind that you always want to purchase and use products which are easy to use, easy to learn, and contain a minimum of errors. The goal of any instructional package is to get information to the user by the most effective means. When using a software package, never forget to ask yourself: Is this the best possible way of teaching this particular topic? If your answer is "no," skip the software and use some other approach; when the answer is "yes," take advantage of the power that this tremendous means of instruction has to offer.

References

1. Lagowski, J.; Rodriguez, C., Abstracts of Sept. Meeting of the American Chemical Society, 1966, F(22).

2. Siegel, M.; Davis, D. *Understanding Computer-Based Education,* Random House: New York, NY, 1986.

3. Smith, Stanley, G.; Jones, Loretta L., *Comprehensive Chemistry Curriculum,* Falcon Software: Wentworth, NH, 1988-1993.

4. DOS and MS-DOS are products of Microsoft Corporation, One Microsoft Way, Redmond, WA 98052.

5. Smith, Stanley G.; Jones, Loretta, L., *J. Chem. Educ.* 1989, *66*, 8.

6. Russell, Arlene, A.; Chapman, Orville L., *FT-NMR Problems,* Alpha-Omega, Inc., 3930, Mandeville Canyon Rd., Los Angeles, CA 90049.

7. Although not discussed because only available through the author, a good source of expert systems in chemistry: Larrechi, M. S.; Rius, F. X., *J. Chem. Educ.,* 1991, *68,* 659.

8. Eggert, A.; Middlecamp, C.; Kean, E., *J. Chem. Educ.,* 1991, *68,* 403.

9. Burke, J., *J. Chem. Educ.: Software,* 1990, *IIIB,* (2).

10. Windows is a product of Microsoft Corporation, One Microsoft Way, Redmond, WA 98052.

11. Whisnant, D.; McCormick, J. A., 1992, *VB,* (2).

12. Crook, J.; Weyh, J.; Bruland, J. P.; Gerhold, G.; King, D.; *Inorganic Qualitative Analysis*, Trinity Software: P.O. Box 960, Campton, NH 03223.

13. Vernier Software, 2920 S.W. 89th St., Portland, OR 97225.

14. IBM Corporation, Armok, NY.

15. SCI Technologies, Inc., 1716 West Main St., Suite 4, Bozeman, MT 59715.

16. Hall, T. *et. al.*, *Heath Chemistry Laboratory Experiments*, DC Heath and Company: Lexington, MA.

17. Amend, J. R.; Furstenau, R. P.; Tucker, K., *J. Chem. Educ.*, 1990, *67*, 593.

18. Lotus 1-2-3; Lotus Development Corporation, Cambridge, MA.

19. Vitz, E., *J. Chem. Educ.*, 1993, *70*, 63.

20. Krause, D., *J. Chem. Educ.*, 1989, *IA*, (2)

21. Curtain, T. A.; Wahlstrom, D.; McCormick, J. A., *J. Chem. Educ.: Software*, 1988, *IVB*, (2).

22. Atkinson, D. E.; Brower, D. C.; McClard, R. W.; Barkley, D. S. *Dynamic Models in Chemistry*; N. Simonson: Marina del Rey, CA, 1990.

23. Parker, O. J.; Breneman, G. L. *Spreadsheet Chemistry;* Prentice-Hall: Englewood Cliffs, NJ, 1991.

24. Sundheim, B. R., *J. Chem. Educ.*, 1992, *69*, 650.

25. Edwards, P. A.; McKay, J. B.; Sink, C. W., *J. Chem. Educ.*, 1992, *69*, 648, and references therein.

26. *J. Chem. Educ.: Software*, 1989, *IIB*, (1).

27. MathCAD, MathSoft, Inc., One Kendall Square, Cambridge, MA 02139.

28. Coleman, W. F., *J. Chem. Educ.*, 1990, *67*, A203.

29. Huber, D., *J. Chem. Educ.: Software*, 1991, *IIIC*, (1).

30. Schatz, P. F., *IR Simulator & NMR Simulator*, Trinity Software: P.O. Box 960, Campton, NH 03223.

31. Armatige, D. B., *J. Chem. Educ.: Software*, 1991, *IIB*, (2).

32. Gable, R. W.; McCormick, J. A., *J. Chem. Educ.: Software*, 1991, *IVB*, (1).

33. Rittenhouse, R. C., *J. Chem. Educ.: Software*, 1988, *IIB*, (2).

34. Due to the number of versions available, contact the *Journal of Chemical Education: Software* at this address: Dept. of Chemistry, 1101 Univ. Ave., Univ. of Wisconsin, Madison, WI 53706.

35. Schatz, P. F., *SpectraBook I & II* and *SpectraDeck I & II*, Falcon Software: Box 200, Wentworth, NH 03282.

Teaching Tools In Music

G. David Peters and Darrell L. Bailey

*David Peters is Professor of Music Education
at the University of Illinois
at Urbana-Champaign and a leader
in computer-based music education*

*Darrell Bailey is Director of the IU School
of Music at IUPUI and creator of the
Computer Music Technology Facility*

Computer-Based Music Instruction (CBMI) has evolved into a viable use of technology in teaching music in the classroom, music studio, practice room, and recital hall. Initial investigation of the use of computers in assisting students through instructional tasks dates from the mid- to late 1960s. Projects initiated in 1967 by Kuhn and Allvin (1967) at Stanford University, Earl Hultberg (1979) at the State University of New York at Potsdam, Deihl (1971) at Penn State University, and Peters (1974) at University of Illinois were among the first to use medium-sized to large computers in computer-assisted instruction. During the early 1970s, Hofstetter (1976) at University of Delaware and Taylor (1980) at Florida State University initiated music projects using the PLATO (mainframe computer-based education system developed at the University of Illinois dating from 1960) computer system extending the work initiated at the University of Illinois. By 1975, Hofstetter and others organized the National Consortium for Computer-Based Music Instruction. All of the early work in CBMI entailed the use of mid-sized to very large computers. The PLATO computer allowed faculty from Indiana University, University of Delaware, Florida State University, University of Illinois, University of Georgia, and a number of other colleges to work together in sharing the development of instructional music software.

As microcomputers became available in the late 1970s, several small companies emerged to publish instructional software in music for the Apple II and Commodore-64 computers. Programs also existed for the Atari and Radio Shack computers in these early days of the microcomputer. The basic research initiated on large university campuses was slowly transferred to the smaller microcomputer environments by university faculty, teachers, and publishers. The dissemination of instructional software was slow, however, because of the initial high cost of microcomputers.

Teachers successfully used both large computer systems such as PLATO and small microcomputers such as the Apple II to improve students' musical knowledge and skills. Consequently, musical learning has been greatly enhanced by the existence of computer-based equipment. Since 1980, and each year thereafter, more and more of these technological "musical components" have emerged for use by the music teacher and music student alike. The cost continues to decrease for the peripheral equipment required for high-quality computer-based music instruction. Critical hardware and software components were outlined by both Hofstetter (1977) and Peters (1977).

This chapter focuses on components, i.e., hardware and software, as well as classroom learning environments for optimum delivery of instruction to music students.

Components

Components which enhance music instruction and learning through CBMI include high-quality digital sound, music input devices such as keyboards and microphones, and high-quality music graphics.

The requisite components for successful computer-based music instruction are much the same as the arsenal of electronic gadgets now considered as multimedia technology. The ability to digitize sound, store sound, and retrieve sound through direct computer communication has greatly enhanced the power of electronic learning. Components which were created in the 1980s were precursors to the multimedia platform which can be successfully used by teachers in a contemporary teaching environment.

Cognitive learning "about" music can be presented in much the same way as other fields of instruction. Actual information about composers, music notation, music instruments, periods of music, and musical form can be presented and learned without high-quality sound equipment. By adding instruction in various musical skills such as reading music, hearing and discriminating musical pitches, and playing musical instruments, high-quality sound equipment must be added to the music "learning station." The use of digital synthesizers, electronic keyboards, CD-ROM playback devices, and videodisk equipment greatly enhance the students' learning environment through visual and auditory presentations.

In learning musical values, students are discriminating the "quality" of music performances. The student needs a broad selection of music literature and music performances for learning examples. The random-access of auditory information was one of the most recent problems solved in the multimedia puzzle. The use of CD-ROM and various digital compression techniques have made digital sound quite "transportable."

Learning Environments

Musicians and music teachers use different types of music "classrooms." When one envisions a mathematics classroom or an English literature classroom, one typically envisions a standard classroom occupied by 20-30 public school children or perhaps 30-50 college students. However, music teaching takes place in several different types of "classroom" environments.

The **music studio** is a setting where private or small group lessons are administered by an instructor teaching musical skills such as piano playing, instrumental performance, or singing. The music studio once consisted of a piano, a metronome, and a teacher. The contemporary music studio has a computer, synthesizer, sampling device, music printing device, and sophisticated software to assist the student and teacher in honing the students' performance skills. The "music-minus-one" concept allows the teacher to have prerecorded MIDI (Music Instrument Digital Interface) accompaniments which can be played at a moderate or quick tempo under computer control. The same music workstation can be used to digitally record the students' performance and allow the students to hear digital recordings of themselves to compare to pre-recorded digital models. The sophistication of digital samplings and the power of microprocessors in comparing music performances have never been better.

The **practice room** is a basic but vital part of the music classroom scenario. Not only do music students receive tutoring individually or in small groups, but they are also expected to practice individually or in small groups for hours each week. Often such practice is unsupervised, with little or no feedback for a hard-working student. Traditional practice rooms typically contained an acoustic piano and music stand. The contemporary practice room is now equipped with a computer very similar to the music studio. Students can also use computer-controlled accompanying devices which assist them in preparing for music performances. These same computer modules assist the students in playing or singing "in-tune" through direct and immediate feedback on computer screens or peripheral devices. The study of keyboard instruction, for instance, can directly result from attaching a digital keyboard to a computer through a MIDI interface and allow students to get feedback directly from the computer screen.

The **music classroom**, typically found in elementary schools or middle schools, can now be equipped with a "multimedia" computer to allow the teacher immediate access to CD audio disks, videodisks, or computer graphics presentations in front of the entire classroom. Using a computer console in the front of the music classroom, teachers can invite students to participate in solving musical problems as part of class participation. Music teachers experimented with these teaching techniques early in the 1980s using Apple II computers and large computer monitors in front of the classroom. The interaction between the teacher and the computer, plus the students and the computer, greatly enhanced presentations in areas of music acoustics, sound waves, and electronic sounds made by digital synthesizers.

The **electronic music classroom** has evolved from two models. First, the traditional computer laboratory used in many other subject fields has been enhanced with music keyboards for each computer station. The electronic or computer-music classroom typically has 12 to 30 computers, each with an individual music attachment such as a digital keyboard, microphone, and music tone generating device such as a Roland Sound Canvas, Korg MT-300 or a Proteus II sound module. Such computer music laboratories emerged in the early to mid-1980s and replaced the music classroom, or in some cases the music rehearsal room. Students were able to use CBMI music materials to create music and learn music through individualized instruction. This model still is viable and is used in K-12 education as well as many college and university settings. A computer-music laboratory is particularly effective in teaching listening skills, music theory rudiments, and basic compositional techniques.

The second type of electronic music classroom evolved from early "group piano" laboratories. Dating from the 1960s, teachers attempted to teach large groups of students the fundamentals of piano performance. Piano laboratories were commonplace in most university settings and many public school settings. The equipment developed in the 1960s consisted of primitive electronic musical sounds, and rather insensitive keyboard action. Students were able, however, to play keys, hear sounds, and interact with the classroom teacher through an audio network consisting of headphones and a series of microphones, one for each student and teacher. The concept of the piano laboratory has been greatly refined through the use of MIDI technology and more sophisticated digital sound. Many companies, including Korg, Roland,Yamaha, Baldwin, and Kawai now have developed sophisticated digital keyboard laboratories. The tone quality of each digital sound is highly sophisticated and the "touch" of the piano key is very similar to an acoustic piano. Within the last few years, Korg, Yamaha, and Baldwin have developed digital keyboard laboratories capable of presenting music instruction through a computer network which uses only one controlling, server computer for up to 24 keyboard students. The computer is located at the teachers piano keyboard and allows for LCD display of music examples as well as computer collection of student performance data.

A growing number of public schools are very interested in piano laboratories to either enhance their music program or replace failing music programs in the 1990s. Laboratories are being custom-designed for very young children (K-3) as well as middle school and high school. Universities and colleges have long used the piano lab concept to teach piano skills and fundamental theory performance. The same materials are now being redesigned for younger children to adapt into this relatively new electronic music classroom. Innovative design teams such as Cannon IV have provided solutions to the problems of equipment integration in the music laboratory. Figure 1 profiles a well-designed music laboratory module for K-12 or university application.

The **lecture hall** is perhaps best seen as a lecture or lecture-demonstration format with a college professor making a presentation to a very large number of students. Music appreciation and music history classes are ideal for such presentations. The adept music lecturer can now have a multimedia platform available on the podium to control videodisk performances of opera, CD audio disks of jazz performances, computer graphics of music notation and music analysis, then immediately play a digital sequence of music using a MIDI keyboard.

The Multi-media Instructional Portable System (MIPS) equipment developed by Indiana University Purdue University Indianapolis researchers has been effectively used by Bailey (1993) and Gass to teach up to 65 music students music appreciation classes. Classroom presentations implemented videodisk, CD-ROM audio programs, videotape, and computer-controlled graphic displays, in addition to audio CDs which would normally

Figure 1 An electronic music laboratory module

Photo by L. E. McCullough

be used in such a teaching situation. Bailey and the music faculty have developed a library of usable videodisks and videotapes to teach courses entitled History of Jazz, Music for the Listener, American Popular Music, History of Rock Music, and Music of the Beatles. These courses have been designed to attract the non-music major to arts and music appreciation classes at IUPUI.

Bailey and the music faculty at IUPUI have created a curriculum model for hypermedia learning for the listener, which was centered on large group presentation initially. Students are then able to extend their music listening in a laboratory of an extensive audio library.

A revolutionary audio library system is being created at Indiana University at Bloomington which will revolutionize the access to sound media. The system, Variations Project, Fenske (1993), was initiated in the fall of 1993 as a feasible hardware retrieval system. The project will allow a student or faculty listener to receive digital audio, full-motion video, and other multimedia sources over a communications network. Included in the holdings of such a system will be analog sources such as long-playing records, audiocassettes, videocassettes, and CDs. These sources will be digitized for transmission to remote sites within the Indiana University extended communications system and beyond.

A growing number of community colleges, colleges, and universities are equipping large lecture halls and auditoriums for such multimedia presentations. One of the authors teaches three classes each week in such an environment. Students can immediately connect a Shakespearean character from literature with a particular singer's role in opera. The visual presentation of the opera is enhanced by full-screen color video and high-quality digital sound.

Software Tools

Components and learning environments are useless without particular software tools to integrate instruction such as software for the development of performance skills and music accompaniments. Programs such as "sequencer" software and "music-minus-one" programs assist teachers in giving students feedback during their lessons. Programs which give feedback as to pitch accuracy and tone quality are also available to the studio teacher. Current examples include the Amadeus II (Pygraphics), Pitch Explorer (Advantage Technologies), and Vivace (Coda Music Technology).

In a music practice room, students should be able to use the same type of music software and hardware as they have available in the music studio. In other words, the students should be able to "practice" with the same high-quality feedback in a private practice situation that they receive in a music teacher's studio. Current examples of these programs include Instant Prodigy (Instant Pleasure Corp.) and Piano Works (Temporal Acuity

Products). These programs tend to focus on skill development within a musical context.

The electronic music classroom was developed as a computer laboratory with music keyboards and other peripheral devices to allow students to study music. Bailey (1991) defined the use of computer and a comprehensive software curriculum used at IUPUI. The use of commercially available software was enhanced by the addition of a network, server, and router/curriculum index system created by the IUPUI staff. The combination of software and hardware was the first large-scale, networked installation of such a music laboratory using DOS-based microcomputers and digital synthesizers which subsequently upgraded to a comprehensive Windows environment.

Over 80 music lessons were selected as instructional programs from various software companies. Included, however, were tools for the creative musician and student. Music notation software such as Music Printer Plus (Temporal Acuity Products), LIME (Electronic Courseware Systems) and the sequencer program Cakewalk (Twelve Tone Systems) added to the power of student tools. A laser printer allowed students to actually print music they developed during class and lab sessions. Figure 2 shows high-quality music notation output.

Students were also able to develop music keyboard skills playing scales, chords, and simple music composition, all under computer control. Music theory and ear training skills were developed in music fundamentals classes using network software.

A major accomplishment of technology is the large lecture presentation. The immediate recall of video and sound information for lecture presentation has finally been solved. In music lectures, the professor must be able to rapidly access examples of specific points within a music composition. The use of CD-ROM and videodisk has now reduced this access time to about 30 milliseconds. This new presentation capability has revolutionized the music lecture hall. With the CD Timesketch (Electronic Courseware Systems) software created by Short (1992), a professor can quickly create unique music charts of musical form through time. Synchronized text and hot words allow the teacher to display lyrics in original and translated languages, definitions of musical terms, and even music notation where needed; and all under immediate computer control. Full-motion video of opera, orchestral performances and vocal works can be programmed into this windows environment as well using Multimedia Express (IBM). This "hypermedia power of random access" permits an interactive exploration of the entire content of these disks — certainly a welcome evolution from "dropping the needle." Figure 3 shows sample screens of timesketches of Beethoven's *Symphony No. 5* and Bach's *Goldberg Variations.*

The use of hypermedia languages such as Hypercard and Toolbook are noteworthy for music applications. Specific sets of software drivers have been developed for music peripheral devices. The protocol for music hardware has been standardized through the use of multimedia to a level that Windows 3.1 now serves as an archway for teachers to use nearly any

Figure 2   LIME™ print of "beethoven"—"Score" at 6:23 on 10/22/93

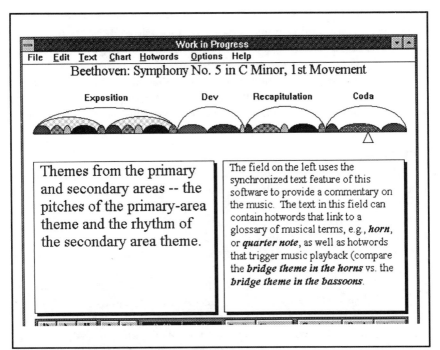

Figure 3a   *CD Timesketch of Sonata-allegro form*

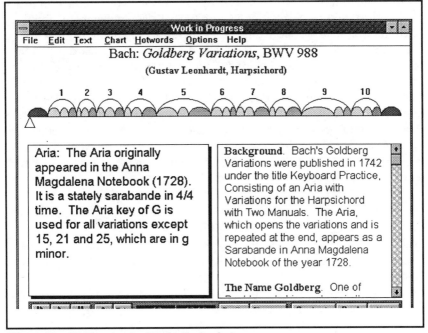

Figure 3b   *CD Timesketch of Umbrella Analysis*

music device they choose. Examples of hypermedia publications for consideration include publications by Voyager and Warner New Media including Beethoven's *Ninth Symphony*, Schubert's *Trout Quintet*, Brahms' *Requiem*, and Stravinsky's *Rite of Spring*.

The CD Timesketch program authored by Doug Short allows the teacher to use any CD audio disk with the multimedia MS-DOS platform to create inventive presentations of music analysis. The Clip Creator by Charles Boody offers an additional set of tools for the Macintosh computer.

The Future

In the music industry, music software publishers are adding multimedia instruction titles to their catalogues each month. Companies such as Dr. T's have released a program titled Composer Quest, Electronic Courseware Systems released the CD Timesketch, and Aabaca Software released the Clip Creator. Voyager and Warner New Media continue to create exciting new materials for presentation in the classroom and lecture hall alike. The use of digital equipment has brought the music teacher into the electronic classroom with an exciting array of tools. Moving from the PLATO computer in 1969 to the Apple II computer in 1979 to powerful Macintosh, MS-DOS and Windows computers, the music teacher has entered the 1990s with incredibly powerful tools, even as prices for the tools continue to drop.

Clearly, musicians, teachers, and students are learning to use technology. The digitization of sound has changed the way that we transport music (CD audio). Recent developments in compact disk interactive technology hold great promise for accessing large amounts of multimedia information from a small storage format. The standardization of keyboard, wind, and string controllers of MIDI require the development of new musical skills by performers and students. These skills have now become part of the new, emerging music curriculum. A growing number of universities are taking the steps needed to assist students in acquiring these skills. The Computer Music Technology Facility at IUPUI is one of the innovative centers which is developing the pedagogy for teaching these new music skills. Other universities are following this model as students search out programs which embrace today's technology and today's music.

References

Bailey, Darrell (1991). "Music Cluster to Open in January" in *Integrated Technologies*. No. 1, January-February, Indiana University Purdue University at Indianapolis.

Bailey, Darrell (1993). "Music" in *Technology Success Stories*. Indiana University Purdue University at Indianapolis.

Deihl, N. (1971). "Computer-assisted Instruction and Instrumental Music:

Implications for Teaching and Research" in *Journal for Research in Music Education* XIX, University of Illinois, Urbana, Illinois.

Fenske, D. (1993). "School of Music Library Variations Project," unpublished manuscript, Indiana University School of Music, Bloomington, Indiana.

Hofstetter, F. (1976). "Results of the 1975 Delaware PLATO Project" in *Proceedings of the Association for the Development of Computer-Based Instructional Systems.*

Hofstetter, F. (1977). "Music Dream Machines: New Realities for Computer-Based Musical Instruction" in *Creative Computing*, III No. 2.

Hultberg, M. L.; Hultberg, W.E.; and Tenny, T. (1979). "Project Clef: CAI in Music Theory, Update 1979" in *Proceedings of the 1979 Conference of the Association for the Development of Computer-Based Instructional Systems*, San Diego, California.

Kuhn, W. and Allvin, R. (1967). "Computer-assisted Teaching: A New Approach to Research in Music" in *Journal for Research in Music Education*, XV, University of Illinois, Urbana, Illinois.

Peters, G. D. (1974). "Feasibility of Computer-Assisted Instruction for Instrumental Music Education," University of Illinois, University Microfilms No 74-14.598.

Peters, G. D. (1977). "The Complete Computer-Based Music System: A Teaching System—A Musician's Tool" in the *Proceedings of the 1977 Winter Conference of the Association for the Development of Computer-Based Instructional Systems.*

Short, Douglas D. (1992). "Instruction in a Postliterate Culture: Multimedia in Higher Education" in *Journal of Information Systems Education*, Purdue University, West Lafayette, Indiana.

Taylor, J. (1980). "Activities at Florida State University" in *ADCIS News*, XII, No. 6.

Teaching Visual Analysis Using CAV Interactive Videodisk Technology

Suzanne Regan

Suzanne Regan is Professor of broadcasting at California State University in Los Angeles, CA

Interactive Video: The Interface of Videodisk and Computer

Interactive video has been used in many instructional settings from corporate to university (see Hoelscher, this volume, and Copeland,[2] Florini,[3] Wilson[7]). Usually the disk is programmed with specific instructions and exercises designed to offer individually paced, independent learning in a specific field (see Hoelscher, this volume, and Copeland,[2] Glenn et al.,[4] O'Sullivan et al.,[5] Wilson.[7] This traditional use of disks is not appropriate for media analysis. Chen[1] points out that interactive video allows for creative applications using faculty and student ingenuity. In the case of film analysis, the technology presents an extremely powerful tool for analyzing the classic and contemporary films that are commercially available on videodisk. This in-depth analysis develops students' analytic and critical thinking skills and increases their ability to decode visual messages.

Problems

Media study has long been held hostage to the technological limitations of the media analyzed. Early film analysis was limited to examination of original 35mm prints and 16mm copies, available either from archives or rental houses. The delicacy of film stock meant that multiple viewings created increasing risk of scratching or burning. Close textual analysis that utilized frame by frame review, or the repeated viewing of a particular section of a film required special equipment (a Steenbeck editor or Athena

130

analysis projector) and a copy of the film that was dispensable, so that wear and tear was not an issue.

These requirements were difficult to meet in all but limited circumstances. Individual research at a film archive or in a graduate seminar offered at a university that could afford and was willing to support the effort was among the few opportunities for close textual analysis. Only a few major archives and universities had the resources. This held back scholarship and teaching throughout most of the country.

Solutions

The introduction of videocassette technology and the development of extensive film libraries on video meant a whole new set of possibilities for film research and teaching. The inexpensive cassette ($29 to buy, $2.50 to rent, as opposed to $350 per viewing 16mm film rental) allowed researchers to view a sequence several times to assure accuracy in analysis. Students who missed class screenings could rent the video of the film or check it out of the library and watch it at home or in a media lab. Student research papers could incorporate extensive film viewings previously impossible to all except those whose schools held extensive film libraries available to undergraduates.

For teachers attempting to set up a series of specific shots or sequences for examples in lectures, videocassettes remain problematic. Cassettes take time to fast-forward and numerical counter settings are imprecise.

With the advent of cassette technology also came a whole myriad of new problems in the area of copyright. Copyright law forbids the public screening of many films on videocassette unless royalty payments are made or permission is granted for the specific educational use. Individual use of films on videocassettes is acceptable, and indeed the intent of cassette sales and rentals. Short clips are, for the most part, exempt from extra costs for public screening.

While some faculty argue that not-for-profit educational use is a gray area of the law, a final negotiation that will meet the needs of both educators and distributors is yet to be satisfactorily achieved. Academic organizations such as the University Film and Video Association and the Society for Cinema Studies are actively involved in resolving the issues that copyright creates for the film educator.

The latest development in media technology that allows for further sophistication in media analysis is the laser videodisk. Laser disks offer a quality of playback far superior to videocassettes. The cost of a CLV (extended play) videodisk is comparable to videotape, but like tape, the issue of copyright for some videodisk projection to groups is a concern.

Videodisks are far more durable than videocassettes for archival purposes. The information on videocassettes starts to deteriorate seven to 10 years after it has been laid down. Cassettes are vulnerable to changes in climate and to magnetic fields. Disks are far less vulnerable to climate, store easily, and are predicted to last 100 years without serious deterioration. Until CD-ROM technology advances, similar archiving of visual images in computer memory takes up prohibitive amounts of memory.

It is in the development of full feature format (CAV) videodisks that visual analysis of media has truly made a giant advance. CAV provides the clarity of videodisk technology plus frame-by-frame capabilities. CAV disks assign a frame number to every frame of the film. (Films are made up of a series of still pictures running at the rate of 24 frames per second.) Disks can be further organized into chapters or sequences as appropriate. A computer program and proper connections allow the computer to control the operation of the videodisk machine. The faculty or student operator can then call up any frame of the disk and receive exact and immediate retrieval. An individual frame can be held frozen indefinitely. A specific sequence can be run at regular speed with sound, or in silent slow motion. As with CLV, the laser reads the information embedded in the videodisk without physically touching the disk. Laser videodisk technology allows the union of videodisk and the computer so that information can be analyzed frame by frame and sections can be viewed multiple times without harming the disk. Also, sections can be viewed in new sequential order, repositioning the elements and allowing for closer semiotic analysis of the syntagmatic structure of the film.

The software allows for recording of information for later retrieval. Example files are developed to organize information, record analysis, and label specific sequences or shots in assigned categories. Categories can be cross-referenced and individual examples reordered to present the information within the frame from another vantage point. The disk system allows for close frame-by-frame analysis of the organization of the visual information in the film. Structure can be systematically explored and thematic development traced. The research information can be developed for formal presentation, using examples from the film to support the arguments developed by the analysis.

CAV is a format that meets the needs of the individual student. Since CAV takes up a great deal more disk space than CLV, using CAV disks for playback is cumbersome. Either the disk must be turned over several times during the screening of a feature length film, or, two separate videodisk players must be used, with considerable coordination on the part of the person projecting the film. Choosing to playback CAV, however, invokes the same problems with copyright as the simpler-to-use CLV and videocassette formats.

Student presentations to their class of short clips from the film they are analyzing seems to fall under the fair use areas of the copyright law and would not, unless quite extensive, be considered an infraction. Films on CAV videodisks are priced at around $100.00. The possibilities of interactive exploration and multiple use without damage to the disks make the investment worthwhile.

The Teaching of Media Aesthetics

My class in Media Aesthetics is an undergraduate class which is optional in a major that requires both Critical Theory and Theories of Mass Communication as well as an introductory course in Film Analysis. In order to make this class challenging and valuable to students well-versed in media theory and to attempt to teach a close textual analysis not available in other classes, I changed Media Aesthetics from a traditional aesthetics theory class to a course of study emphasizing interactive media analysis.

The class consists of close textual analysis of classic films, using CAV laser videodisks with a computer interface, to better understand their underlying aesthetic modes and practices. As was pointed out in Peters and Bailey (this volume), the ability to access work in a high-quality format is very useful. In fact, it is essential to teaching visual analysis.

The classroom in which media aesthetics is taught is a multipurpose lecture facility that holds up to 40 students. Since the majority of film and television critical studies classes are taught in this classroom, it has been set up for 16mm film projection and 3/4 and VHS videocassette playback. It has a large screen monitor that allows for easy viewing by all students. For the revised aesthetics class a videodisk playback system has been added along with a 386 computer with monitor. The computer is connected to both the videodisk player and to the campus computing system through an Ethernet connection. Information from the computer can be shown on either its own monitor or the large screen projection system. The monitors can also be used separately so that the students can study the Video Windows menu on their computer monitor while looking at the film that is played by the videodisk player.

The hardware necessary for this class consists of a videodisk playback unit compatible with a DOS-based computer, the computer, and appropriate connection cable. Software consists of CAV videos of classic cinema, available through Criterion Video and several other sources, Microsoft Windows, and Video Windows, developed by Stephen Mamber of the University of California at Los Angeles (UCLA) School of Film and Television. Similar projects have also been done by linking videodisk players to Macintosh computers and using Hypercard stacks.

The class consists of a series of lectures discussing the nature of art and the bases by which we consider film an art form. Films are screened for the class and the class is divided into groups, each group to develop a video project analyzing in depth one film available on CAV videodisk.

Everyone in a group is required to do an extensive research paper on the film which is analyzed. This paper is required to be finished at mid-term, so that the analysis of the individual videodisk is informed by research into the background of the film's director, contemporary reviews of the film, scholarly analysis and thought into the psychological, sociological, and corporate background of the film as well as its aesthetic bases. This is explained in the syllabus as follows:

> Each student will team up with two other students and develop an interactive video analysis of a feature film. The team will have 30-45 minutes of class time to describe their analytic techniques and goals and to present their analysis of the film in a demonstration to the class.

> Each individual in the group will hand in a 10-15 page research paper with bibliography analyzing the film that is being looked at for the group's presentation.

> Required to be explored in the analysis:

> • the life of the director and other creative works
> • how the film fits into its genre
> • the value of the film as a work of art

> Choose one of the following to discuss in depth:

> • mise-en-scene
> • camera style
> • editing style
> • use of color/the gray scale
> • use of sound
> • historic representation
> • societal and psychological representation
> • narrative construction
> • fantasy construction/deconstruction
> • construction/deconstruction of the real
> • portrayal of the hero
> • portrayal of the other (women, minorities)

The middle portion of the class is taken up by myself as teacher working with individual groups, instructing them in the operation of the equipment and software and helping them develop video examples of the basic principles of aesthetics and the individual contributions which their film represents.

For example, the power relationships in *Citizen Kane* are expressed both in the narrative development and in the visual organization within the film frame. Kane dominates the frame as he dominates the storyline and the lives of those with whom he is professionally or emotionally involved.

Kane is continually in the dominant position in the frame, as a figure in the foreground, the subject of a close-up or the apex of a triangular relationship with two or more people. His shadow obliterates his second wife Susan as she reads her negative dramatic review by Jed Leland. His figure appears as a reflection in a window over the heads of Leland and Bernstein as they discuss his acquisition of new journalists at the party welcoming them to the staff of the *Inquirer*. There are many examples that show Kane as dominant in the frame and support the social and political thrust of the film. To be able to look at the film over and over, isolate examples, review them and cross check them with others is to utilize a powerful learning tool geared to independent analysis and increased understanding. To show examples such as those above clarifies the student's analytic argument to the class far more solidly that mere description.

Videodisk analysis allows for analysis across the body of a director's work. Hitchcock uses females as both the source of his heroes' troubles and as the mechanism by which heroism is validated. This can be explored by examining several of his films. Eve Kendall of *North by Northwest* can be compared to Marnie and other duplicitous females in manner, visual presentation, and other discrete visual and aural patterns that support or undercut the basic Hitchcockian paradigm.

The last few weeks of the class consist of student presentations utilizing CAV videodisk technology.

The class final exam is based on research papers written by the students and the information offered in their presentations. Papers are made available as part of a computer conference on our campus Bestnet computer node. (For a discussion of the Bestnet computer conferencing system see the chapter by Arias and Bellman in this volume.) A computer conference is a series of electronic postings. Unlike e-mail, which is distributed to individuals, anyone with permission to participate in a conference can make entries and view all entries made. By making the papers available via computer conference, they become widely available free of charge. In the past papers were bound and sold in the bookstore (an added expense that proved a burden for some students) or left on reserve in the library (problematic when several students share a limited number of copies).

The students are graded according to their performance on their research papers, the shared grade for their class presentations, and the final exam.

Presentations of the student groups' research material utilizing their video example files for support are the highlight of the course. Students benefit from the group interaction necessary to master the technology of the disk/computer configuration, and also from debating and negotiating the research material to be presented. The presentations are class "events." Students even dress for the presentations: one predominantly female group discussing *North by Northwest* wore men's suits and ties, hair slicked back, in homage to Cary Grant's '50s Hitchcock hero, Roger Thornhill. The ability to support their assertions with instantaneous examples proves very compelling. Many students go far beyond the material published on their film and filmmaker to show relationships in color, design, and sound as they relate to the film's narrative development. Social and psychological developments are debated. Others feel very comfortable supporting or debating the arguments of major critics, with proof readily available from the video examples they have set up.

A number of students volunteer to help train the next year's class in the use of the videodisk/computer technology. Several continue their analytic projects as "independent studies" to further explore the technology and the films.

This technique for close visual analysis is being used in several film study programs across the country, including the University of Southern California (USC) and UCLA. Study centers are being developed on several campuses where information about a specific film can be collected in a Hypercard stack or using Windows. Students can combine film viewing with immediate access to contemporary reviews and scholarly analysis. Also accessible within the computer's files are previous researchers' comments on the film and space for students or faculty to add their own analyses for future scholars to consider.

The Future of Interactive Videodisk Analysis in Media Courses

The future possibilities of this technology are both exciting and impossible to predict definitively. Format will change. Disk size is not yet finalized. New means of interface between the computer and the laser disk reader are being developed. Interactivity will become more complex and sophisticated (see Scorge et al.,[6]).

Interactivity is being built into some contemporary story/entertainment disks on an experimental level. The viewer is allowed choices that help develop the story at several junctures.

Virtual reality will have an impact on modes of interactivity and could in effect allow us to be in *Casablanca* with Bogart, or take on Rocky Balboa in a heavyweight champion fight. The ability to re-edit material, rework the camera angle, and reorganize the film set elicits very exciting possibilities in film and video education.

Conclusion

To take classic films, dissect them, and manipulate them via computer disk interface increases the student's understanding of structure and motivation, how and why creative decisions are made. Whether students are interested in careers in film production, in going on to graduate study, or simply in becoming more literate viewers, the ability to take control of the mode of visual analysis empowers them as learners.

Inexpensive computer manipulation of visual media is in its infancy. Future possibilities are limited only by imagination, cost of technology, and the ability of copyright law to deal equitably within the new territories being charted.

Bibliography

1. Chen, Lin Ching, "Interactive Video Technology in Education: Past, Present, and Future," *Journal of Educational Technology Systems*, 1990, v. 19, n. 1, p. 5.

2. Copeland, Peter, "Interactive Video; What the Research Says," *Media in Education and Development*, June 1988, v. 21, n. 2, p. 60.

3. Florini, Barbara M., "Teaching Styles and Technology," *New Directions in Continuing Education*, Fall 1989, n. 43, p. 41.

4. Glenn, Allen D.; Sales, Gregory C., "Interactive Video Technology: Its Status and Future in the Social Sciences," *The International Journal of Social Education*, Spring 1990, v. 5, n. 1, p. 74.

5. O'Sullivan, Mary; Stroot, Sandra; Tannehill, Deborah, "Interactive Video Technology in Teacher Education," *Journal of Teacher Education*, July 1989, v. 40, n. 4, p. 20.

6. Sorge, Dennis; Campbell, John; Russell, James D., "Evaluating Interactive Video: Software and Hardware," *Techtrends*, April 1, 1993, v. 38, n. 3, p. 19.

7. Wilson, Kathleen S., "The Interactive Video Research and Development Project of the Museum Education Consortium," *Visual Resources: vr.* 1991, v. 7, n. 4, p. 395.

Instructional Technology in the Military

J. D. Fletcher

*Dexter Fletcher is a researcher in the Science
and Technology Division of the Institute for
Defense Analyses, Alexandria, VA*

Military operations are infused with technology. We seek advantage in fast tanks, stealthy airplanes, powerful sensors, precise ("surgical") fire control, robotic weaponry, robust communications, and so on. This investment in technology does not stop with combat systems. Just as the military seeks advantage by developing and applying advanced technologies to warfighting, it also relies on the application of technology to meet its training requirements.

Military organizations are not established and supported to train, however. Their primary mission is successful warfighting, and training, vital as it is, remains a means to this end. There is, therefore, great interest in seeing that military training funds are spent wisely and that they take advantage of the best training and educational practices that are known. Each of the three Services supports a major laboratory for applied research in education and training and each supports a vigorous contractual program of basic and applied research carried out by universities and firms specializing in the development of training systems and devices. Annually, the military spends about $40 million for research and development in education and training and an additional $260 million for research and development of simulation and training devices. These expenditures have a significant impact on the development of instructional technology in both Defense and non-Defense applications. The Office of Technology Assessment has reported that, "The military has been a major, and occasionally *the* major, player in advancing the state-of-the-art" (*Power on!*, 1988, p. 158).

Historical examples of military contributions include the development and use of examinations for personnel selection and classification by the Army and Navy as early as 1814 (Zeidner and Drucker, 1988), introduction of chalkboards at West Point in 1817 (Olsen and Bass, 1982), development in 1917 of individual ability tests with parallel forms for administration to groups using simple, standard procedures (Yerkes, 1921), early development and implementation of training films (McKown and Roberts, 1949), simulation for flight training (Mahler and Bennett, 1949) and aircrew training (Hudson and Searle, 1944), development of training devices (Blaiwes and Regan, 1986), and applications of computer technology to instruction (Fletcher and Rockway, 1986).

Many current initiatives in instructional technology have their roots in the military research and development community. Some examples include the following:

- The University of Illinois PLATO project, a large and influential computer-based instruction effort begun in the late 1950s, was initiated and supported for its first 5-6 years by the three Services under an Army Signal Corps contract (see Fletcher and Rockway, 1986, for more details).

- The first 2-3 years in the development of LOGO were supported by the Office of Naval Research as part of a longer term ONR-funded effort to develop new computer systems for teaching complex concepts (*Power On!*, 1988).

- Interactive videodisk functionalities, which include surrogate travel, microtravel, and interactive movies, were developed under the direction of the Cybernetics Technology Office in DoD's Advanced Research Projects Agency (ARPA).

- Many early, influential systems (e.g., SOPHIE, STEAMER, IMTS, BUGGY, WEST, GUIDON, QUEST) for applying artificial intelligence to computer applications in instruction were supported by the three Services and ARPA (see Fletcher, 1988, for more details).

- Most of the development, implementation, and institutionalization of instructional system design (ISD) were supported by military research on systems analysis and its applications to instruction (see O'Neil, 1979, for examples).

- The massive connectivity that is the backbone of the internationally emerging "information highway" used by schools to support Kids Network, Global Lab, and similar activities (see Hunter, 1993) has been based on ARPA development of packet switching technology for networking and wide ranging experience with the ARPANET.

Electronic technology would probably have found its way into classrooms sooner or later. But without work by the military research and development community on computer-based instruction, computer-based equipment simulation, intelligent instructional systems, computer networking, cognition and learning, cooperative (team) learning, and other issues, it is unlikely that the electronic revolution in education would have progressed as far as it has. This is not to suggest that the revolution is complete. Most probably it has barely begun, and we should prepare for what may be next. Initiatives in military training technology have affected civilian applications in the past and may do so again. Two of the most immediate and likely of these initiatives can be discussed in the space available here. They are networked simulation and courseware portability.

Networked Simulation

The absence of a true criterion test—performance in warfighting—and the cost, complexity, and variety of military materiel causes military instruction and its technology to rely increasingly on simulation as an instructional strategy. Much of the current interest in military applications of simulation for training center on the development of synthetic environments based on simulator networking. Work on simulator networking was begun by ARPA as a major development and demonstration project in February 1983, developed jointly by ARPA and the U.S. Army, and is now being pursued by ARPA and all the Services (Thorpe, 1987; Alluisi, 1991). It arose from a culmination of technologies that cross many disciplines and include computer image generation, realism keyed to specific training objectives (i.e., "selective fidelity"), computer networking, distributed computing, and the emerging principles of object-oriented design.

Networked simulation joins in a single distributed network a large number of fully crewed simulators that, in military applications, engage (fight) one another on a common electronic battlefield. Computer graphics and distributed processing ensure that participants in the simulators see through their viewing ports and receive from their electronic sensors what they would see and sense on the actual terrain. The engagement outcomes are strictly determined by the capabilities of the participants—not by umpires, battlemasters, or military controllers outside the engagement. The simulators and their crews may be physically located anywhere in the world—all that is needed is a connection to a network (i.e., the Defense Simulation Internet). For instance, during an engagement on the electronic battlefield, a tank crew in a simulator located in Germany under attack from the crew of a helicopter simulator in Alabama can call for support from a pilot in an aircraft simulator in Nevada—all of which might occur on a common electronic terrain model of a location in the Middle East.

"Time travel" is also possible. All the data packets that are transmitted on the network during an exercise are saved. Using these data, participants can choose some earlier point in the exercise, back up to it, and re-start the engagement from that point making different decisions, using different tactics, or incorporating different capabilities in their vehicles, sensors, or weapons in order to assess the impact of these changes on the outcomes of the engagement.

Some entities may not be crewed, but aggregated into military units under a (human) commander and individually controlled through the use of knowledge based techniques—they are intended to be indistinguishable from simulators with (human) crews and capable of passing something like a Turing test. This capability allows many more participants, or entities, to engage one another on the simulator network than available personnel or actual simulators would permit. Currently, networked simulation can support engagements involving 1,000 entities. Engagements of 100,000 entities are planned for the year 2000.

Networked simulation additionally provides training applications with all the benefits of simulation. These include safety, economy, controlled visibility, and reproducibility. Lives can be hazarded, materiel destroyed, view-points and perspective changed, and events played and re-played in ways that range from impracticable to unthinkable in the "real world" using real equipment.

Candidate applications in the non-military world for networked simulation used to train crews, or "collectives," can be imagined. Cannon-Bowers, Oser, and Flanagan (1992) cited 21 examples of collectives that need training and are commonly found outside the military. These include quality circles, management teams, maintenance crews, product development teams, cockpit crews, surgery teams, negotiating teams, instructor teams, and athletic teams. Fire fighting teams, well-drilling crews, police SWAT teams, ship crews, disaster emergency teams, ground-air control teams, and others could easily be added to their list.

Applications in school-based group problem solving might also be added. These might include cooperative exercises in surrogate travel to exotic locations such as the surface of Mars or Venus, in building items such as the Wright brothers' original airplane using materials available in 1903, or in re-designing biological entities such as wetlands to survive drought, biological threats, or (simulated) relocation to other environments. Through networked simulation, physically dispersed and/or isolated students can engage in cooperative activities that require them to develop and exercise higher level cognitive and social skills to solve concrete problems posed by intrinsically motivating experiences. Applications of networked simulation are just beginning to emerge, but they may significantly expand the roles played by classroom technology—and classroom teachers—in the not-distant future.

Courseware Portability

Each year the military Services invest millions of dollars to develop interactive courseware, which is instruction that responds to individual student input in determining the pace, sequence, style, difficulty, content, etc., of instructional presentations. Interactive courseware is a catch-all phrase that includes applications such as computer-assisted instruction, computer-managed instruction, interactive video instruction, and tutorial simulation. Interactive courseware is used in all military instructional settings including initial skill training, advanced skill training, garrison training, job-site training, officer education, and Reserve Component training. If the courseware is not designed to be portable, different versions of the same material will have to be prepared for operation on different computer systems that may differ only in such minor aspects as a graphics card, monitor, or pointing device. It will have to be re-programmed, or "re-purposed," to operate in these different computer environments, and the general development and use of this technology will be limited.

For this reason, the military has developed technical standards for preparing interactive courseware (ICW) that is portable, i.e., that will operate on a variety of delivery systems other than the one on which it is originally developed. These standards increase the sharing of interactive courseware by providing ICW programs that operate with little, if any, reprogramming across a full range of within-Service and between-Service instructional settings.

The standards settle some major issues by their choice of what should be standardized. Four possibilities for standards are those based on 1) hardware, 2) operating systems, 3) authoring software, or 4) the interfaces between these components. The issue is to establish standards for portability without stifling creativity and innovation among developers. The military has pursued the fourth of these approaches through development of what might be called a virtual device interface. In this approach, neither the devices nor the application programs that use them are standardized, but the ways the application programs communicate with the devices are.

Standards of this sort establish common techniques for application programs, such as courseware programs and their authoring software, to communicate with system resources such as display, storage, and input devices (Lewis, 1991). The burden of standardization is thereby borne almost entirely by authoring systems, not by the courseware, since authoring systems control access to system resources for instructional programs. Once the necessary changes are made in an authoring system, most courseware developed using the authoring system will comply with the standard. The virtual device interface allows upward compatibility and migration to new systems without requiring extensive modifications in the standard or its structure; it allows developers freedom to exercise creativity in choosing and developing cost-effective combinations of hardware, software, operating systems, and authoring systems; and it preserves competition among potential suppliers.

This approach has been embraced by industry and is being expanded by industry groups. Eventually it should result in the "plug-and-play" portability we enjoy for high fidelity audio productions. When that occurs, we can expect the interactive courseware enterprise to break out of its current cottage-level confinement, begin to realize its potential as a multi-billion dollar market, and raise its standards for quality to levels that benefit all education and training enterprises.

These standards also encourage transfer of instructional software from Defense to non-Defense entities — including civilian educational institutions and industrial training organizations. They provide a technical foundation for the military to meet Congressionally mandated requirements for training technology transfer with minimum impact on the resources needed to perform its operational missions (see Fletcher, Wienclaw, Boycan, Bosco, and O'Neil, 1992, for details). Notably, they can be used by any organization. Other federal agencies that adopt the military's portability procedures should benefit similarly. If non-government developers begin to use these standards, transfer across non-military applications will be considerably facilitated.

Final Word

Military instruction differs from instruction provided in non-military environments and especially in civilian schools in a number of key ways. Among these are emphases on (1) preparing students to perform specific, identifiable jobs; (2) instruction and performance of collectives in addition to instruction and performance of individuals; (3) equipment maintenance and operation; and (4) instructional simulation. However, there is little in these emphases to suggest that military instructional technology is irrelevant to instruction outside the military. To the contrary, the military's historical contributions to instructional technology suggest that military instruction research, development, and practice have much to offer all who are concerned with instructional applications of technology, especially electronic technology. Budgets for research and development in all sectors of instruction are too limited to duplicate relevant information. More should be done by investigators on both sides, military and non-military, to locate this information and make it readily accessible.

References

Alluisi, E. A. (1991). "The Development of Technology for Collective Training: SIM-NET, a Case History." *Human Factors*, 33, 343-362.

Blaiwes, A. S. and Regan, J. J. (1986). "Training Devices: Concepts and Progress."

In J.A. Ellis (Ed.), *Military Contributions to Instructional Technology*, New York, NY: Praeger Scientific.

Cannon-Bowers, J. A.; Oser, R.; Flanagan, D. L. (1992). "Work Teams in Industry: A Selected Review and Proposed Framework." In R.W. Swezey and E. Salas (Eds.) *Teams: Their Training and Performance*, Norwood, NJ: Ablex Publishing.

Fletcher, J.D. (1988). "Intelligent training systems in the military." In S.J. Andriole and G.W. Hopple (Eds.) *Defense Applications of Artificial Intelligence: Progress and Prospects*. Lexington, MA: Lexington Books.

Fletcher, J.D.; Wienclaw, R.; Boycan, G.; Bosco, J.; and O'Neil, H.F. (1992). *Defense Workforce Training Programs* (IDA Paper P-2743). Alexandria, VA: Institute for Defense Analyses.

Fletcher, J. D. and Rockway, M. R. (1986). "Computer-based training in the military." In J.A. Ellis (Ed.) *Military Contributions to Instructional Technology*. New York, NY: Praeger Publishers.

Hudson, B. B. and Searle, L.V. (1944). *Description of the Tufts Tracking Trainer* (OSRD Report No. 3286). Washington, D.C.: National Defense Research Committee, Applied Psychology Panel.

Hunter, B. (1993). "Internetworking: Coordinating Technology for Systemic Reform." *Communications of the ACM*, 36, 42-46.

Lewis, D. S. (1991). "Introducing the IMA Recommended Practices for Multimedia Portability." In P.V.W. Dodds (Ed.), *IMA Compatibility Project Proceedings*. Annapolis, MD: The Interactive Multimedia Association.

Mahler, W. R. and Bennett, G. K. (1944). *Special Devices in Primary Flight Training: Their Training and Selection Value* (Technical Report No. SPECDEVCEN 151-1-18). Jamestown, RI: Navy Special Device Center.

McKown, H. C. and Roberts, A. B. (1949). *Audio-Visual Aids to Instruction*. New York, NY: McGraw-Hill.

Olsen, J. R. and Bass, V. B. (1982). "The Application of Performance Technology in the Military: 1960-1980." *Performance and Instruction*, 21, 32-36.

O'Neil, H. F., Jr. (1979). *Issues in Instructional Systems Development*. New York, NY: Academic Press.

Power On! New Tools for Teaching and Learning, Washington, D.C.: Congress of the United States, Office of Technology Assessment, 1988.

Thorpe, J. A. (1987). "The New Technology of Large Scale Simulator Networking: Implications for Mastering the Art of Warfighting." In, *Proceedings of the Ninth InterService/Industry Training Systems Conference*, Arlington, VA: American Defense Preparedness Association, 492-501.

Yerkes, R. L. (Ed.) (1921). "Psychological examining in the U.S. Army." In, *Memoirs of the National Academy of Sciences*, Volume XV. Washington, D.C.: National Academy of Sciences.

Zeidner, J. and Drucker, A. J. (1988). *Behavioral Science in the Army: A Corporate History of the Army Research Institute*. Alexandria, VA: U.S. Army Research Institute for the Behavioral and Social Sciences.

Extending the Classroom: Regional Networks

Computer Networking in Distance Education

James D. Lehman

James Lehman teaches educational computing in the School of Education at Purdue University, West Lafayette, IN

Computer networks are not new, but the proliferation of personal computers is rapidly accelerating the process of linking computers with one another. Local and regional networks are springing up all over the United States and around the world. The Internet, a conglomeration of various networks that ties together computers all over the world, is growing at an astonishing rate. This large-scale networking of computers offers many opportunities, one of which is the opportunity to use computer networks for distance education.

Several years ago, Purdue University, Indiana University, the Indiana Department of Education, IBM Corporation, and participating school systems in Indiana launched an initiative called the Electronic School District (ESD) project. In broad terms, the goal of the project was to investigate the potential of a large scale computer network for enhancing the educational process. The project established a wide area computer network within Indiana that created numerous links: links among computers in a school building, links among different schools, links between schools and outside agencies, and links between schools and universities. The objective was to explore how these links might be exploited to improve education.

As one part of the ESD project, a computer–based distance education learning effort was initiated. That effort sought to determine the feasibility of using the ESD computer network for remote delivery of a university course to practicing teachers in participating schools. Computer–mediated distance education, while relatively new, is growing and seems destined to become even more important in the future. This chapter will examine computer–mediated distance education, in general, and the lessons learned from the ESD project and subsequent efforts.

Computers in Distance Education—Modes of Use

Efforts to use computers as "teaching machines" date back at least as far as the early 1960s when the first explorations of computer-assisted instruction began. This view of the computer as a deliverer of instruction continues to dominate many people's thinking today, even though technological advances and changing perspectives have expanded the realm of possibility considerably.

Computer–based delivery of instruction has been, and continues to be, used in distance education. In the typical scenario, computer–based instruction (CBI) is provided to the distance learner to supplement or perhaps replace more traditional forms of distance learning such as print, audio, and video. The CBI software itself can be supplied to the distance learner by means of a network or on a diskette that is mailed from a central site. The learner then uses the software on his or her home computer to acquire the content. The interactive nature of computer–based instruction offers the potential for greater effectiveness than more traditional techniques such as print–based correspondence study. However, this approach maintains a narrow view of the computer as a deliverer of instruction only.

More recently, the growth of computer networking has opened the possibility of using the computer as a facilitator of interaction in distance education. In this mode, the computer is a tool that mediates the instructional process. It creates what has been dubbed the "virtual classroom."[1] The computer re-creates the elements of a traditional classroom in an electronic environment. Distance learners, separated not just by space but also by time, can participate in the virtual class almost as if they were in the same room in a school building.

In this approach, the computer serves both as an information delivery vehicle and as the mediator of an interactive environment for learning. An electronic version of the traditional class discussion can take place using computer conferencing. Private communication is facilitated by electronic mail (e–mail). In addition, the computer serves as a repository of content information and maintains a complete history of class discussion. For the learner, this methodology offers both convenience and an opportunity for extended dialog.

In a typical situation, the learner participates by using a personal computer or terminal, from home or work, to access the class discussion at any time that is convenient. The contents of the discussion may consist of lecture notes, questions or discussion starters from the instructor, and the comments of other members of the class. The learner can peruse this discussion at his or her own pace. Whereas the give and take in actual classrooms can be limited, computer–mediated distance education gives participants the opportunity to carefully examine the comments of others, backtrack to previous relevant entries, and frame thoughtful contributions to the discussion. This methodology has a number of positive attributes that make it an interesting alternative to more traditional methods.

Advantages and Limitations of Computer–Mediated Distance Education

Figure 1 compares computer–mediated distance education to the traditional classroom. This comparison suggests both the advantages and the limitations of this method of distance education.[1,2,3]

Traditional Classroom	Computer–Mediated Distance Education
• Students travel to class site	• Students take class at local site
• Class times and schedule are fixed	• Class times and schedule are flexible
• There are live, interpersonal interactions	• Interactions are computer–mediated
• Content delivery occurs via lectures, class discussions, laboratories, readings, etc.	• Content delivery occurs via computer conferencing, on–line discussions, self–study, readings, etc.
• Class discussions are limited in time and may be dominated by a few individuals	• Class discussions have unlimited time and provide opportunities for wide participation
• Unless recorded, class sessions are inaccessible after they have occurred	• All class exchanges are maintained in the computer and can be accessed at any time
• Access to instructor occurs in class, via office hours, etc.	• Access to the instructor is through electronic mail at any time
• Students interact with one another inside and outside of class	• Student interactions occur via electronic mail and computer conferencing
• Assignments and examinations are submitted in person	• Assignments and examinations are conducted on–line or submitted via electronic file transfer

Figure 1   *A Comparison of the Traditional Classroom with Computer–Mediated Distance Education*

Advantages

- Eliminates travel time and expense
- Permits flexible scheduling
- Provides convenient (potentially 24 hour per day) access to course materials and instructor
- Provides learners with access to expert instructors as well as to group knowledge and support
- Enhances opportunities for class interaction
- Provides an egalitarian class atmosphere
- Stores communications for convenient access, reflection, and response
- Provides instruction relatively inexpensively (once the necessary infrastructure is established)

Limitations

- Lacks the visual and verbal cues of face–to–face or video instruction
- Requires the use of equipment that is unfamiliar to many learners
- Requires computer familiarity and acclimatization to the computer conferencing system for effective participation
- Requires structure to facilitate learning and foster interaction
- Can create information overload and difficulties tracing interchanges because of the sheer volume of information generated
- Can place extra burdens on both the instructor and the learners
- Is subject to problems including, but not limited to, computer hardware, computer software, and telephone or network lines
- Initial costs are high and may be compounded by continuing costs such as computer maintenance and telephone line charges

Computer–Mediated Distance Education Systems

Computer–mediated distance education systems rely on a central computer operating special computer conferencing and electronic messaging software. Class participants use local terminals or personal computers connected via modems to telephone lines to access the virtual class at any time and from any place convenient to them. As long as the host computer is operating, there is no restriction on when an individual may participate. The host system maintains correspondence and the class "discussion" for access at any time.

The first systems designed especially for computer–mediated distance education were developed in the early 1980s. Much of the development took place at Canadian institutions and, in the United States, at places like the New Jersey Institute of Technology (NJIT) and the New York Institute of Technology (NYIT). Today, popular systems include CONFER, CoSy

(Conferencing System), EIES (Electronic Information Exchange System), and FORUM.[3] These are distinguished by their particular capabilities and the hardware platforms upon which they operate. In the U.S., NJIT uses the EIES system, while NYIT uses CoSy. In the ESD project, a derivative of CONFER was used for computer conferencing. See the chapter on networked collaborative teaching and learning by Arias and Bellman for more information about the roots of computer–mediated distance education and its classroom applications.

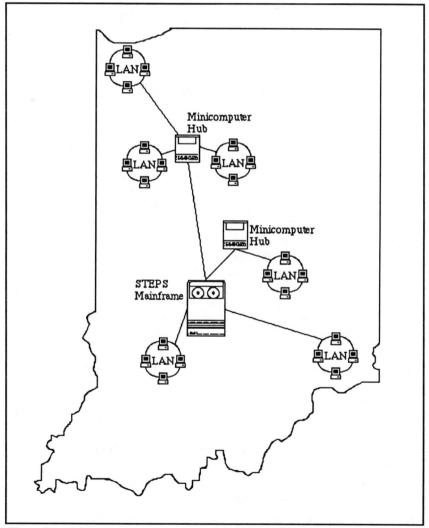

Figure 2 *A diagrammatic representation of the STEPS wide-area computer network as it was originally configured*

The Electronic School District System

The ESD project established a wide area computer network within Indiana that interconnected a number of public schools and two major state universities, Purdue University and Indiana University. This network was dubbed STEPS, Student and Teachers Electronic Productivity System. The STEPS network was anchored by an IBM mainframe computer located on the main campus of Indiana University. As originally configured, minicomputers served as regional hubs that connected to the STEPS mainframe. These hubs, in turn, were connected via dedicated telephone lines to local area networks (LANs) of personal computers in the participating schools. This arrangement allowed teachers or students in the participating schools to work locally or to connect to the STEPS network to perform network tasks such as electronic mail exchange or computer conferencing. For individuals outside of the participating schools, dial–up access to the STEPS network was supported. Figure 2 shows a diagram of the network.

The STEPS network provided the basic elements necessary for computer–mediated distance education: electronic mail (via IBM's PROFS software), computer conferencing (via IBM's Grouptalk CONVENE software, a derivative of CONFER), and support for file transfer. To make the system more user-friendly, a menu system modeled on a school building was created. It allowed users to visit the school's mail room to send or receive e–mail or visit the science classroom, for example, to participate in one of several computer conferences concerning science education.[4]

Teachers and students used the STEPS network in a variety of ways in the classroom. One project involved a writing exchange. Students in high school English classes electronically submitted writing samples to college students majoring in English Education at Indiana University. The college students critiqued the writing samples and returned them to the high school students; both groups of students benefitted from the exchange. The chapter by Schwartz concerning cross–cultural team teaching describes a similar writing exchange. Students in science classes accessed a STEPS information database established by staff at the Indianapolis Zoo, among others, containing fact sheets about all of the animals at the zoo. If the fact sheets were not enough, the students exchanged electronic mail with the zoo's education staff to get more information. Teachers used the network to keep in contact with other teachers and to consult with university faculty. Of course, as already mentioned, the network was also used to conduct a computer–mediated distance education class for teachers in the participating schools.

The Computer–Mediated Distance Education Class

In the ESD project, an introductory level computer course for educators was offered through Purdue University as a computer–mediated distance education class. Teachers from four ESD school sites enrolled. A grant from the Indiana Department of Education provided tuition support for the distance class participants. A regular, on–campus section of the course was offered in parallel to the distance class to facilitate comparisons.

The computer–mediated distance class and the traditionally taught, on–campus class differed in the ways already described. Students in the traditional, on–campus class attended lectures and laboratories according to a fixed schedule, had personal access to instructors, and directly submitted assignments. Participants in the computer–mediated distance class used computer conferencing, contacted the instructor via e–mail, and submitted assignments electronically. Both groups used the same print–based materials and supplemental computer tutorials. To assess the computer–mediated distance education method, several variables were tracked including achievement, attitudes, student time–on–task, and dropout and incompletion rates.

Results

In field studies, plans often go awry. At two distance class sites, network technical problems effectively prevented participants from reliably connecting to the STEPS network. As a result, participants at these sites were forced to adopt a print–based correspondence course approach. Therefore, comparisons were made among three groups of participants: a computer–mediated distance education group, a correspondence–based distance education group, and the traditional, on–campus group.

A brief summary of the results follows; a fuller accounting has been reported elsewhere.[5] Except for the final examination, there were no statistically significant differences in the achievement of the three groups. Interestingly, the correspondence group scored the highest on the final examination while the computer–mediated group scored the lowest. Several factors may have contributed to this particular result. But, it is perhaps more important to note that all other indicators suggested that there were no achievement differences among groups.

Time–on–task differences among the groups were observed. The correspondence group, on average, spent the most time on the course—about nine hours per week. The computer–mediated group spent about seven hours per week. The on–campus group spent about five hours per week.

Attitudes toward computers improved equally in all groups. However, both the correspondence and computer–mediated group participants were somewhat less positive toward the course itself than were the on–campus students. Finally, consistent with some other reports of distance education, there were higher rates of attrition and failure to complete the course among the distance education groups.

Several other findings emerged serendipitously. A group cooperative atmosphere spontaneously arose at one of the computer–mediated sites. At this site, all participants successfully completed the course in timely fashion. At the other computer site, however, there was no such cooperation, and the course completion rate was poor. This suggests that on–site cooperation could be a valuable component of some computer–mediated distance education. Electronic mail was very well received and led to an openness of exchanges between students and instructors not typically seen in the classroom. However, e–mail contributed to a very heavy instructor workload. The computer–mediated distance class required much more than the normal amount of instructor time because of the need to respond to extensive e–mail and to download assignments for grading. Finally, the nature of the course, a beginning-level computer education class, proved largely inappropriate for the format. Opportunities for generating real dialog among participants were limited, and there were numerous problems. Participants in the distance groups were too computer-inexperienced to work through problems without hands–on instructor assistance.

Is Computer–Mediated Distance Education Viable?

A number of different trials at various universities have established that computer–mediated distance education can be a viable alternative approach in certain instructional situations. The ESD project test, though marred by some problems, did succeed. For the most part, achievement of the computer–mediated class was at a level on par with the traditionally taught class. Although time–on–task was greater for the distance education group, when travel time was taken into consideration, the trade–off was reasonable. From this experience, a more recent computer–mediated distance education class offered via IDEAnet (the Indiana Department of Education Access Network) and others sources[1],[2],[6] some general statements regarding this methodology can be made.

What Works and What Does Not?

- Content involving extended discussion, dialog, and decision–making seems best-suited to this methodology.
- Reliable operation of the computer system and orientation of the users to it is important. Participants can be "turned off" by technical problems or their own inabilities to perform functions. The approach may not be suitable for beginning computer users.
- Cooperative or collaborative learning at remote sites may be of benefit to participants. Some isolated participants may suffer.
- Electronic mail is a valuable communication tool that

may foster a more open and egalitarian atmosphere, and computer conferencing may provide for a more extended dialog than found in the traditional classroom.

- Supplemental materials are of benefit. The system itself supports interaction. Supplemental materials can provide a common basis for discussion.
- Participants strongly support the flexibility and reduced travel demands of this approach.

The Future

With the recent passage of national legislation to begin to develop a high-speed national data network akin to the interstate highway system, it seems certain that opportunities for using computer networks will only expand in the coming years. Computer–mediated distance education has a bright future. One day, it seems likely that distance education will be available on demand at any time from home, on the job, and in the classroom. To prepare for that day, educators today must continue to explore the possibilities and push the boundaries of distance education via computer networks.

References

1. Hiltz, S. R. (1986). The "virtual classroom": Using computer–mediated communication for university teaching. *Journal of Communication, 36* (2), 95–104.

2. Harasim, L. (1987). Teaching and learning on–line: Issues in computer–mediated graduate courses. *Canadian Journal of Educational Communication, 16*(2), 117–135.

3. Cheng, H–C.; Lehman, J.; & Reynolds, A. (1991). What do we know about asynchronous group computer–based distance learning? *Educational Technology, 31*(11), 16–19.

4. Lehman, J. D.; Campbell, J. P.; Halla, M.; & Lehman, C. B. (1992) Doing science in the electronic school district. *Journal of Computers in Mathematics and Science Teaching, 11*(2), 193–198.

5. Cheng, H–C.; Lehman, J.; & Armstrong, P. (1991). Comparison of performance and attitude in traditional and computer conferencing classes. *The American Journal of Distance Education, 5*(3), 51–64.

6. Quinn, C. N.; Mehan, H.; Levin, J. A.; & Black, S. D. (1983). Real education in non–real time: The use of electronic messaging systems for instruction. *Instructional Science, 11*, 313–327.

Teaching and Learning in the Extended Classroom: Nursing Telecourses

Diane M. Billings

*Diane Billings is Professor of Nursing
and Assistant Dean of Learning Resources
at Indiana University School of Nursing
in Indianapolis, IN*

Health care in the United States is changing from acute-care, crisis-oriented to community-based and client-centered, with a health care system focused on prevention as well as treatment. In response to these changes, nurse educators are revitalizing curricula to prepare nurses at entry levels for community-based primary health care and at graduate levels for advanced practice. Goals have been established to increase access to nursing education, support geographical distribution of graduates for varied practice settings, promote educational mobility, and use limited faculty resources wisely (AACN, 1992; NLN, 1993). One strategy to accomplish these goals is to extend the classroom using telecourse (videoteleconferencing) technologies.

The use of video-based technologies for nursing course delivery is increasing as nursing courses and programs are being broadcast by way of cable, microwave, or satellite on closed or open circuits using one- or two-way video and two-way audio (Billings & Bachmeier, 1994; Billings, Frazier, Lausch, & McCarty, 1989; Boyd & Baker, 1987; Colbert, 1988; Limon, Spencer, & Henderson, 1985; Major & Shane, 1991; Shoemaker, 1993; Tribulshi & Frank, 1987). Telecourses with classes videotaped for viewing in health care agencies or homes are used for continuing nursing education (Clark, 1989). In addition, several nursing professional organizations and health care companies regularly broadcast telecourses to member agency sites. In light of these recent developments, it is apparent that

156

the nursing classroom can no longer be traditionally defined. When teleconferencing technology is introduced, however, modifications must be made in the instructional interchanges that occur between student and faculty. These interchanges have been explained by Jafari (1990) as technology interfaces. According to Jafari (1990), instructional interfaces in the traditional classroom occur between teacher and student, but in the high-tech classroom such as occurs with telecourses, there are also added communication interfaces between faculty and technology, and between students and technology. The goal is to maintain traditional teacher-student communications while limiting barriers of technology to achieve curricular and course goals.

The purpose of this chapter is to identify the modifications required to manage the changed instructional interfaces and suggest pedagogical strategies for supporting classroom communications in the extended nursing classroom.

Teaching and Learning in the Extended Classroom

Teaching and learning in the extended classroom involves a reconceptualization of both teaching and learning. While the technology facilitates access, both teachers and students must modify longstanding communication patterns to accommodate the technology interfaces.

The Instructor-Technology Interface

The instructor-technology interface in the telecourse classroom involves the presence of cameras, technicians, and directors in the classroom, as well as the absence often times of face-to-face student contact. Faculty must adapt to these changes by modifying preferred teaching and evaluation strategies to accommodate the technology and students at a distance. These modifications, in turn, increase the teaching workload and require additional support from administrators and colleagues. Finally, for nursing faculty there is the additional challenge to provide clinical practice experiences for students at distant sites.

Teaching and evaluation

Using telecourse technology requires adaptation of teaching and evaluation strategies, because 1) technical barriers preclude the use of some teaching strategies, 2) large class sizes or lack of two-way interactivity may limit discussion and interaction, and 3) faculty may need to develop acceptable visual aids or seek copyright clearance for using commercially prepared instructional materials (Billings, Frazier, Lausch, & McCarty, 1989; Billings, et al., (in press); Gehlauf, Shatz, & Frye, 1991; Major & Shane, 1991; Shoemaker, 1993). Faculty also need to develop or emphasize a teaching style that projects warmth and interest to overcome the barriers of distance (Parkinson & Parkinson, 1989). Finally, faculty must adapt evaluation strategies to assure exam security and timely feedback for students at a distance. This may mean using multiple-choice tests that can be quickly graded and decreasing evaluation activities that necessitate immediate feedback. Strategies to assist faculty manage the technology include faculty orientation and instructional design or redesign of courses.

Workload

Teaching on television increases faculty workload due to the necessity of adapting course materials, teaching styles, and evaluation procedures (Boyd & Baker, 1987; Fulmer, Hazard, Jones & Keene, 1992). Most schools of nursing compensate for this increased workload by reducing workload the semester before the course (Boyd & Baker, 1987), adding workload credits for teaching television courses, and/or providing release time or teaching assistance support while teaching the course.

Faculty support

Shoemaker (1993) suggests that teaching on television is innovative and risk-taking, and that faculty need a strong support system to avoid isolation and to achieve a sense of satisfaction. Furthermore, lack of reward or incentives detracts from faculty willingness to risk teaching on television (Dillon & Walsh, 1992). Several sources of faculty support have been identified, including administrators, colleagues, telecourse production staff, and reception site coordinators (Billings, et al., in press). Having a comprehensive program of support systems motivates faculty to accept teaching assignments for televised courses. Teaching awards, merit raises, and revised promotion and tenure standards which include criteria for innovative teaching are other strategies to support faculty who teach in a telecourse classroom.

Reception site management

Telecourses create an extension of the classroom for faculty, and relationships at the reception sites must be developed because faculty depend on operational support at the sites to maintain communications with distant students (Billings, et al., 1993). This support can include student registration, distribution of course materials and exams, and orientation of students to the reception site and use of technology. For large classes, this support also includes monitoring the classroom to assure an environment conducive to learning.

Clinical practice supervision

A final consideration in relation to the faculty-technology interface is managing the clinical practice component of the nursing courses. Several clinical supervision models have been used, both of which have some drawbacks. One is to employ on-site clinical faculty (Viverais-Dresler &

Kutshke, 1992), thus extending the classroom to include the health care community. However, it requires considerable time to orient clinical faculty to a course or program. Clinical practice supervision can also be managed by nursing faculty who travel to distant sites (Major & Shane, 1991). While assuring faculty continuity, faculty travel is expensive and time consuming. No differences in clinical outcomes between these two approaches have been reported.

The Student-Technology Interface

The telecourse classroom also changes the classroom communication dynamics for students. Administrators and faculty responsible for telecourses must assure adequate outcomes and learner support. The nursing literature is reassuring about outcomes of academic achievement, student satisfaction, and degree completion for students enrolled in telecourses. These outcomes are generally positive and comparable to those in traditional classrooms (Billings & Bachmeier, 1994).

Learning outcomes

Classes offered by teleconference have been compared with traditional on-campus lecture versions of the same course. Allowing for methodological inconsistencies among the research studies, **course achievement** in telecourses as measured by course grades has been found to be comparable or higher than that in traditional courses for Licensed Practical Nurse (LPN) programs (Parkinson & Parkinson, 1989), BSN programs (Fulmer, Hazard, Jones, & Keene, 1992; Luchinger, 1990; Moser & Kondraki, 1977), and MSN programs (Keck, 1992).

Students generally report **satisfaction** with telecourses and seem to be willing to trade the inconveniences of the technology interface for the savings in travel costs and time (Billings, et al., 1993). However, Fulmer, Hazard, Jones, & Keene (1992) report that students prefer not having multiple teachers in the telecourse, and Parkinson & Parkinson (1991) found that students were less favorable toward faculty teaching on television than toward "live" instructors. Billings, et al., (1993) also found differences in satisfaction between undergraduate and graduate students. For example, undergraduate students reported that they would prefer a proctor at the site because classmates at the reception sites are disruptive to learning, while graduate students reported that classmates facilitated learning. Graduate students also perceived a relatively greater opportunity to participate in class discussions.

Since one of the purposes of telecourses is to promote access to courses and degrees, nurse educators must continue to monitor outcomes of **course and degree completion**. For degree programs, graduation rates appear to be comparable or higher for students in telecourses as compared with students on-campus (Boyd & Baker, 1987). However, students in off-campus programs may take longer to complete the degree (McClelland and Daly, 1991).

Student support services

Assisting students to manage the technology interface requires well-developed support services. Recruitment and advisement are essential components of a nursing telecourse program. Students need information about courses and degrees, as well as easy access to faculty advisors and academic counselors. Toll-free telephones, computers, fax, and voice-mail systems can be used to support access (see chapter by MacBrayne and Russo).

Students also benefit from an orientation to the telecourse broadcast and reception site communication technology. This can be accomplished by distributing information about the reception site and studio classroom prior to the course, developing student handbooks to explain telecourse procedures, and having personnel at the reception site provide needed technical support (Billings, Frazier, Lausch, & McCarty, 1989; Clarke & Cohen, 1992). Faculty must also orient students about the use of the technology, how to participate at reception sites, how to respond to cameras in the studio, and how to adapt their presentations for the medium of television. The time spent in orientation is beneficial because student class participation increases following adequate orientation (Fulmer, Hazard, Jones, & Keene, 1992).

Learning effectiveness in general involves complex interactions among the student, faculty, setting, and instruction. These relationships are even more critical when traditional instruction is modified for students at a distance (Billings, 1991). Students may need to adapt their preferred learning style to that necessitated by the telecourse. For example, telecourses can eliminate peer support when a student is the only person at a reception site or limit the structured support for studying often emphasized by faculty in traditional classrooms. As a result, students must be relatively independent and self-directed. Student support systems must compensate for these restricted learning styles by working with students to identify ways to adapt. For example, faculty can assist students to identify study groups, or they can develop study guides and ancillary course materials to provide students with needed structure for studying.

The Student-Faculty Interface

Interpersonal communication between faculty and student—the student-faculty interface—is often considered the hallmark of effective instruction, but interactions in electronically mediated classrooms tend to be relatively shorter and impersonal (Ritchie, 1991). Telecourse faculty have been shown to miss formal and informal face-to-face contact with students (Billings, et al., in press), and it is likely that students also miss it. The challenge, therefore, is to promote student-faculty communications in spite of the technical barriers of the extended classroom.

Student-faculty interaction

Student-faculty interactions are decreased by both distance and technology. Informal relationships are difficult and intentional strategies are required to support them. Faculty can foster student participation in the extended classroom by calling the students at the reception sites by name and making students at the reception sites a part of the class by using photographs of them on air as they speak (DuGas & Casey, 1987; Wurzbach, 1993). Interactive teaching strategies such as discussion, debate, and ice-breaker exercises also encourage student participation in the extended classroom.

Informal student-faculty relationships can be accomplished by having students meet on campus prior to the beginning of the course, having students attend at least one class in the studio, and/or having an end-of-course party. Scheduling telephone calls or having on-air office hours also foster student-faculty communication. For clinical courses, faculty visiting students at practice sites allows opportunities for mentoring and feedback. Faculty must make an effort to maintain the important teacher-student relationship and use the technology to facilitate rather than detract from this relationship.

Socialization

Professional practice has an affective component and most nursing courses and programs include objectives related to socialization into the profession. When large portions of the curriculum or entire programs are delivered by television, faculty must build student-faculty communication channels that promote mentoring and socialization. Socialization strategies include encouraging students at reception sites to form peer support groups, linking students to other professionals in their own community, and using other electronic supports (computer conferences, electronic mail) to encourage student-faculty collaboration such as writing for publication.

Summary and Conclusion

Telecourses are one way to assure access to education and promote geographical distribution of nurses educated to meet current and future health care needs. However, telecourse technology in the nursing classroom complicates the traditional student-faculty classroom communication and places demands on all involved to create a classroom environment in which positive teaching and learning outcomes can occur.

It is clear that teaching on television requires additional faculty time and modifications to traditional teaching and evaluation strategies. Furthermore, the rewards to faculty for innovation and risk-taking are often limited. At the same time, teleconferencing is one effective way to make education for geographically dispersed and diverse learners accessible and once the students are oriented to the technology and adequate support services are in place, student achievement and satisfaction are comparable to those found in traditional classrooms. Finally, it is important to nurture the student-faculty interface in the electronic classroom in order to achieve professional values.

As administrators, faculty, students, and funding agencies become aware of the benefits as well as the limits of telecourse teaching, the future holds promise. To fulfill this promise however, nurse educators must continue to establish learning environments that support effective classroom communications. First, educators must prepare students and faculty for changing roles as teachers and learners in the extended classroom. Faculty roles change from instruction-giver to facilitator and designer of instruction and learning environments, while students must become active participants in the learning process and assume increasing responsibility for managing their own learning.

Secondly, there must be local, national, and international infrastructures that promote communication in health care agencies and community-based facilities. These infrastructures should support clinical instruction and development of clinical databases as well as promote closer links between education and clinical practice. In fact, the extended nursing classroom supports health care reforms and community-based initiatives as community-based learning maintains nurses in the community and promotes a model of client-centered health care.

Finally, nurse educators must continue to monitor the extent to which telecourses are facilitating goals of establishing cost-effective, articulated, and community-based educational systems. While questions regarding course outcomes, course and degree completion, and student satisfaction, for the most part, have been answered, issues of cost-effectiveness, use of appropriate teaching-learning models, and the health policy implications of a community-based nursing education system need further examination.

Teaching and learning in the extended classroom of nursing telecourses requires nurse educators to be creative in managing the changes in instructional communication interfaces between student-faculty, student-technology and faculty-technology. When instructional communications are supported to accommodate the technology, offering nursing telecourses in the extended classroom is one strategy to support nursing education for community-based health care.

References

American Association of Colleges of Nursing (1992). *Position statement for addressing nursing education's agenda for the 21st century.* Washington, D.C.

Billings, D. (1991). Student learning style preferences and distance education: a review of literature and implications for future research. *The Second Symposium on Research in Distance Education*. The Pennsylvania State University, May 22-24.

Billings, D.; Frazier, H.; Lausch, J.; & McCarty, J. (1989). Videoteleconferencing: solving mobility and recruitment problems. *Nurse Educator*, 14 (2), 12-16.

Billings, D. & Bachmeier, B. (1994). Teaching and learning at a distance: A review of the nursing literature. In Lois Allen (Ed.). *Review of Research in Nursing Education*. New York: The National League for Nursing.

Billings, D.; Boland, D.; Durham, J.; Finke, L.; Smith, C.; & Manz, B.; (1993). Assessing the effectiveness of videoteleconferencing and the nursing telecourse program at Indiana University School of Nursing: Views of the stakeholders. *Proceedings and abstracts of the 11th Annual Conference on Research in Nursing Education*. New York: National League for Nursing.

Billings, D.; Boland, D.; Durham, J.; Finke, L.; Smith, C.; & Manz, B., (in press). Teaching on Television: Nursing Faculty Perceptions. *Journal of Professional Nursing*.

Boyd, S. & Baker, C. M. (1987). Using television to teach. *Nursing and Health Care*, 8 (9), 523-527.

Clark, C. E. (1989). Telecourses for nursing staff development. *Journal of Nursing Staff Development*, May/June, 107-110.

Clarke, L. M. & Cohen, J. A. (1992). Distance learning: new partnerships for nursing in rural areas. *Rural Health Nursing*, 359-388.

Colbert, C. D. (1984). Nursing management in the 80s: a seven-part teleconference series. In L.A. Parker and C.H. Olgren eds. *Teleconferencing and Electronic Communications III*. Madison, WI: Center for Interactive Programs, University of Wisconsin Extension.

Dillon, C. L. & Walsh, S. M. (1992). Faculty: The neglected resource in distance education. *The American Journal of Distance Education*, 6 (3), 5-21.

DuGas, B. W. & Casey, A. M. (1987). Teleconferencing. *The Canadian Nurse*, 22-25.

Fulmer, J.; Hazzard M.; Jones, S.; & Keene, K. (1992). Distance learning: an innovative approach to nursing education. *Journal of Professional Nursing*, 8 (5), 289-294.

Gehlauf, D. N.; Shatz, M. A.; & Frye, T. W. (1991). Faculty perceptions of interactive television instructional strategies: Implications for training. *The American Journal of Distance Education*, 5 (3),20-28.

Jafari, A. (1990). Designing and Engineering a Teacher-Friendly High-Tech Classroom. *Ohio Media Spectrum*, 42 (4),22-26.

Keck, J. F. (1992). Comparison of learning outcomes between graduate students in telecourses and those in traditional classrooms. *Journal of Nursing Education*, 31 (5), 229-234.

Limn, S.; Spencer, J. B.; & Henderson, F. C. (1985). Video-teleconferencing by nurses—for nurses. *Nursing & Health Care*, June, 313-317.

Luchsinger, B. (1990). Distance education in the mountain plains states for associate degree nursing programs. *Journal of Adult Education*, 19(1), 13-18.

Major, M. B. & Shane, D. L. (1991). Use of interactive television for outreach nursing education. *The American Journal of Distance Education*, 5 (1), 57-66.

McClelland, E. & Daly, J. (1991). A comparison of selected demographic characteristics and academic performance of on-campus and satellite-center RNs: Implications for the curriculum. *Journal of Nursing Education*, 30 (6), 261-266.

Moser, D. H. & Kondracki, M. R. (1977). Comparison of attitudes and cognitive achievement of nursing students in three instructional strategies. *Journal of Nursing Education*, 16 (1), 14-28.

National League for Nursing (1993). *A Vision for Nursing Education*. New York, NY.

Parkinson, C. F. & Parkinson, S. B. (1989). A comparative study between interactive television and traditional lecture course offerings for nursing students. *Nursing & Health Care*, 10 (9), 499-502.

Ritchie, H. (1991). Interactive, televised instruction: What is the potential for interaction? *Proceedings of the Second American Symposium on Research in Distance Education*. College Station, PA: The Pennsylvania State University.

Shoemaker, D. (1993). A statewide instructional television program via satellite for RN-to-BSN students. *Journal of Professional Nursing*, 9 (3), 153-158.

Tribulski, J. A. & Frank, C. (1987). Closed circuit TV, an alternate teaching strategy. *Journal of Nursing Staff Development*, Summer, 110-115.

Viverais-Dresler, G. & Kutschke, M. (1992). RN students' satisfaction with clinical teaching in a distance education program. *The Journal of Continuing Education in Nursing*, 23 (5), 224-230.

Wurzbach, M. E. (1993). Teaching nursing ethics on interactive television: fostering interactivity. *Journal of Nursing Education*, 32 (1), 37-39.

The Tools of Self-Direction: Student Services in the Electronic Classroom

Pamela MacBrayne and Jane Russo

*Pamela MacBrayne is Dean of
Telecommunications and Academic
Development at the University of Maine at
Augusta, ME*

*Jane Russo is Executive Assistant to the
President at The Education Network of Maine
at Augusta, ME*

One Student's Story

It took Jen more than a year to make up her mind to enroll. When her tiny island community was first wired to the Education Network of Maine, the University System's statewide telecommunications network, most people welcomed the opportunity for higher education; others worried the subject to death for months. But now college had settled into the life of this windswept rock almost 25 miles off the Maine coast.

Jen grew up here, was married early in life to a man who fished and trapped lobster; they now had three kids. College had been somewhat of a mystery to her—a thing that people from away did before they grew up, she imagined, to prepare for the fast track of mainland life. The idea of leaving her beloved island to go to school had never occurred to her. But island life was changing. New people, new ideas, new jobs seemed to be rolling in with the tide. And then one day, without a word to anyone, her friend Donna called the University in Augusta and enrolled in a history course scheduled for broadcast at the island school that fall. Michelle and her sister Lisa signed up too, and soon the talk in the market began to spin off in the direction of English Lit or Algebra or even Art History. Art History—in South Haven.

165

Jen was early for her first class at the sprawling Community School, the site of countless PTA meetings, teacher conferences, and bake sales. One of the teachers, Gail Greene, worked part-time as the site coordinator; they chatted as she distributed the class syllabus, switched on the TV and slipped a tape into the VCR. From the screen, the professor grinned, greeted the class, then asked South Haven to call in. Jen touched the button on the portable phone and soon found herself in lively discussion with the instructor and with students watching from distant classrooms in towns hundreds of miles away.

Jen was ready for college now, but she hadn't always been. She'd graduated from high school more than 20 years ago, and was far from convinced that she could formally learn anything anymore. And what about this interactive TV?

That nagging uncertainty, and the prompting of her friends, finally caused Jen to pick up the course guide she found in the mail and call the toll-free number connecting her to the University's Teleservice Center. A woman introducing herself as Alice listened carefully to her concerns, calmed her fears and systematically answered the questions Jen recited from the notes she had scrawled on the back of an envelope. Alice promised to mail her a catalog and course schedule. After Jen pored through these at least twice, she phoned Alice again. She had decided to enroll in College Writing, she told her. She didn't tell her that writing was a subject for which she harbored a secret, passionate interest, or that later, if she could cut it, she might apply to one of the four degree programs offered through the Network.

Alice told Jen that she'd have to take a placement test in English before she could enroll in the course, but that she could take a Computerized Placement Test right there, at the island school. If she didn't pass this time, Jen could always take it again after honing her knowledge on the developmental English software newly available at the school. Jen received the news with considerable dread, her anxiety at the thought of taking a test dwarfed only by her fear of negotiating a computer. But a review of the testing videotape and manual and some practice at the terminal under Gail's gentle guidance revealed that the process was straightforward, even fun; she took the test and, in a week, discovered she had passed honorably. With renewed courage, she phoned Alice and registered for the course, ordering, on the spot, all of the books she'd need for the course.

But she still wasn't ready. So when several of her friends mentioned that they were planning to attend an orientation to college scheduled for broadcast on ITV that evening, she decided to join them. Later in the semester she took part in the "College Plus" series, workshops designed to help students develop the habits that would make them successful scholars. Jen found the program on study skills helpful, but she knew the program about procrastination would save her. These informal, interactive TV sessions, and the support of her college-going friends, boosted Jen's confidence in her ability to learn and allowed her to practice the protocol of ITV, including the rather intimidating task of calling the campus and listening to her voice ring out in a distant classroom.

She was particularly proud of her easy mastery of the URSUS system. Alice had mailed her a slim brochure that explained how to use this friendly, on-line library catalog to scan the indexes of libraries in Maine and across the country. With URSUS she could order library books and journal articles directly from her computer terminal and find them stacked neatly in her mailbox several days later.

As Jen progressed through the semester, she visited the regional center during excursions to the mainland to meet with a counselor to get career or personal advice, or to evaluate her career choices through the SIGI+ Computer Guidance System. At the center she could find a tutor, take a workshop, or join in a number of student activities. One day, she phoned Alice to say that she had decided to apply to the University's associate degree program in Liberal Arts. Soon, a one-page application, tailored to the adult student, and a "viewbook" containing all the information about her program, appeared in her mail, along with a warm note of encouragement in Alice's neat script.

The complexities of the financial aid form were finessed with the help of a step-by-step videotape, which she paused and rewound at strategic points along the way. Audio tapes, available at the school or with a call to the Teleservice Center, provided basic information about prior learning assessment, CLEP, DANTES, and Challenge exams. When Jen was assigned a faculty advisor, they communicated at will on the school's computer and modem, or through toll-free phone, voice-mail, and fax notes.

Academic Programs in Place in Maine

This account of a fictional student's experience at a distant site on a Maine island illustrates how many University students living in Maine's remote regions are supported in college today. Academic and student support services, traditionally campus-based, have eased students' adjustment to college, assisted in their intellectual and personal growth, and contributed to their academic successes. But just as faculty have begun to harness the information technologies of the electronic classroom for instruction, academic and student services staff have restructured their programs to take advantage of these new technologies. While applications of technologies have often resulted in improved instruction and services to students on campus, they have also been used to serve new populations of students—students previously precluded from the college experience by barriers of time and distance.

These students are having a profound effect on the ways in which both instruction and support services are delivered. Many of them are adults whose family and job responsibilities and distance from a college campus make it impossible for them to conform to a campus' course schedule.

Using an interactive television system that reaches more than 85 locations in this rural state, student services staff at the University of Maine at Augusta offer a general college orientation session for all new students. Both new and returning students may enroll in the "College Plus" program which covers such topics as financial aid, stress management, physical fitness, sexual harassment awareness, the job search process, term paper writing, time arrangement, study skills, and test taking skills.

Career planning, admissions counseling, and academic advising for all available degree programs are also offered.

Many students attend these 75-minute workshops at their local site to interact during "real-time" with the facilitator and other students, while some prefer the convenience of borrowing a videotape of the sessions to view at home. Plans are underway to offer much of this information on audio cassette tapes for the convenience of students who travel frequently in their cars.

Students who want more information about subjects critical to college success can enroll in a three-credit seminar, delivered via interactive television, entitled "Introduction to the College Experience." The major topics covered in the course include:

- Introduction to the university
- Academic policies
- Student support services and resources
- Time management
- Stress management
- Study skills
- Introduction to the library: library resources and the research process
- Decoding your professors
- Critical thinking
- Involvement in college: curricular, co-curricular, extra curricular
- Word processing
- Values clarification
- Career planning: strategies and resources
- Personal health: nutrition, exercise, weight management
- Chemical dependency
- Higher education and technology

Technologies can help promote students' development by giving them direct access to wide and varied sources of information and resources. At the University of Maine at Augusta, staff are developing a comprehensive student database and an interactive advising system that will allow students to build a portfolio of their academic progress, conference with their faculty and peers, and seek necessary information, about topics from careers to course schedules, directly from their homes or offices. This computerized system will:

- establish a database for faculty advising
- provide a bulletin board, on-line catalog, and personal access for students to use 24 hours a day
- offer computer conferencing capability to support asynchronous communication among students and faculty
- deliver self-paced services and instruction

Some institutions have begun to use information technologies to serve the needs of an off-campus urban population. The Extended Learning Institute of Northern Virginia Community College offers these students a unique range of support services that includes:

- counseling videos aired over cable television, covering topics such as registration, career planning, and the veterans affairs program
- placement and tips for successful distance education study
- a voice-mail system containing prerecorded information on faculty office hours, financial, aid and over 20 other student services topics
- information kiosks, accessible by computer and modem, providing information on a variety of student services topics
- "Homework Help" videos aired on cable television and voice-mail for call in questions or problems.

Further west, Rio Salado Community College has developed a computer conferencing system to support distant students. Through the "Rio Electronic Forum," students discuss career planning topics, resume-writing and job-hunting skills, along with an array of personal topics. Counselors initiate the process by asking questions electronically; students respond or generate their own questions.

The efforts of these three institutions highlight a small part of the variety of technology-based services becoming available to students on campus and off. Programs using interactive television as their primary medium strive to integrate video and computer graphics, experiment with cooperative learning, case studies, and other means to enhance interaction. Computer and audio conferencing, fax, voice-mail, audiographics, videotapes, videodisks, audio cassette tapes and the more familiar telephone and print-based materials may be used alone or in combination to meet the academic, career, and personal needs of students. These tools offer a new range of alternatives to institutional-based services, adapting effectively to the particular learning preference, schedule, or special challenges of today's college student.

As educational institutions necessarily reach out to busy adults, students with disabilities, and those living far from campus, technology will increasingly be employed as a cost-effective avenue of access to the institution's programs and resources. Because they demand active participation and require particular skills on the part of students who use them, these tools provide more than specific information; they also promote confidence in the ability to seek, from many sources, the information and support they need. Programs that employ information technology to support students' development are modeling, whether consciously or not, a profound shift from relative passivity to increased self-direction as students become skillful manipulators of the tools that connect them to the burgeoning world of information.

Further Extending the Classroom: Global Networks

Cross-Cultural Team Teaching: Electronic Mail for Literary Analysis

Helen J. Schwartz

*Helen Schwartz is Professor of English
at Indiana University Purdue University
Indianapolis*

Communication via computer networks—whether local-area or wide-area—is now fairly common in American higher education (Mabrito, 1990; Harasim, 1990; Hiltz, 1990; Berge and Collins, in press). However, international exchanges at the college level, with the notable exception of BESTNET (Arias and Bellman, in this volume), are still comparatively rare (see also Cohen & Miyake, 1986; Payne, 1987). Students in K-12 classes have been using electronic mail for cultural exchange and collaboration, especially through programs with national or vendor support. At the college level, however, although contacts through international networks are more available as part of the computing infrastructure, the need for disciplinary richness plus the limited time students are involved in one class have apparently kept down the number of cross-cultural exchange. This chapter reports on the pedagogical philosophy, the activities and the results of exchanges when an introductory literature class at an American university studied drama in conjunction with a master's-level class at a Finnish university.

Electronic mail made possible the planning, coordination, and exchange between the two classes and the two instructors: Professor Aarre Heino and Professor Helen Schwartz. This collaboration, between two teachers who were not to meet face-to-face until three months into the semester, put into practice a number of theoretical assumptions emerging in composition theory and literary analysis:

173

1. Having a real audience and authentic purpose helps students understand and meet audience needs better than in the situation of students writing solely to the teacher as expert.
2. Interpreting literature is a constructive act, not simply a decoding of meaning. During this constructive act, the reader interacts with the text to create a meaning that is based in individual and cultural experience, so that different people will have varying interpretations, as will people from different cultures. During this constructive act, the text exerts constraints on the reader so that universal constants in literary response are also possible.

Logistics

Two instructors in widely disparate locations met each other on electronic mail, introduced by a mutual colleague because of their known interests in both literature and computer applications in the humanities. In addition to their shared computer-mania, both professors were interested in research on the differences in literary interpretation—with Schwartz studying variations among individual readers and Heino interested in differences between cultures as well as systems for distance learning and life-long education. Therefore, both were eager to attempt intercontinental team-teaching, despite important differences and difficulties. The time was short, with only two months to plan before the beginning of the courses and with important questions to answer and differences to deal with creatively.

The students were at different levels of preparation, with the American students enrolled in English L203, Introduction to Drama, and the Finnish students enrolled in a master's-level course, preparing to write a long master's thesis.

The American students did all of their writing and all of their reading in English. Finnish students, who were comparative literature majors, *not* English majors, wrote in English and read in English, Swedish, and Finnish.

The writing requirements were very different for the two classes, with American students writing many journal entries and several short essays, whereas Finnish students tended to write medium-length formal essays that sometimes included responses to American comments. However, the reading list was shared, chosen mainly on the basis of the book order already submitted by Schwartz, but with the addition of a Finnish play, *Snow in May*. Another Finnish play, Jarner's *Eva Maria*, was read optionally by American students and by all the Finnish students. Schwartz unwittingly made the Finnish students' task even more difficult because she was unaware that Jarner's play was in Swedish (one of Finland's two official languages), even though Tampere is in a region in which people's native tongue is the linguistically unrelated Finnish language.

Neither the American nor the Finnish students had direct access to Bitnet, so both the teachers had to be the technicians who sent, received, and distributed student texts. The five Finnish students created their own texts using word processing, but Schwartz had to retype student essays from the 26 students in her class, sometimes "editing" by omitting passages, but otherwise allowing students speak in their own voices. The transmitted material came from student journals, turned in on a rotating schedule, so that some student journals had not been turned in by the time the student texts had to be transmitted. Student participation was broad for Miller's *Death of a Salesman* and the Finnish play, Männer's *Snow in May*, but thereafter, American students participated on a volunteer basis with essays on *Antigone, The Misanthrope,* and the Finnish play (in Swedish), Jarner's *Eva Maria.*

Results

Although many problems limited the scope of achievement, intercontinental team-teaching produced evidence that the potential both teachers saw could in fact be realized—even more fully with more advance planning and improved student access to computer facilities. Students in both classes enjoyed the exchange and expressed strong support for continued inclusion in courses. In their autobiographical statements sent to their distant peers, many included their addresses and phone numbers. On a questionnaire, American students rated the exchange and the journal entries which provided texts for the exchange as the most worthwhile activities in the class.

Short autobiographies showed clear differences in the two student populations. American students represented a wider range of ages (from 19 to 41, as opposed to Finnish students from 21 to 31). Almost all the American students worked many hours per week, unlike the full-time Finnish students whose tuition and expenses were paid by the government for about 6 years. Americans represented a more ethnically and socially diverse group (single and married, with and without children). However, Finnish students showed the greater sophistication one would expect of advanced students.

Student texts showed evidence that the first hypothesis underlying our experiment was valid: a real audience helped writers understand what to include. For example, Minna-Kristiina Linkala included responses from American students along with documented sources in her essay on *Snow in May.* And Finnish students writing on the place of Swedish literature in Finland and reporting an interview with author V. V. Jarner had a real audience, whereas these topics might seem simply academic if the students had not been in the rhetorical situation of interpreting their culture to a foreign audience.

American students included information about themselves to explain how they were "locating" themselves in their responses to the American play, *Death of a Salesman*; they did so to an extent not usually seen, even in journal entries. For example, Mark Gibson included his own experience as a fast-food clerk and aspiring creative writer as a contrast to *Death of a Salesman's* Willy Loman's search for upward mobility:

> Willy [Loman] . . . ignores the little things in life to con-
> centrate on the big prize—elusive success. He becomes
> an empty man chasing empty dreams—tragic in his
> pathetic pursuit. This play touches upon many things in
> my own life. . . . My major is creative writing, and it is not
> exactly a lucrative field unless you're extremely talented.
> I work two low level jobs (PizzaHut and a video store)
> that I enjoy very much. I'm good at most jobs I take on
> and I love the people I work with. Maybe I'll end up as a
> college educated pizza cook who spends his life getting
> rejection slips from publishers. . . . I have dreams of
> wealth, success and world fame/love, but they aren't the
> ends that justify any means. If I don't become rich and
> famous, I'll settle for happiness and still be worth far more
> alive than dead.

For another student, her response to Willy led her toward an assessment of her own father:

> I think I can understand how Mr. Loman feels. My father,
> who is self employed, often feels that we kids MAY not
> respect him as much because he was so busy working try-
> ing to raise a family of 7 and meeting the demands of his
> customers. In reality, he is an extraordinary father who
> has given so much to his family.

I believe the presence of a non-American audience made these students see the relevance of their experience, value it and include it, to an extent that the assignment to speak from their own values does not normally elicit.

Student texts also supported the idea that cross-cultural exchange would help students explore what was universal and what was culturally-bound in literary interpretation. Students commented on the national characteristics evident in their literature while also arguing, by the very act of interpretation, that interpretive communities could be established through literary analysis. For example, Kirk Smith consciously brought in ideas from his

American Studies course:

> On p. 520 we are given Willy's "key" by Hap when he
> says, "Dad is never so happy as when he's looking for-
> ward to something." We as Americans are taught to never
> be content. We always have to strive for better, always on
> the go. It's much like the JFK administration from my
> American Studies class in that they were always "doing
> something," always on the go, but never accomplishing
> anything.

And Finnish student Minna-Kristiina Linkala delineated cultural differences between American and Finnish lifestyle and society in her essay on
Snow in May:

> "a typical Finnish character differs from American one
> quite a lot. It is well known, that Finnish people (in gen-
> eral) are introvert, shy, melancholy and they can control
> their feelings very well. The Finns also love to deliberate
> different questions. In spite of Americans (as far as I know
> them!) are open, noisy, always smiling." (The stereotype
> seems to have occasioned one American student's irony in
> his later autobiographical statement: "I am not always
> loud nor do I always smile, which is a common stereotype
> about Americans.")

American students also showed awareness that cultural differences
should be considered when interpreting a play. For example, David Black,
a 37-year old creative writing major, asked about Finnish perceptions of
juvenile delinquency in relation to *Eva Maria*, perhaps because of his full-
time job as a deputy bail commissioner at the county jail, setting conditions
of pre-trial release for defendants in criminal cases:

> The scenes involving the gang make me wonder if you
> have the same perception of and problems with juvenile
> delinquency that we do in the United States. In the US
> their behavior might be construed by some people as
> delinquent and by others just normal youthful behavior.
> How do you view it?

A number of problems, however, limited the effectiveness of this
exchange. There were technical problems (lost files, problems with
uploading and downloading), but they were remarkably unimportant.
More important was the need, realized from experience, for much more
careful planning and timing of exchanges. The problems occurred, in part,
because the teachers were the conduits and technicians. If students had

direct access to a Bitnet electronic conference, they could load their texts themselves and also read whenever they could access, rather than relying on teachers finding time to send out files and get printouts of incoming files. Thus, for example, Paula Korhonen's invitation for exchange about Chaim Potok's work and Johanna Javanainen's query whether any of the Americans played the flute remained unanswered. Although some question-answering was possible, other more sensitive exchanges (such as the American student's dig against stereotypes) were probably inhibited by the indirectness of exchange among students. In addition, students sometimes found the names confusing (with Ms. Linkala assuming Kari Scott was male). An earlier exchange of captioned photographs would probably have been advisable.

Even with greater student responsibility for creating, sending, and reading texts, however, the timely scheduling of discussions needed to be more finely tuned, allowing for some delays, even though electronic mail had much faster turnaround time than airmail. As a concrete example, David Black's questions about cultural differences were finished on February 4, but formal essays on Jarner's reputation, cultural background, and interpretation were already drafted and arrived, with only indirect response to Black's questions, within the week. And Finnish essays on *The Misanthrope* arrived after we had already finished discussing the play in Indianapolis.

American students felt that the difference in genre (informal journal entries versus formal essays) made them uncomfortable, although they did not seem to mind the difference in the level of sophistication between the two groups. The Indiana students, who said the journal entries were their favorite activity in the class, even volunteered to write formal essays, but then decided that a better strategy would entail using a software program, SEEN (written by Schwartz and used in the class), that would elicit responses to the literature and store it as electronically transmittable (ASCII) textfiles.

Professor Heino confirmed the benefits of more direct student access, embedded in an educational philosophy that encourages students to take responsibility for their own learning and to set the terms and needs of collaboration. For future collaborations, he envisioned students having direct access to Bitnet: "[Finnish students could then] discuss directly with your students. And perhaps without papers only via terminals from (Finnish) heart to (American) heart." Instructors could set topics beforehand for their groups, with SEEN or a list of relevant questions.

References

Berge, Z. and Collins, M. *Computer-Mediated Communication*. (in press).

Cohen, M. & Miyake, N. (1986). A worldwide intercultural network exploring electronic messaging for instruction. *Instructional Science*, 15, 257-273.

Harasim, Linda. (1990) *Online education: Perspectives on a new environment*. NY: Praeger.

Hiltz, S. R. (1990) Collaborative learning: The virtual classroom approach. *T.H.E. Journal*, 17, 10, 59-65.

Mabrito, Mark. (1990). Annotated Bibliography of Resources in Computer Networking. *Computers and Composition*, 7.3, 23-40.

Payne, D. (1987). Computer extended audiences for student writers: Some theoretical and practical implications. In L. Gerrard (Ed.), *Writing at century's end: Essays on computer-assisted composition*. NY: Random House. 21-26.

Networked Collaborative Research And Teaching

Armando A. Arias, Jr. and Beryl Bellman

*Armando Arias is Dean of Academic Planning,
Instruction and Assessment, California State
University, Monterey Bay*

*Beryl Bellman teaches in the Department
of Communication Studies, California
State University, Los Angeles*

The applications of communication technologies in higher education are leading to new conceptions of the research setting, as well as the classroom as a social form.[3] Until recently, the basic organization of the classroom changed little since the advent of the modern university. The teacher assumes the role of "font of knowledge," and he/she has only minimal interaction with students. Likewise, discussion between students is usually considered disruptive and discouraged. Even "quality circles" as promoted by more recent academic disciples of the "TQM" (Total Quality Management) movement discussion sessions, conducted as break-out groups from large lecture sections, are run by student group leaders or teaching assistants who interpret the words of the faculty member (font of wisdom). Seldom do TAs encourage any form of sustained interaction. According to Arias & Bellman[2] there is minimal student participation for classes of less than 20 and very little student participation for large lecture classes. And these participations are primarily requests for clarification or repeating of information, which, according to Flores, Fernando, and Winograd,[8] is not the same type of intellectual participation as when discussing technical matters, such as, when is the next test.

Sometimes faculty collaborate and jointly teach courses. Such courses mostly involve faculty teaching in tandem. When faculty teach at the same time they normally interact only with each other, and student participation

180

is even more constrained than in the single faculty situation.

Teaching, Learning, and Computer Conferencing

One consequence of this pedagogical style is a clear distinction between teaching and learning, and strongly defined roles of student and teacher. This social form promotes competition for grades rather than collaboration in the pursuit of knowledge.[6] It is a social form that leads to alienated and disinterested students, and faculty who set up barriers between their pedagogical and research interests.[2,3]

The uses of computer communication technologies are having a major impact on this academic culture. These technologies are used in a variety of ways, ranging from methods to augment and supplement regular coursework to distance education applications. As Arias & Metes[4] have pointed out:

> The distinction between distance learning and networked learning is important: while distance learning attempts to replicate the classroom ambiance across geographic space, networked learning involves the acceleration of interactions between teachers, researchers and students through electronic networks. Of course, the network learning model does encompass distance learning as well. (p.1)

The use of computer conferencing and electronic mail introduces writing across the curriculum and teaches essential computer concepts as an integral part of every course. Students engage each other and the faculty in discussion groups like conferences, which improves critical thinking and promotes learning. When used in distance education, computer conferencing lessens the distance and alienation of the student with the professor and other students in the course.[9]

Students log on to a host computer either at their own university or by accessing a data packet switching network. Students read or download all waiting items in one or more computer conferences for the class. They then respond by writing their comments on what was read, very often after having taken time to reflect and do research on their electronic class contributions. These mediated or "virtual" classrooms differ from face-to-face classes in that students are required to be much more active, and to interact not only with the faculty member teaching the class but also with the other students enrolled.[12] In this way, on-line education is less competitive than traditional methods and is more of a collaborative learning experience.[10]

Evolving into Computer Conferencing for Teaching

One of the first courses ever to incorporate computer communications as a form of "conferencing" to encourage collaborative thinking between students was applied in an English course offered at The Colorado College in the fall semester of 1991.[2] By coincidence and at the same time, the Western Behavioral Sciences Institute had established an executive training program, or the School of Management and Strategic Studies, and began conducting advanced seminars (while performing human factors research for the Digital Equipment Corporation) using computer conferencing.[7] A distinguished faculty from major international universities conducted seminars for senior-level executives, who participated from around the world. In 1984, Starr Roxanne Hiltz[10] evaluated the effectiveness of computer conferencing by introducing courses in engineering and sociology into the curriculum of the New Jersey Institute of Technology. These courses were the first such that were offered for credit and a grade. As a result of that project, Hiltz and Turoff (the developer of the Electronic Information Exchange System computer conferencing system at the NJIT) and his colleagues published a series of monographs and essays demonstrating the effectiveness of the technology, both for the delivery of educational programs and for decision making in electronic meetings in corporate and academic settings.

Within the past few years, a number of institutions have introduced computer conferencing as a regular method to augment existing lectures. In 1987, the Fielding Institute developed its own conferencing system to encourage faculty and student interaction for distance learning in order to compliment its face-to-face program, which was non-traditional in nature. Professors at California State University, Los Angeles and Texas A&M University-Kingsville regularly team-teach courses in Chicano Studies utilizing computer conferencing on their Vax System. Students are actively engaged in rewriting the final chapters of numerous Chicano novels in a collaborative (albeit, on-line) manner. These campuses have found that the distance learning environment allows campuses with few Chicano professors/students to benefit from those campuses that do have more. California State University, Dominguez Hills, uses conferencing in their International External Degree Program in seminars in the Division of Extended Education. Like California State University, Los Angeles, they are developing their conferencing software and introducing it to a number of other universities in the United States and the world. The Ontario Institute for Studies in Education has operated a program in which students take graduate level seminars in virtual and actual settings. In some of the latter, students are asked to engage in both face-to-face and on-line projects in groups of various sizes.[17]

Conferencing has also been used extensively at the University of Arizona for electronic meetings in both university departments and research institutes, as well as for instruction in several departments, including Spanish, English, and Education. Their president, Manuel Pacheco, worked with the faculty in setting up a committee to use computer conferencing for reducing the budget. It turned out to be a successful exercise inasmuch as faculty were able to make contributions and suggestions, yet remain anonymous when they wanted. Given the amount of money they had to cut, plus the short time-line given them by the state, this method proved to be extremely effective. Also in Arizona the Maricopa Community College Office of Instructional Technologies has been offering computer conferencing-delivered courses in English composition and other subject areas along with the use of other mediums, especially telephone conference calls between student groups. The New York Institute of Technology's Open University and the British Open University have also used computer conferencing to supplement existing media programs.[17]

Having studied firsthand numerous projects (as above) in 1984, we drew upon several of these experiments to create the Binational English and Spanish Telecommunications Network, BESTNET (for details see chapter by Metes, et al.). In our evaluation of the project, we learned that students were particularly responsive to the computer conferencing interactions and did not need as much formal presentation of lecture materials by video as we originally believed. As a result, we began to rely more heavily on computer conferencing interactions for both the presentation and discussion of materials, and to use video and other materials to supplement or present information for those discussions. Because we found conferencing to be so effective as the dominant or stand-alone form of course delivery, we then explored applications of computer conferencing in different kinds of courses.

Forms of Computer-Mediated Courses

We are now involved with three kinds of computer communications-delivered courses. The first form is one in which students do not see the instructor but communicate with him/her in computer conferences or virtual classrooms, during synchronous on-line office hours utilizing the computer phone or chat utility and with private electronic mail messages. In the second format, faculty make formal video lecture presentations to complement the discussions in computer conferences. In the third course format, faculty members conduct part of the course on-line and also have face-to-face interaction with the classes. These courses are team-taught among several institutions. Students participate on-line with faculty and students at other campuses, with the elected option of a local faculty member offering a section of the course on his/her campus.

One alternative to the use of computer conferencing is utilization of electronic mail distribution lists, or listserves that function either on the Internet or Bitnet.[11] These distribution lists are managed by each participant writing either new mail or replies, which are then sent to a central server and distributed to all other members of the list.[1] There are several hundred such listserve conferences that students can join. Very often several faculty members at different universities arrange for their students to have campus accounts, and thereby encourage their participation in specific lists. For example, in the XCULT-L or inter-cultural newsletter listserve there are three different university classes involved in addition to several hundred individual members in the discussion. In this manner, students interact with faculty and students from diverse institutions on a large range of topics. The difficulty with listserves is the tremendous amount of mail that each member receives each day. Also, topics get intertwined and often confused. The discussion group is also very open, and it is often difficult to follow the course of a topic's development. Because of the large number of discussants the conversations are sometimes a bit tense and full of debate.[13]

The culture of a computer conferencing system is quite different.[5] The topics in a computer conference are maintained on the server, and can be reread and searched for various subject strings. A computer conference has a defined membership, and even for those which are open to all members of a network, it tends to support group solidarity. Consequently, the discussions tend to be more polite and mutually supportive than the listserves. In addition, computer conference discussions are able to sustain a topic longer, as any given topic can be added to at any time by searching it out and adding a reply to it. Most conferencing systems have both a topic and reply structure.[16] In this way a participant can add a reply branch to any topic at any time. This helps keep topics organized and continually updated, while allowing other topics to be introduced as the conference evolves.

The Virtues of Distance Learning

In either form, the implementation of these technologies is radically altering the classroom as a social form.[4] Again, rather than the faculty member assuming the role of font of wisdom, he/she is a facilitator and guide. Rather than being passive recipients of lecture materials, students are assuming an active role in the educational process. Instead of student participation being relegated to requests for clarification or more information, they engage the professor and each other in creative dialogue and develop ideas. Rather than faculty occasionally collaborating in teaching, the new computer communications-mediated classroom promotes cooperative work. No longer is there a clear distinction between the roles of student and teacher, as every participant in networked computer-mediated classes is concomitantly both teacher and student.[3] As students become active participants in the learning process, their alienation decreases; and likewise as faculty themselves become learners, learning from the comments of students and other colleagues (located at dispersed sites), the boundary between teaching and research is less distinct.[14,15]

Bibliography

1. Alberti, Bob; et al., (1992). *The Internet Gopher Protocol.*

2. Arias, Armando and Bellman, Beryl, (1990). "Computer-Mediated Classrooms for Culturally and Linguistically Diverse Learners" in *Computers in the Schools*, Vol 7, Nos 1/2 1990, pp 227-242, Special Issue on Language Minority Students and Computers.

3. Arias, Armando and Bellman, Beryl, (1993). "Pedagogical and Research Uses of Computer Conferencing" in *Successful Cultural Diversity.*

4. Arias, Armando and Metes, George, (1993). "BESTNET: A Laboratory for Networked Learning" in *Proceedings of the MacBeth National Conference On Computing in the Liberal Arts.*

5. Champine, George, (1991). *MIT Project Athena: A Model for Distributed Campus Computing.* Digital Press.

6. Egido, Carmen; Galegher, Jolene; and Kraut, Robert (Eds.), (1990). *Intellectual Teamwork: Social and Technological Foundations of Cooperative Work.* Erlbaum Associates, New Jersey.

7. Feenberg, Andrew, (1988). "The Planetary Classroom" published in *Message Handling Systems and Distributed Applications*, edited by Stefferud, Lacobsen, and Schicker, North Holland Press/The Hague.

8. Flores, Fernando, and Winograd, Terry, (1991). *Understanding Computers and Cognition: A New Foundation for Design.* Addison-Wesley Publishing Co., Inc.

9. Harasim, Linda, (1986). "Computer Learning Networks: Educational Applications of Computer Conferencing," *Journal of Distance Education.*

10. Hiltz, Starr Roxanne, (1986). *Online Communities: A Case Study of the Office of the Future.* Ablex, New Jersey.

11. Kehoe, Brendan, (1992). *Zen and the Art of the Internet: A Beginner's Guide to the Internet.*

12. Ringle, Martin (Ed.), (1992). *Computing Strategies in Liberal Arts Colleges.* Addison-Wesley Publishing Co., Reading, MA.

13. Slavin, Robert; et al., (Eds.), (1985). *Learning to Cooperate, Cooperating to Learn.* Plenum Press, New York.

14. Sproull, Lee and Kiesler, Sara, (1991). *Connections: New Ways of Working in the Networked Organization.* MIT Press.

15. Teich, Albert (Ed.), (1993). *Technology and the Future.* St. Martin's Press, New York.

16. Truxal, John, (1991). *The Age of Electronic Messages.* MIT Press.

17. Zimmerer, Loel, (1989). "Computer Conferencing: A Medium for Facilitating Interaction in Distance Education" in *Educational Media and Technology Yearbook*, Vol 14.

Electronic Student Response Systems in Corporate Distance Education

Barbara J. Garvin-Kester
Thomas A. Kester
Alan G. Chute

Barbara Garvin-Kester is a district manager for Executive Education and Management Training at AT&T in Cincinnati

Thomas Kester is a training manager for the AT&T Network Systems Group

Alan Chute is the manager of the AT&T National Teletraining Center in Cincinnati

As corporate demand for workplace skills accelerates, demographic, economic, and technological pressures are creating human resource shortages that affect both new and experienced employees. In addition to basic job competencies, skilled workers now must have a broader set of problem-solving, communicating, and negotiating skills to facilitate learning on the job. Couple this with an additional concern: our pool of entry-level workers is shrinking as the post WWII baby boomers shuffle toward retirement. An increasing number of new employees is coming from culturally deprived areas where potential workers have historically lacked entry-level skills. Faced with the pragmatic needs for developing competent workers and the reality of rising education costs, businesses are choosing to re-train their existing workforce rather than hire new employees.

With the attendant costs of corporate education surpassing $44 billion annually, many institutions now are turning to the telecommunications industry to provide training through lower-cost, alternative technologies. Through the ability to simultaneously transmit voice, data, graphics, and video to their constituencies anywhere in the world, institutions can link people electronically through teletraining.

Teletraining

As a specialized application of the broader communication tool called teleconferencing, teletraining combines the productivity gains of advanced training with advantages of teleconferencing: it enables groups to communicate with no limitations on distance. Generally, three delivery media are used to provide teletrained programs: audio-only teleconferencing, audio-graphic computer teleconferencing, and video teleconferencing.

Audio teletraining uses conventional telephone lines to provide a relatively brief, interactive, shared-audio space between instructor and students.

Audiographics teletraining provides users with the capability to interact through two-way voice and interactive graphic communication that presents images simultaneously on high-resolution, color monitors at all sites. The screen images are annotated with the aid of graphics tablets that further enhance the participants' ability to interact. Students also interact with instructors via electronic student response systems.

Video teletraining adds the motion video medium to the training experience. Two types of technology are in widespread use today. One-way video broadcasts use satellite transmission and provide for interactive voice communication, with students calling in questions from a regular telephone. Interactive video teletraining systems use codecs and high-capacity digital lines to compress video signals and enable two-way visual, as well as two-way audio, communication among multiple locations.

Teletraining Users

Though corporations have only recently begun to capitalize on the benefits of teletraining—timely instruction, reduced training expenses, access to subject matter experts, increased productivity, and increased flexibility—the teletraining concept is not new; educational institutions have been successfully using teletraining for years. The first teletraining program began in 1939 with a curriculum for home-bound and hospitalized students in rural Iowa. By 1941, this service reached more than 1,000 registered participants at a monthly cost of $15 per student. In the 1980s, corporations including Aetna, American Airlines, AT&T, GE, Honeywell, Merrill Lynch, and Xerox expanded the concept. Their collated cost-efficiency data has convinced these firms that teletraining in its many guises produces significant savings. However, hard data on efficiency is not enough. In their 1988 article *"Enhancing the Appeal of Teletraining,"* Graham and Wedman find that these cost measures, although compelling, are insufficient to ensure that the training will be well-received, or that the "teletrainees" will participate in the future. Appeal is equally important to consider in business environments where training success is partially dependent on how much satisfaction the student anticipates from the experience. The appeal is enhanced when interaction among course participants is increased. Although teletraining is an efficient, effective, and affordable alternative to classroom training, interaction remains a persistent concern for trainers. With an increase in popularity, the audience size per program for corporate clients has grown dramatically. One teletrained program may reach over 100 students in a single program with multiple locations on line. Keeping all participants involved has become a major interest, one that can be solved through technical application.

Electronic Student Response Systems

How do student response systems improve teletraining? Student response systems can significantly enhance learner attention and the appeal of the teletraining medium. In the past, these electronic devices have been used largely to supplement nonverbal communication in traditional classroom environments. Twenty years ago, the University of Texas and Ball State University recognized a need to increase class interaction in large lecture halls, and adapted the use of electronic student response systems. These systems are electronic teaching aids that support progressive learning environments. While some systems are electronically operated, others are electronically based. Typically, the system includes student response pads with labeled buttons or a conventional computer keyboard that allows students to key responses. In teletraining, where nonverbal cues do not exist, this technology does more than augment training; it provides an alternative channel for nonverbal communication to increase student motivation, student attention, and media appeal.

Until recently, most research related to student response systems focused on technical features, perceived instructional values, and their impact on cognitive learning gains. These gains were tracked by several colleges and universities that reported using these devices in large lecture hall courses 25 years ago. Researchers Whitehead, Bassett, Corrigan, and Roush also noted that the FBI Academy, the Air Force Academy, and the U.S. Army Infantry School at Ft. Benning, Georgia, have effectively used student response systems to process trainees through their respective programs. Horowitz linked these systems to traditional business training at IBM and BMW of North America. In addition, the Ford Motor Company and McDonald's "Hamburger U" have reported using student response systems as well.

One of the largest audiographic teletraining networks to utilize electronic student response systems is the AT&T Audiographic Teletraining Network headquartered in Cincinnati. Over 100 sites across North America have been equipped with the system and, on average, 2,000 students a year complete sales and technical courses. Each site is equipped with a personal computer, large screen monitor, writing tablet, speaker phone, and 15 student response keypads. The complete system costs $13,000. Additional keypads may be connected. Student acceptance of this network with its student response system has been overwhelming. The network saves nearly $1.3 million each year in travel and related expenses.

Effectiveness Research

Research reveals that special design and delivery methods in teletraining are essential to understanding how student response systems enhance effectiveness and appeal. Specifically, the absence of nonverbal cues leaves instructors unable to assess listener attentiveness, the disposition and intentions of learners, and student comprehension. Additionally, teletraining instructors cannot rely on gestures to clarify what is being communicated, and their ability to control communication channels limits the way participants speak and listen during these sessions. Without nonverbal cues for "feedback" and channel control, questioning techniques become more important and more difficult to assure in teletraining than in face-to-face instruction. These systems ensure that students remain attentive; they provide visual cues regarding student comprehension level, attitudes, and intentions. Response systems also provide methods for students to interrupt comfortably for questions while giving student progress information to instructors electronically.

In order for the applications to function properly, Yao (1988) states that most student response systems nominally have some or all of the following features and capabilities:

1. A student panel or keypad with labeled buttons for response entry and other functions (e.g., transmitting the response and calling for the instructor's attention)
2. The capacity to allow the instructor to activate the student panel to solicit responses
3. A display screen for students to see the responses they just made
4. The capacity to allow students to change their responses or to allow only one response
5. The ability to judge the correctness of responses
6. An indicator that shows whether the student's or group's response is correct or not
7. The capacity to indicate the percentage of the class responding to each of the alternatives
8. The ability to indicate the performance of each individual or the group as a whole

9. The freedom for the instructor to set the time span for accepting responses
10. The capability for the instructor to assign different weights or value points to different questions
11. The capacity to display, store, and print the results

Student response systems can be used only for objective questions (i.e., multiple choice, matching, or true/false selections) and for questions that require a Likert scale. These question formats are used as: questions that test actual student comprehension, questions that ask students their impression of their own comprehension, or questions that probe students' attitudes, opinions, and feelings.

Brown (1963) states that some student response systems allow participants to send a signal to the instructor to clarify an issue or to raise questions. This is an important feature for distance learning environments in which students experience microphone shyness and would prefer a less intimidating way to gain channel control. Analogous to raising one's hand in class, this function of student response systems compensates for missing nonverbal cues in teletraining environments.

Horowitz (1988) found that the application of this technology in group settings creates a competitive environment through peer pressure that encourages a higher level of attentiveness among participants. Individual and group responses can be either "tagged" or anonymous as well. In tagged systems, answers are recorded separately from each seat in the room. Anonymous systems merely tabulate the total number of responses in each category. Littauer (1972) argues that tagging may further intimidate students while smothering the instructor in a mass of data. However, Littauer also states that the benefits of tagging include:

1. Providing maximum information about each student
2. Monitoring student activities and attendance
3. Giving students a feeling of being treated as individuals

Question Design

Empirical research by Garvin-Kester (1990) demonstrates that the frequent use of high-order questions increases learner attention and perceived relevance of the instructional material. Based on David Merrill's Performance-Content Matrix, high-order questions focus on concepts, procedures, and principles that require complex levels of mental processing. The application of problem-solving skill is labeled as the "Use" level in the Merrill model. In contrast to this complexity, the low-order question is concerned with facts, simple concepts, procedures, and recall. Merrill has tagged this basic category as the "Remember" level of question design.

Garvin-Kester's research explores the use of higher level questions whenever student response systems are employed in a teletraining environment:

- What type of questions used with student response systems elicit and sustain learners' interest?
- How often should student response system questions occur?
- Where, within the delivery of the program, should student response system activities occur in order to achieve sustained interest?
- Does improved learner interest correlate with the appeal of the teletraining medium?

Her research demonstrates that students exposed to frequent, high-order student response system questions will show higher scores on the variable of interest than those exposed to less frequent, low-order student response system questions; and that a combined measure of frequency and level of question (intensity) will positively correlate with student interest (attention and relevance).

The frequent use of high-order questions increases performance, while immediate and constant feedback as learners move through instruction increases learners' comprehension of instructional content. Separate motivational studies by Robert Gagne (1985) and Roger Keller (1983) have also substantiated the use of questions for gaining and maintaining student attention and thereby improving performance. In particular, Keller outlines three strategies for stimulating and sustaining learner attention, and for increasing student performance: perceptual arousal, inquiry arousal, and variability. Perceptual arousal represents the gaining and maintaining of student attention by use of novel, surprising, incongruous, or uncertain events in instruction. Inquiry arousal stimulates information-seeking behavior by posing or having the learner generate questions or a problem. Variability maintains student interest by varying the element of instruction.

Implications and Recommendations

From the theories and studies reviewed, it is reasonable to argue that performance and appeal is positively affected by the design and delivery of student response system questions and activities that adhere to guidelines developed by Keller and to principles uncovered by Garvin-Kester's research in the use of questions. Student response system and teletraining research shows that student response questions and activities overcome problems from missing nonverbal cues when the following guidelines are employed:

1. To gain student attention, use frequent student response system pre-questions and post-questions to present novelty, surprise, or unexpected events in the instruction (Keller, 1985).

2. To maintain student attention and increase perceived relevance, use student response system post-questions at the "use" or application level (Garvin-Kester, 1990).

3. To maintain student attention and provide variety in programs use post-questions frequently at both the "Remember" and "Use" level (Garvin-Kester, 1990).

4. To humanize and personalize the distance learning environment, present student response system questions through the auditory channel (vocally) in addition to graphically depicting them on the computer or video monitor (Monson, 1978).

5. To humanize and personalize teletraining experiences, as well as improve student retention, provide instructor follow-up and feedback to the student response system activities used (Schloss, et al., 1986).

6. To enhance interaction and facilitation in telelearning, and to increase student retention, allow for some student response system activities that provide students with opportunities to construct responses (completion items) to questions (Yao, 1988).

7. To provide variety in instruction and increase student attentiveness, use student response systems questions to solicit responses from groups (Horowitz, 1988; Keller, 1983).

8. To facilitate two-way (student to instructor) and three-way (student to instructor and to other students) interaction, design student response system technology to include a question key for signaling the instructor and other students for clarification or elaboration (Yao, 1988).

9. Carefully weigh the arguments for and against disclosing student identities in the questioning process. Anonymity may encourage students to interact more freely (Littauer, 1972).

10. Arrange the physical conferencing facilities to expedite maximum interpersonal interaction (problem solving, decision making, and negotiation) among students both within and across locations. Equipment must be highly accessible, easy to use, and strategically placed for viewing and for interactive communication (Chute, 1984; Svenning & Ruchinskas, 1986).

11. Provide participants with pre-training instruction on the use of both the teletraining and student response system hardware (Chute, 1984).

12. Ensure that on-site coordinator assistance is immediately available for troubleshooting the system when problems occur (Chute, 1984).

Summary

Corporations using electronic classrooms for distance education have discovered more efficient and effective ways for facing a growing demand to provide training and education to the adult work force. Researchers, designers, and practitioners can profit from a keen understanding of the capabilities of student response systems for improving interaction and participation in technology-driven environments to make these experiences more personalized, more human, and more appealing. Trainers who use questioning techniques with learner input devices enhance interaction, bring surprise and novelty to the class, and establish relevance for their students.

References

Brown, J. W. (1963). Student Response Systems. *Audiovisual Instruction,* 8, 214,219.

Chute, Alan G. (1984). "Guidelines for implementing teletraining systems." Paper presented at the International Teleconference Symposium, Philadelphia, Pennsylvania on April 3, 1984.

Corrigan, R. E. (1963). Student Response Systems: A defense of the concept. *Audiovisual Instruction,* 8, 599-601.

Gagne, R. M. (1985). *The Conditions of Learning and Theory of Instruction.* New York: Holt, Rinehart & Winston.

Garvin-Kester, B. J. (1990). *The Effect of Student Response System Questions on Learner Attention and Performance in a Distance Learning Environment.* Ann Arbor: UMI.

Graham, S. W. & Wedman, J. F. (1988). Enhancing the appeal of teletraining. *Journal of Instructional Psychology,* 16 (4), 183-191.

Horowitz, H. M. (1988). "Student response system: Interactivity in a classroom environment." Paper presented at Sixth Conference of Interactive Instruction Delivery for the Society for Applied Learning Technology (SALT) on February 24, 1988.

Keller, J. M. (1983). Motivational Design of Instruction. In C.M. Reigeluth (Ed.), *Instructional Design Theories and Models: An Overview of Their Current Status.* Hillsdale, NJ: Lawrence Erlbaum Associates.

Littauer, R. (1972). Instructional implications of a low-cost electronic student response system. *Educational Technology,* 12 (10), 69-71.

Merrill, D. M. (1987). A lesson based on the component display theory. In C. M. Reigeluth (Ed.), *Instructional Design In Action* (pp. 201- 244). Hillsdale, NJ: Lawrence Erlbaum Associates.

Monson, M. (1978). *Bridging the Distance: An Instructional Guide to Teleconferencing.* Wisconsin: Regent of the University of Wisconsin System.

Roush, D. L. (1968). Army Student Response System. *Educational Technology,* 8, 12-13.

Schloss, P. J.; Sindelar, P.T.; Cartwright, P.; & Schloss, C.N. (1986). Efficacy of higher cognitive and factual questions in computer assisted instruction modules. *Journal of Computer-Based Instruction,* 13 (3), 75-79.

Svenning, L. L., & Ruchinskas, J. E. (1986). Decision factors: Why people choose to video conference. In L.A. Parker & C.H. Olgren (Eds.), *Teleconferencing and electronic communications V: Applications, technologies and human factors,* (pp. 258-266). Madison, WI: Center for Interactive Programs.

Whitehead, J. L. & Bassett, R. E. (1975). Providing feedback through student response systems. *Audiovisual Instruction,* 20, (8), 22-24.

Yao, K. (1988). "A needs analysis: Student response system features for teletraining." Unpublished manuscript and workshop. August 8, 1988. AT&T National Teletraining Center, Cincinnati, OH. (AT&T Proprietary)

BESTNET International: A Case Study in the Evolution from a Distance Education Experiment to a Virtual Learning Environment

**George S. Metes, Rodrigo Gutierrez S.,
Vicente Lopez Rocher, Armando Valdez,
and Ricardo Jimenez**

*George Metes is President, Virtual Learning
Systems, Inc., Manchester, NH*

*Rodrigo Gutierrez S. is Director de la Escuela de
Ingenieria, and Vicente Lopez Rocher is
Director de Proyectos Especiales, both at the
Centro de Ensenanza Tecnica y Superior
(CETYS), Tijuana, B.C. Mexico*

*Armando Valdez and Ricardo Jimenez both
teach at Instituto Tecnologico de Mexicali
(ITM), Mexicali, B.C. Mexico*

Introduction: The Coming of the Virtual, Boundaryless Environment

There is general agreement that distance education techniques and technologies have effectively surmounted time and distance barriers to education. But as we all know, distance is only one of many barriers to learning. Communications links do enable information and knowledge to pass between physically separated people and places; but such links provide only the first levels of connectivity that the future will demand. The

195

realities of the emerging "virtual society," with globally involved economies, ubiquitous communication technologies, "distributed" knowledge workers, fluid populations, international information flows, and accelerated change in many dimensions have foregrounded a new crop of learning and work "boundary" challenges in both the educational and commercial sectors. These are boundaries between perspectives, cultures, organizations, and disciplines, to name just a few (Grenier & Metes, 1992; Hirschhorn & Gilmore, 1992; Lipnack & Stamps, 1993).

In learning environments from K-12 through higher/adult education, today's professionals are applying modern techniques and technologies to overcome limiting boundaries such as media channels (multimedia), artificial subject and grade structures (interdisciplinary/student-designed curricula), student capability categories (mainstreaming), learning styles (individualized instruction), cultural perspectives (multicultural pedagogy/cross-cultural communications), and the traditional four-walled classroom (distance education, situated and virtual learning) (Hawkings, 1991; Hiltz, 1990; McLellan, 1993).

In the industrial, or organizational, sector management development models now favor "virtual" teams whose membership, linked in their work by computer and telecommunications technology, transcends the traditional boundaries of function (designers, process engineers, customer services representatives), discipline (chemical engineer, environmentalist, economist), corporations (telecommunications company, entertainment company, computer manufacturer, advertising agency), and even sectors (insurance company, university, engineering company, recycling plant). These alliances are flexible, have beginnings and ends, and often include international and multicultural membership. By design, not by reaction or exception, companies temporarily cross organizational boundaries to bring together the competencies needed to quickly produce highest quality products and services (Davidow & Moore, 1992).

The term "virtual," then, describes communities that transcend historical boundaries of buildings, structure, beliefs, perspectives or bureaucracy, being unified instead through technology supported networks of people and information resources, working toward a common purpose (Hiltz, 1990). Indeed, even the too-long-standing distinctions between "work" and "learning" are dissolving under the pressures of complexity and rapid change, as workers seek the continuous learning they require to keep up with science, with development and manufacturing processes, with challenges in cross-cultural communication, and with shifting market demands.

The good news is that we are discovering how to apply the rich conceptual bases, the body of experience, the pedagogy and communications technologies of distance education to these further boundaries of work and learning. In the perspective on BESTNET that follows, we describe how an international distance education initiative pursued its destiny to become a virtual learning environment; in some ways the ontogeny of BESTNET has prefigured the phylogeny of future virtual learning capabilities. Of necessity, this account is much neater and more structured than were the experiences behind it; but we think the BESTNET story holds some instructive lessons in meeting significant international work and learning challenges with collaborative solutions.

BESTNET: Phase 1—Addressing Boundaries of Distance, Time, and Language Through Video

BESTNET (The Binational English and Spanish Telecommunications Network) is an international community of universities in the southwest U.S. and northwest Mexico, linked by common educational goals and processes, as well as by computer and telecommunications technologies. BESTNET originated in the late 1970s, as a distance education experiment led by Dr. Armando Arias, a Dean at the Imperial Valley Campus (IVC-Calexico) of San Diego State University (Arias, 1992). Dr. Arias, wishing to tap more of the resources of the main campus in San Diego, helped establish an ITFS link between the campuses, bringing live courses taught at the San Diego campus to various sites in Calexico. While the ITFS courses were welcomed, many students at the remote sites felt marginalized by professors' apparent focus on the live San Diego classroom audience. Not only was there no opportunity for interaction, but students didn't even feel part of the learning community. More importantly, most of the students were of Mexican origin; many would have preferred courses in Spanish.

Dr. Arias spent a good deal of time working on curricula and the language issue with universities across the border in Mexicali, Mexico. This work eventually led to a collaborative FIPSE proposal with the Instituto Tecnologico de Mexicali (ITM) to fund the development of bilingual video tapes at Mexicali for use in engineering and mathematics courses at IVC. Students could learn, say, algebra in English, Spanish, or both, at their own pace and on their own time. In fact, while the first courses were delivered periodically over local cable, soon students were making their own copies of "the classes" and reviewing them in ad hoc groups at each other's homes (Arias, 1992).

Even with progress made on the language problem, students still felt constrained by the video approach. The pace of the presentations was fixed, and there was no capability for student/teacher interaction. Clearly, something besides video was needed. One possible solution was suggested by Dr. Beryl Bellman, a consultant on the ITM/IVC project who was on the faculty of the Western Behavioral Sciences Institute, a pioneer in computer conferencing-based learning networks. Dr. Bellman suggested using the same computer-mediated communication (CMC) approaches that were so successful in WBSI's School of Management and Strategic Studies (SMSS).

BESTNET: Phase 2—Building Knowledge Interactively Through Computer-Mediated Communication

In late 1980s, results were coming in on successes in technology-augmented interaction in education. In the SMSS program executives from a variety of disciplines—industry, the military, universities, the creative arts—were linked with experts through computer conferencing. These computer conferencing "courses" examined such global issues as environmental threats, economic theory, philosophy, and leading-edge management strategies (Feenberg & Bellman, 1990). The value of interactions in the learning community of teachers, students, and outside experts was perceived to augment, if not surpass, the learning created by teachers in the more traditional roles of information and knowledge deliverers.

Behind this phenomenon were three major factors. First, students were becoming older and more experienced, bringing valuable knowledge to learning situations. Second, computer and telecommunications technologies were available to support continuous synchronous and asynchronous interactions in networked learning communities (Hiltz, 1990; Dede, 1991; Hawkins, 1991). Finally, it is in the nature of networks that links between, in this case, learners, have an exponential relationship to the number of learners. A teacher can maintain 15 two-way learning links with 15 students; in a networked environment, 105 links may be in place. This shift in perspective from "one-to-many" to "many-to-many" learning indicated that physical distance was no longer the key indicator for computer conferencing, networking solutions; technology-supported interactive learning was just as valuable within a single room or building as across a continent.

A few global businesses had already developed extensive networked learning capabilities to support their far-flung resources (although they generally considered theirs to be "work" rather than "learning" systems). One such enterprise was Digital Equipment Corporation, with headquarters in Massachusetts and worldwide research, development, manufacturing, and customer service resources. For many years Digital had done its work through an electronic mail and computer conferencing network; every employee in the corporation could interact with every other employee electronically, regardless of location, division, or place in the corporate hierarchy. With the support of these networking technologies, Digital was able to develop products using information and knowledge drawn from all over the world, with minimal need for face-to-face communications.

It seemed natural for BESTNET, with its binational focus, constituency of non-traditional, older students, and access to CMC expertise, to explore the possibilities of networked learning.

In 1990 Dr. Bellman sought support from Digital's Drs. John Gundry, Ulf Fagerquist, and George Metes, who were championing networked learning within Digital and with leading Digital commercial customers (Gundry, 1992; Gundry & Metes, 1991). By mid-1991 a BESTNET collaborative research project involving Digital and six U.S. and Mexican Universities coalesced and was approved. The primary institutions were Centro de Ensenanza Tecnica y Superior (CETYS), Tijuana; Instituto Tecnologico de Mexicali (ITM); San Diego State University (SDSU); California State University at Los Angeles (CSULA); Sonoma State University (SSU); University of New Mexico (UNM); and Texas A&I, where Dr. Arias was now Dean of Liberal Arts.

Briefly, Digital would provide dedicated people, computer conferencing, electronic mail, and networking software as well as hardware to support a collaborative action research program in networked learning pedagogy and technology. Dr. Frank Medeiros, Associate Vice President of Academic Affairs at San Diego State University, was selected as BESTNET Director, with Dr. Gundry of Digital, U.K., as Research Director. Participating institutions on both sides of the border all were given basically the same challenges:

1. Build campus BESTNET nodes, consisting of Digital's Vax Notes computer conferencing system, electronic mail, and a synchronous "chat" facility on Digital hardware.
2. Negotiate telecommunications services with local providers for Internet access to connect the nodes.
3. Conduct joint research in networked learning pedagogy and networking technology, by designing, delivering, and evaluating computer conferencing-based courses. As much as possible, courses were to be conducted across the boundaries of department, campus, university system, language, and culture (San Diego State University, 1992).

BESTNET: Phase 3—Going Virtual Through International Computer Networking

Some of the most energetic and rewarding work accomplished over the duration of the research project occurred, fittingly enough, in the border area that was the original BESTNET focus. Working very closely with San Diego State University, both CETYS and ITM quickly built local area BESTNET networked learning systems, linked to BESTNET systems at San Diego State University, Sonoma State University, and the University of New Mexico through Internet.

The driving force for building BESTNET at CETYS was Ing. Rodrigo

Gutierrez. He knew that investment in something as dramatic as an international learning network held political, as well as technological and pedagogical, challenges. He dedicated his time to organizational and technical issues, while his colleague, Professor Vicente Lopez Rocher, took on responsibility for developing the curriculum, pedagogy, and research approach.

Over the next two years, this division of labor proved to be most effective. In the end, CETYS's administration embraced the BESTNET model, while the CETYS faculty developed and successfully delivered computer conferencing-based courses in philosophy, the sciences, and anthropology locally at the CETYS campus, and virtually within the larger BESTNET system.

At ITM, a similar approach accelerated the development of BESTNET. In Mexicali, Professor Armando Valdez played the organizational and political cards, over time not only winning approval for ITM to engage in the BESTNET community, but also gaining the commitment of all 70 members of the nationwide IT systems to explore the opportunities in BESTNET. ITM's Professor Ricardo Jimenez carefully designed BESTNET courses in computer science, including Logic Design, Speech Processing Chips, and Telecommunications Theory. Jimenez combined computer conference assignments and discussions with classroom meetings in which students used PCs to show their proficiency at various module design tasks.

San Diego State University, meanwhile, played a dual role in the BESTNET project. Dr. Medeiros represented BESTNET at high levels of the California State University system and helped build and cement relationships with ITM and CETYS administrative officials. At the same time, SDSU pursued its own aggressive BESTNET research agenda in networked learning pedagogy and technology. Additionally, SDSU provided the center of gravity for the program, building the most robust node in the system and providing a BESTNET menu and user support to other universities as they came online.

At SDSU, one BESTNET course was "Media Technology," taught by Professor John Witherspoon. This course was "virtual" in its entirety; no class meetings were held. Presentations by Professor Witherspoon and guest lecturers were accessible on videotape at the library's reserve desk; assignment texts were online or at the library; discussion was conducted through computer conferencing, and office hours by electronic mail. Guest experts could make online contributions throughout the duration of the course. Digital's Dr. Gundry not only was featured in a videotaped panel on future trends in technology, but actively participated in the BESTNET course conference throughout the semester via his office PC in Reading, U.K. Because of the open nature of the course and the ease with which conferences could be accessed, such outside experts were frequent and highly regarded members of the learning community.

Not only were most BESTNET course conferences open to students and faculty at other campuses in the network, but institutions designed and delivered collaborative courses and even programs. Dr. Mark Resmer, who directed the development of BESTNET at Sonoma State University, contributed a library facility that gave BESTNET institutions menu-driven access to University library catalogs around the world. CETYS, CSULA, and the University of California at Irvine co-hosted a cross-cultural awareness course that brought Mexican and Anglo students together alternately in each other's home communities, and electronically through personal journals shared in the course conferences. At this writing, CETYS and California State University, Dominguez Hills, were collaboratively delivering a BESTNET-based Humanities Degree Program, in English and/or Spanish, depending on student's desires and capabilities.

We should note that one specific kind of computer conference has thrived at every campus on both sides of the border. This is the informal, electronic meeting place in which students can discuss whatever subjects they wish. Self-policed and open to all BESTNET students at any node, these virtual meeting places, whether called *TELEPUB, EN LINEA, CAFE,* or *DIALOGOS,* help build the interstudent relationships that enhance interaction and learning within the actual course conferences and stimulate the larger BESTNET-wide community of learners. No barrier exists between socializing and learning in the networked community.

Further Boundaries

Today, BESTNET continues to seek boundaries to cross. Initiatives are under way with universities in Africa, Eastern Europe, and Latin America. San Diego State University, CETYS, and ITM, in recognition of potential new business relationships between Mexico and the U.S. as a result of initiatives such as the North American Free Trade Agreement, are reaching out to the "boundaryless" border business community—Maquiladoras—offering BEST-NET as the vehicle for situated learning (McLellan, 1993), including the delivery of distance education, and access to the real-time consulting expertise—knowledge—that is essential to the success of virtual business teams. Today grants are in place from the Center for International Business Education and Research and the Public Service Satellite Consortium to develop and support data communications and databases.

These new directions foreshadow the emerging role of the university as the "knowledge stakeholder" in virtual business initiatives (Baldwin, 1992). Integrating higher education and the business world through the medium of knowledge will be a significant milestone in the evolution of the virtual paradigm. But, much like the futile search for the end of a recursive fractal chain, crossing boundaries will lead not to conclusions, but to further boundaries, and the assurance of the continual evolution of networked learning applications.

References

Arias, A. (1992). Higher education and borderlands telecommunications in Texas, California and Arizona. *Rio Bravo: A Journal of Research and Issues,* Spring.

Baldwin, L. V. (1991). Higher-education partnerships in engineering and sciences. *The Annals of the American Academy of Political and Social Science, 514,* 76-91.

Davidow, W. H. and Moore, M. (1992). *The Virtual Corporation: Customization & Instantaneous Response in Manufacturing & Service: Lessons from the World's Most Advanced Companies.* New York: Harper.

Dede, C. (1991). Emerging technologies: impacts of distance learning. *The Annals of the American Academy of Political and Social Science, 514,* 146-158.

Feenberg, A. and Bellman, B. (1990). Social factor research in computer-mediated communications. In Linda M. Harasim (Ed.), *Online Education: Perspectives on a New Environment.* (pp. 67-97), New York: Praeger.

Grenier, R. and Metes, G. (1992). *Enterprise Networking: Working Together Apart.* Bedford, MA: Digital Press.

Gundry, J. (1992). Understanding collaborative learning in networked organizations. In Anthony R. Kaye, *Collaborative Learning Through Computer Conferencing—The Najaden Papers* (pp. 167-178), New York: Springer-Verlag.

Gundry, J. and Metes, G. (1991). *Working by Wire.* Maynard, MA: Digital Equipment Corporation.

Hawkins, J. (1991). Technology-mediated communities for learning. *The Annals of the American Academy of Political and Social Science, 514,* 159-174.

Hiltz, R. S. (1990). Evaluating the virtual classroom. In Linda M. Harasim (Ed.), *Online Education: Perspectives on a New Environment.* (pp. 133-183), New York: Praeger.

Hirschhorn, L. and Gilmore, T. (1992). The new boundaries of the "boundaryless" company. *Harvard Business Review,* May-June 1992, 104-115.

Lipnack, J. and Stamps, J. (1993). *The Teamnet Factor: Bringing the Power of Boundary Crossing Into the Heart of Your Business.* Essex Junction, VT: Oliver Wight.

McLellan, H. (Ed.). (1993). Situated learning [Special Issue]. *Educational Technology, 3.*

Ohler, J. (1991). Why Distance Education? *The Annals of the American Academy of Political and Social Science, 514,* 22-34.

Quinn, J. B. (1992). *Intelligent Enterprise: A Knowledge and Service Based Paradigm for Industry.* New York: The Free Press.

San Diego State University. (1992). *BESTNET: A Home for International Communities of Interest.* San Diego, CA.

Monitoring the Electronic Classroom

It's Too Late to Dig the Well When Your House is on Fire: Using Formative Evaluation to Increase the Educational Effectiveness of Technology Products

Karen J. Hoelscher

Karen Hoelscher teaches at Western Washington University in Bellingham, WA

A n old proverb warns of the danger of delaying important decisions. Similar problems exist when evaluation activities are delayed until the end of the development of educational technology products. *Formative* evaluations answer important questions while a product is still being developed:

- Is there a need for the product? Who is the audience? What are the goals?
- What media will be used to deliver the content?
- What specific content, behavioral objectives, and instructional strategies should be included?
- How can pilot materials be more user-friendly, appealing, comprehensible, persuasive, and instructional?
- How can the program be more effective with its target group?

These questions, if examined *during the development* of products, can help increase the overall educational effectiveness of final products. This

205

chapter will explore the use of formative techniques during the development of technology products for higher education (e.g., computer software, instructional videodisks, and telecourses). Examples from a videodisk for higher education will illustrate how the four phases of product development (planning, design, production, and implementation) correspond to the four phases of formative evaluation (needs assessment, preproduction, production, and implementation).

The purpose of this chapter is to share knowledge gained from developing and implementing formative evaluation plans to improve educational technology products. To judge the educational effectiveness of programs, evaluation techniques are designed to help program developers test and modify the materials at different stages in the development process. In this chapter, four phases of formative evaluation—and specific techniques used at each stage—are illustrated, with examples from a recent series of formative evaluations conducted at Harvard Law School. The first section defines formative evaluation terminology and provides a context for understanding how formative phases relate to the phases of product develop-

	PRODUCT DEVELOPMENT PHASE	**EVALUATION PHASE (AND OBJECTIVES)**
PHASE I	Planning phase (Define proposal for product)	Needs Assessment (Determines need for product)
PHASE II	Design phase (Produce design document)	Preproduction Formative Evaluation (Guide content decisions, develop program objectives)
PHASE III	Production phase (Produce prototype program)	Production Formative Evaluation (Guide revisions, develop prototype program)
PHASE IV	Implementation phase (Produce fully operational program; use in setting)	Implementation Formative Evaluation (Guide limited revisions, develop accompanying print materials)

ment. Examples describe the data collection procedures at each phase (i.e., needs assessment, preproduction, production, and implementation). The second section summarizes the characteristics and expected outcomes of formative evaluation of products for higher education.

Formative Evaluation: Excavating the Well While Framing the Castle

Innovative learning technologies, especially those permitting complex instructional designs, pose unprecedented challenges for instructional designers. It is not always apparent which instructional strategies make the best use of the features of a particular technology. And, when technology is used to meet *new* learning objectives (see, for example:[1],[2],[3]), inventive instructional strategies must be devised. As a result, formative evaluation strategies have evolved to keep pace with the demands of testing and improving increasingly complex designs for educational technology products.

In a definitive work on the use of formative evaluation to improve electronic learning materials, Flagg[4] describes the application and value of formative methods to improve final products:

> Formative evaluation helps the developer of a product during the early development stages to increase the likelihood that the product will achieve its goals in its final implementation. "Evaluation" in this definition means the systematic collection of information for the purpose of informing decisions to design and improve the product. The term "formative" indicates that information is collected during the formation of the product so that revisions might be made cost-effective. (pp.9-10)

Formative evaluation is a practical sequence of techniques that correspond to the major phases of product development (i.e., planning, design, production, and implementation). In each product development phase below, the outcome is listed in terms of a level of understanding about the developing product that allows a development team to move forward with confidence to the next development phase [5, p. 12], as shown in the table on the previous page.

Each of these phases, with examples relevant to the growth of a case development videodisk for law school students, will be explored in the following four parts of this section.

1. Needs Assessment: Do We Need a Well? Where Should We Locate It?

During this phase the feasibility of actually producing the product is studied. Generally, this is the stage at which existing products are surveyed to determine the need for creating a particular new product. If the need is justified, other areas are studied, such as the type of content and its level of difficulty, the type of delivery system to be used, and the overall scope of the project.

In the past 15 years, educational researchers have examined the learning benefits of computer technology. There exists considerable evidence of the benefits of computer-based instruction designed to simulate experience beyond textbook and lecture learning.[6,7,8] For example, computer-based simulations allow medical students to develop diagnostic skills before meeting a real patient; simulations allow engineering students to conduct stress-testing on computerized model bridges before designing the structural plans for an actual bridge; they can enable future NASA scientists to employ rocket-launching techniques. Thus, the computer environment provides simulated career experiences that enhance the traditional classroom environment.

In law schools, process-oriented skills such as establishing client-attorney relationships, interviewing witnesses, and evaluating evidence are difficult to learn merely through reading cases or listening to another's experience. At the needs assessment phase, several groups of people with expertise in legal education and technology evaluation collaborated to study the possibility of producing a computer-based product to meet these needs:

- Harvard Law School (faculty, students, and interactive video project staff members)
- The American Video Institute, at the Rochester (NY) Institute of Technology (instructional designers and programmers)
- Harvard University Assessment Seminar (a group supporting projects designed to study issues in teaching and learning)

When the group became convinced that this type of independent experience was both desired and not in existence in law school curricula, they considered various ways of designing such an environment. For obvious reasons (i.e., potential to offer very life-like video, and to store a large amount of written and pictorial information that could be accessed almost instantaneously), interactive videodisk became the medium of choice. The product would use a visual and textual database to complement traditional curriculum by simulating the experience of a junior partner in a law firm. To exploit the storage capacity of the videodisk medium, the design team suggested the use of still photographs containing a small amount of text at the bottom, versus moving video. This would enable a much larger amount of information to be stored on the disk (motion video requires 30 frames per second), as well as providing a greater level of control for students of the movement between screens.

These and other types of planning decisions created the framework for the eventual design of the product (later to be named "Litigation Strategies"). The overall goal: to bridge the gap between the theory students learn in law school classrooms and the practice they enter as legal professionals. Based on careful consideration during the needs assessment phase, the "Litigation Strategies" development team moved into the design phase—and preproduction formative evaluation— confident that the product was needed and that its general direction was on-target.

2. Preproduction Formative Evaluation: What Shape the Well?

This phase builds on the knowledge gained during the needs assessment phase. Planning decisions are addressed more specifically and their feasibility reconsidered here. At this point, decisions are made regarding specific content, learner objectives, and instructional strategies. This phase ends with what is often called a "design document," which guides the subsequent development of the product. This document may outline the content, learning objectives, and expected general audience characteristics. It may also provide a flow chart showing the major directions of the program, and perhaps include some typical treatments of the objectives (i.e., examples of how the information might be presented on-screen).

With videodisk technology, this phase offers a chance to test ideas for possible program interfaces (i.e., the relationship between what is on the screen and what is expected of the learner using the program). In the "Litigation Strategies" project, preproduction activities involved two broad areas relating to the interface. The first area involved determining the types of categories to include in the section used to interview witnesses; the second area involved matching the facial expressions of witnesses to the textual sequence of the story they told. (The photos, in addition to a color picture of a person with a particular facial expression, contain a few lines of text at the bottom.)

Using a section called "Line of Questioning," learners can conduct interviews with any of 28 potential witnesses involved with the civil rights case upon which the disk is based.[1] Questions are posed by selecting menu options such as "What happened?", "How were you involved?", and "Have you ever been arrested?" Used in full, each person tells their story as it relates to the case, including repeated facts, misleading facts, and facts that do not relate whatsoever to the case. It was important that each photo related to the lines of text that accompanied that photo. For example, a sequence in which the client, Donald Boyd, describes his experience being wrestled to the ground by Officer Deaver needed to be accompanied by photos of Boyd that become increasingly agitated as he tells his story. Thus, in the preproduction phase, the development team determined basic outlines for the "story" that would be told by each witness, and planned the process of shooting photographs to accompany those stories. After trying out some of the testimony on each other and on experienced attorneys, the development team was satisfied that the still frame approach would be workable to meet the objectives determined during the needs assessment phase.

The role of the evaluator varies during preproduction formative evaluation, based on the relationship desired by the development team.[9],[10],[11] In this case, the evaluator was not directly involved in data collection. Rather, she synthesized written feedback from team members who participated in various brainstorming sessions, and offered suggestions for design change based on what was working well and what was viewed as problematic. After modifications were decided upon, the team was ready to produce a prototype videodisk program for use in the next phase, production formative evaluation.

3. Production Formative Evaluation: Setting the Tank, Priming the Pump

During this phase, data are collected to guide revision using experimental (not final) versions of a program. These program prototypes are tested with target audience members or content experts for feedback in several areas[4]: user friendliness, appeal, comprehensibility, persuasiveness, and learning. This information is then considered by the development team along with other data (e.g., timeline, costs to implement changes, and the willingness of the team to shift perspectives based on audience reaction).

The "Litigation Strategies" disk was ready to be tried with experienced attorneys and experienced law students. Numerous people who had covered this material using traditional law school methods (listening to lectures and reading about case development) used the pilot videodisk materials, reacted to them, and made a variety of suggestions for improvement. Because the disk was still in the production stage (versus being nearly completed), and because the producers were genuinely interested in testing their instincts and knowledge of the legal process, numerous improvements were made in the program. These included making the program more friendly and easy to use, more understandable, and more responsive to learners. At this point, participants' comments about inaccuracies in content or legal procedure could also be addressed. This same information, collected at a later phase, may have been impossible to use.

Evaluation techniques used to gather these data included direct observation of small groups of attorneys and law students using the disk, followed by focus groups in which participants were encouraged to share their suggestions for improving: (1) the presentation of specific case content, and (2) the overall procedures for the case development experience.

Several changes occurred in the basic design of "Litigation Strategies" during this phase of development. The outlines of witness testimony developed in the preproduction phase were enlarged to full storylines for each character. Still photos were shot and paired with text to achieve the desired effect. A main menu of "Line of Questioning" selections was devised, grouping parts of each story into categories from which learners could choose. The last part of this section describes the use of implementation formative evaluation techniques to fine-tune a near-final product.

4. Implementation Formative Evaluation: Testing and Purifying the Water

During implementation formative evaluation, the program is placed in its intended environment with an appropriate target group. In this phase, several characteristics of a product's use are examined, including appeal, user friendliness, and comprehension outcomes. In this setting a product is tested under near-normal conditions, with developers still expecting to make revisions based on the reaction of the target group. At this point in the development process, only limited changes are still feasible in a product's design. However, this phase is typically used to determine the level of written instruction that accompanies a product.

By the time the "Litigation Strategies" videodisk reached this phase, the development team and several faculty members had targeted its use for novice law students (those in their first year of law school). In this implementation evaluation phase, pairs of first-year law students used the disk and provided feedback regarding two types of written orienting instructions (one set contained minimal information about getting started; another set of instructions provided details and helpful hints about developing a legal case). Thus, this formative study generated feedback about student preferences for written instructions to accompany the videodisk.

As students worked through the case, a variety of methods were used to examine:

- appeal (how much students liked different parts of the program)
- user friendliness (how easy the program was to move around in; how easy it was to use the desktop tools to develop the case; how responsive the program was to students' wishes)
- comprehension (how well students understood the elements of the case)

Appeal and user friendliness were measured using observation and interview methods. Comprehension outcomes were measured using a paper and pencil version of a legal complaint. The complaint form required students to specify several criteria relating to their investigation of the civil rights case on the disk. Complaints were evaluated by outside experts. Finally, the case development performance of students using guided and unguided types of orienting instruction was examined, to determine the effect of orienting instruction on performance.

In this implementation formative evaluation, multiple measures were designed to collect diverse types of data to permit greater understanding of learners' experience. Instruments used in this phase were divided into two categories: (1) measures of student performance, and (2) measures of student perception. Student *performance* data (case development strategies and resulting outcomes) were collected with: (a) an online computer program that tracked student pathways through the case, (b) direct observation, and (c) a paper and pencil test (i.e., the complaint form). Student *perception* data (personal opinions about their use of the product) were collected with (a) a closed- and open-response individual questionnaire, and (b) a brief, structured pair interview.

Based on a systematic analysis of these data, suggestions were developed for improving the use of the *Litigation Strategies* videodisk by its target audience members (i.e., novice law students). For example, student pairs using the more guided instructions not only produced more superior legal documents than the unguided students, but they suggested creating even more specific instructions for their law school peers. It is somewhat paradoxical to impose a mode of use within such an environment based on exploration and discovery. However, the results of this formative study point to the value of providing pre-instruction to familiarize students with the organization and use of a complex computer-based environment. This information, gathered while the product was still being formed, improved the final version of the product.

Reflections: Digging the Well Well

This chapter has outlined the use of formative evaluation strategies to increase the appeal and educational effectiveness of technology products for education. Examples from a videodisk for higher education have illustrated how the four phases of product development (planning, design, production, and implementation) correspond to the four formative evaluation phases (needs assessment, preproduction, production, and implementation). Within each evaluation phase, different questions are asked and different types of data are collected. The process becomes an iterative one, in which several cycles within each phase may be required before a problem is remedied. This is especially true when developing complex products like "Litigation Strategies," which are designed to meet new curriculum objectives. The more lifelike a simulation, the more options a design must include.[12] In such products, the sheer number of avenues for learners to explore makes the formative evaluation process both extremely involved and increasingly important.

Whether the task is to design and conduct formative evaluation of interactive experiences for students of law, business, or the classics, the principles of formative evaluation remain the same. Conducted "well," formative evaluation:

- Provides direction (versus "answers")
- Reduces uncertainty (versus proving superiority)
- Relies on qualitative methods (versus statistical tests)
- Is action-oriented (versus measuring statistical outcomes, and drawing effectiveness inferences)
- Is both proactive and reactive (looks forward and backward)

Because of their ability to provide feedback in early design stages, as well as during prototype implementation in the classroom, formative evaluations give students and faculty a voice in the design process, making the result more appealing, informative, and easy to use.[13] When a development team decides to test their instincts with formative methods during the design and development of an educational technology product, they are, in essence, excavating the well in systematic, parallel steps to increase the potential value of their castle.

Notes

1. "Litigation Strategies" uses factual information from an actual civil rights case, *Hall* v *Ochs*, tried in 1983 in Boston.

References

1. Greenes, R. chapter in this volume.

2. Novak, G. chapter in this volume.

3. Peters, G., and Bailey, D. chapter in this volume.

4. Flagg, B. N. (1990). *Formative evaluation for educational technologies.* Hillsdale, NJ: Lawrence Erlbaum Associates.

5. Hoelscher, K. (1989). "Bridging the classroom and the real world: A videodisc implementation study at Harvard Law School." Doctoral thesis, Harvard Graduate School of Education, Cambridge.

6. Bok, D. (1985, May/June). Looking into education's high-tech future. *Harvard Magazine.* 29-38.

7. Roblyer, M., Castine, W., & King, F. (1988). Assessing the impact of computer-based instruction. *Computers in the Schools,* 5 (3-4).

8. Zollman, D., Nobel, M., & Curtin, R. (1987). Modelling the motion of an athlete:

An interactive video lesson for teaching physics. *Journal of Educational Technology Systems*, 15 (3), 249-257.

9. Bryk, A. (Ed.). (1983). *Stakeholder-based evaluation. New Directions for Program Evaluation 17.* San Francisco: Jossey-Bass.

10. Cambre, M. (1981). Historical overview of formative evaluation of instructional media products. *Educational Communication and Technology Journal*, 29 (1), 3-25.

11. Patton, M. (1986). *Utilization-focused evaluation.* Beverly Hills: Sage Publications.

12. Bergeron, B. (1988, November). Toward more effective learning environments: Strategies for computer simulation design. *Collegiate Microcomputer*, 6 (4), 289-309.

13. Hoelscher, K., & Flagg, B. (1990, September). Evaluating the effectiveness of computer-based instruction. *Technology Window*, Harvard University. V (1).

Working Together with Technology

Linda S. Fowler

*Linda Fowler is with the Network Education
and Training at AT&T in Cincinnati*

NOTE: An asterisk (*) is used to denote other authors who contributed chapters to this volume.

Certain industries revolutionize the way we live: it was computers for the last 10 years; it will be telecommunications in the next 10 years (Dorfman, 1993). The electronic classroom combines computers and telecommunications to reach many more students than ever before possible in novel and hopefully exciting ways. The electronic classroom utilizes technology in many forms to augment existing teaching tools and to provide alternate methods of presenting information. This environment supports independent learning where students operate equipment in media centers and use computer clusters.

Connick and Russo* indicate that throughout history, education systems are redefined to meet the evolving needs of society. Yet, in teaching, changes are occurring sporadically and in relative isolation. What is lacking is not the technology but the widespread understanding of the power and meaning of those tools for the revolution in the classrooms. Connick and Russo* describe Papart's comparison, which says that teachers of 100 years ago could enter a classroom of today and take over. This is vividly contrasted when compared to a surgeon of 100 years ago who attempts to function in a surgical unit today. Multimedia are available but not widely used in today's education process. This book and the experiences described by the authors can give the reader ideas and direction to begin utilizing technology in their classrooms.

Three common issues emerge from the chapters in this handbook. Perhaps the most consistent theme is the need to change the focus of instruction to one of collaborative learning with the teacher functioning as facilitator. The need for appropriate training, documentation, and technical support for both students and instructors was emphasized in the majority of these chapters. The third major theme is the need to plan when formulating new training or when changing from a traditional approach to utilizing state-of-the-art technology. The call is to not just embrace a technology and then try to apply it.

Learning

Information is so broadly based and acquisition of knowledge so complex that new ways of teaching and learning are essential, especially considering the diversity of the students we teach. Steele* emphasizes the problem in education as not just money, but one of using old approaches to new problems. Most of the authors in this book conclude that changes in types of learning and teaching can and must occur for the electronic classroom to succeed. Most methods and equipment require that the student rather than the teacher take responsibility. Billings* gives several examples of how the role of instructors must change to facilitators. In using self-paced methods and formulating their own structures, the students will lead to a "student centered system due to students' ability to address such a vast amount of information." Billings* emphasizes that there will be a change in a relationship from hierarchical with control by teachers, to students collaborating and using student-to-student support.

In many scenarios described by the authors in this volume, patterns of cooperative learning developed. The conceptual framework of Vygotskian theory provides a constructive basis for understanding the functioning in an electronic classroom. One of the key concepts is his "Zone of Proximal Development." Vygotsky (1978, p. 86) defined this as:

> the distance between the actual developmental level as determined by independent problem solving and the level of potential development as determined through problem solving under adult guidance or *in collaboration with more capable peers.* (italics added)

The Zone of Proximal Development expresses Vygotsky's notion that what children can do with the assistance of others might be in some sense even more indicative of their mental development than what they can do alone (Meichenbaum, Burland, Gruson, and Cameron, 1985). Students' achievements in the supportive social environment make the largest contribution to their cognitive development. Even though Vygotsky looked at children's development, the acquisition of knowledge, regardless of age, goes through defined steps. The cooperative learning associated with remote delivery sites and student-centered learning are supported by Vygotsky's theory.

The use of telecommunications and other technologies fits the Vygotskian model of social learning in context with an emphasis on collaboration. Learning is mediated, not only by teachers, but also by peers who are sharing or teaching knowledge and skills. Vygotsky's theory provides support for such a dynamic, interactive structure that forms the basis of successfully using these technologies.

If the collaborative method of teaching is to be successful, a new way of thinking must be supported. The focus in most classrooms today is still one of the teacher in charge and all interactions going through the teacher. The collaborative approach, which is supported by the very logistics of using electronic components in teaching, builds upon a changing paradigm—moving from teaching (teacher focus) to learning (student focus). There are few interactions between and among students. This change in focus from a teacher directed to a facilitated environment has been given some verbal support in many classrooms. The authors' experiences described in this Handbook indicate that they have begun such a paradigm shift.

When T. S. Kuhn (1970) first used the term paradigm, he was describing how "mind sets" of scientists support a given theory. His example of how scientists changed to the concept that the sun, not the earth, was the center of our solar system gives a clear example of what is meant by a paradigm. When one is functioning within a given paradigm, "there seems an attempt to force nature into the preformed and relatively inflexible box that the paradigm supplies." (p. 24) This situation exemplifies education today. Education is ready for and in need of a paradigm shift to support innovation and change. To encourage the widespread use of technology in support of learning, teachers and instructors will need help and encouragement to apply this paradigm shift (Fowler and Wheeler, 1994). Teachers who have taught for years using lecture methods may find it difficult to let go of that role.

Educational change has three components: use of new or revised materials, new teaching approaches, and an alteration of beliefs (Fullan, 1982). Since change is a process and not an event, a paradigm shift in education will not occur quickly. Building on Vygotsky's theory, the role of collaboration in facilitating learning should be stressed. New technology provides activities and an environment that support the facilitation method and acts as a zone of proximal development for students and teachers alike.

Planning

Connick and Russo* describe how confidence and a strong belief in the value of using these tools is critical to a successful advanced technology program. They expressed the need for a committed leadership. Both Hoelscher* and Schwartz* emphasize performing needs analysis at the inception of a new course or project, NOT after development of materials and programs. Before embarking on creating an electronic classroom, outline resources and tools available; define those needed to accomplish your mission—the mission you defined before you actually began to create the electronic classroom. Encourage dialog about a plan's development and implementation. Defining the goals at the beginning provides information on how to improve educational technology products during formation so revisions are more cost effective and the final product is more timely. From Schwartz'* examples, the readers are shown how the lack of planning caused technical difficulties resulting in a loss of messages and extreme time delay.

Results from a Learning Perspective

The examples described in this volume give the reader some idea of the range of possibilities of subject areas that advanced educational technologies can impact. Using technology to teach science using simulations, as Raymond Russo* describes, encourages proper experimental design. Gammon* suggests using instrument simulators to teach chemistry to provide a preview of equipment and also show equipment otherwise not available to many students. Novak* described how experimental information was exchanged in introductory physics classes. A third science example was Russo's* explanation of a simulation of a field trip to a marine bioecosystem. Both Novak* and Gammon* describe using simulations so students can focus on data interpretation rather than hands-on manipulation.

Technology

Dierker* says that the impact of a given technology can be quantified by determining the extent that technology multiplies human capabilities to accomplish the same task. This book provides the reader with a range of technology products that singly or together constitute an electronic classroom. Each example seeks to improve the overall effectiveness of teaching for teachers and learning for students. An electronic classroom can encompass a large assortment of technology products or can simply provide the means for teachers and students in different places and different time sequences to communicate with each other. To effectively utilize technology, Connick and Russo* state that users must have a widespread understanding of the power and meaning of those tools.

Each chapter in this book contains specific examples of how teachers delivered course materials with the aid of multimedia. They used networks linked to projection units and software development facilities, used electronic bulletin boards and searched information archives, and exchanged e-mail with experts and fellow students. Economy of scale is provided when visual teleconferencing is used to connect students at remote locations.

Incorporating More Technology into Teaching

The many examples of different technology products and how they have been used to augment delivery of instructional materials are cited in this volume. Not all achieved the level of results expected. But, even with the diversity of examples, environments and disciplines described here, many common elements emerge. We can learn from their successes, their energy, and their omissions.

The situations described by the authors in this book give the reader many examples in a wide variety of disciplines where electronic media have expanded delivery. From the successes described and the problems shared, an individual new to this environment could embark on this new path learning from others.

The successful implementation of advanced educational technologies requires an examination of current training needs and procedures. The characteristics of the innovative approach along with an awareness of the psychological factors that affect the adopting of a new training system need to be addressed. A strategy for the implementation process is also required. An understanding of these factors will assist the instructor in successfully implementing a new system which addresses student needs.

Training development standards based on recent advances in educational and training technology provide a framework for developing new training materials using various technologies. One example is the SAID (Systematic Approach to Instructional Development) process used to develop training at AT&T.

The steps are:

1. Front-end analysis
2. Project planning
3. Job/task analysis
4. Training design which includes type of technology to be used
5. Materials development
6. Tryout and revision
7. Evaluation
8. Maintenance

Training on the use of the new technology and evaluation are essential components for the successful adoption of a new technology in a classroom or training session. For an innovation to be successful, the instructor must establish a relationship between student and instructor needs and the ability to meet those needs using the new medium. (Bennis, Benne, Chin, and Corey, 1976; Havelock, 1973; Rogers, 1972). According to studies, seven levels or stages of concern are observable during the adoption of any innovative program or project. The stages are:

1. Awareness
2. Informational
3. Personal
4. Management
5. Consequences
6. Collaboration
7. Refocusing

Individuals experience a number of these concerns as they proceed through the change process. Typically, non-users have concerns at the first three stages listed above. As an individual becomes more familiar with an innovation, concerns shift to the management and consequence levels. Experienced users are concerned with the collaboration and refocusing stages (Hall, Wallace, Dossett, 1983; Hall, 1979).

A Working Checklist

A process that can be successfully used to implement new technology into classrooms is recommended. Here are some items to consider:

- Define what you want to teach, including goals and objectives of the training. Remember that technology is a tool.
- Outline the impact of this training including obstacles and cost.
- Perform some type of task analysis on what you want to accomplish and define what it will take to meet these objectives.
- Recognize the change in type of social interaction required by you and the students.
- Make decisions to determine that the medium you select will optimally meet your needs as well as the students' requirements.
- If possible, find someone with experience in using this technology.
- Provide enough support for your students. Technical difficulties have been found to be the most common reason for new technology experiments to fail. Prepare for problems by providing ample reference and supplementary materials and human support so that high levels of anxiety are avoided.
- Use feedback to improve on the training materials and delivery.
- Congratulate yourself on joining the ranks of the pioneers who successfully apply technology to their teaching.

References

Bennis, W. G.; Benne, K. D.; Chin, R.; and Corey, K. E. (1976) *The Planning of Change*, 3rd ed. Holt, Rinehart & Winston, New York.

Dorfman, *USA Today,* August 24, 1993.

Fullan, M. (1982) *The Meaning of Educational Change.* New York: Teachers College Press.

Hall, G. E.; Wallace, R. C.; and Dossett, W. A. (1973) *A development conceptualization of the adoption process within educational institutions.* Research and Development Center for Teacher Education, University of Texas.

Hall, G. E. (1979) "Procedures for adopting educational innovations/CBAM, using the individual and the innovation as the frame of reference for research on change." Paper presented at the annual meeting of the Australia Association for Research in Education, Melbourne, November.

Havelock, B. W. (1973) *The Change Agent's Guide to Innovation in Education.* Educational Technology Publications, Englewood Cliffs, New Jersey.

Kuhn, T. S. (1970) 2nd ed. *The structure of scientific revolutions.* Chicago: University of Chicago Press.

Fowler, L. S. and Wheeler, D. D. (1994) Online from the K-12 Classroom in Z. Berge and M. Collins (eds.) *Computer Mediated Communications and the Online Classroom: An Overview and Perspectives,* Hampton Press: Cresskill, NJ.

Meichenbaum, D.; Burland, S.; Gruson, L.; & Cameron, R. (1985) Metacognitive Assessment in *The growth of reflection in children.* Steven R. Yussen (Ed.) 1985. New York: Academic Press.

Rogers, E. M. (1972) Change agents, client and change. In Zaltman, G.; Kotler, P.; and Kaufman, I. (eds.) *Creating social change.* Holt, Rinehart & Winston, New York.

SAID, Systematic Approach to Instructional Development, (1984) Proprietary Document, AT&T. Cincinnati.

Vygotsky, L. S. (1978) *Mind in Society: the Development of Higher Psychological Processes.* Cambridge: MIT Press.

The Ethics of Teaching and the Teaching of Ethics

Rushworth M. Kidder

*Rushworth Kidder is President of The Institute
for Global Ethics, Camden, ME, and a member
of the Advisory Council of the Character
Education Partnership*

To talk about the ethics of the electronic classroom is to consider two very different bundles of issues: the ethics of teaching, and the teaching of ethics.

The first bundle involves questions of pedagogy. While the questions themselves are unique to the electronic classroom, they belong to an order of inquiry found in any profession. Just as those working in such areas as medicine, journalism, or business face ethical issues peculiar to their specialties, so those teaching in electronic classrooms encounter ethical dilemmas and moral temptations specific to this environment. Among them:

- How do you assure the privacy of the individual and the confidentiality of information? Since every keyboard in each classroom can, theoretically, be tied into software that keeps track of every keystroke by each user, the potential exists for "testing" each user for speed, accuracy, and the ingenuity of his or her solutions—*even when the user is unaware that such testing is going on.* Such testing, aggregated into individual profiles, can easily be used to rank and rate users. Such rating may be useful—especially if gathered secretly, unaffected by pressures that might arise if the individual knew of the testing. But is it ethical to gather that information without alerting the users?

- How do you assure fair compensation to providers of classroom activities? Some of these activities are software-based, which raises all the familiar issues of software piracy and modification that have already come into the courts. But some of them are only tangentially related to software. These include games, lines of questioning, and even extended metaphors that are intended to be used by users who may, for those moments, have their machines switched off. The ethics of using such pedagogical devices is, of course, already a matter of debate in ordinary classroom settings. But when a concept can be circulated instantaneously to vast pools of potential users with no compensation returning to its inventor, what will stimulate other inventors to enter the field? Where will good ideas come from unless there is a legal and ethical framework that assures a fair return for hard creative thinking?

- How can hackers and cheaters be discouraged? When computers are only peripheral to classroom instruction, there is only a marginal interest among a few students in breaking into those systems for personal gain. But when the chip takes center stage, when knowledge of computer technology becomes more widespread, and when the electronic vehicles become both the arbiters of success and the keepers of the academic scorecard, the impetus to break and enter is proportionally increased. Add to this the Nintendo mentality—that winning means beating the electronic system—and the recipe is in place for a disturbing ethical brew. Is it ethical to place substantial new temptations in front of young minds without at the same time creating a moral climate that gives them reason to turn away from cheating and fraud?

- How can instructors be hired with as much attention to content knowledge and interpersonal skills as to technological understanding? The temptation for those establishing electronic classrooms may be to hire the techno-whiz, hoping that he or she will also know a little something about the subject (history, geography, math, or whatever) that needs teaching. The deeper challenge, however, will be to find people who know not only electronics and subject matter but have a lively understanding of people. Here the old adage still operates: If you want to teach math to Mary, it is just as important to know Mary as it is to know math. Unfortunately, the stereotype of the computer nerd may also still operate: Fields requiring profound levels of technological understanding may attract people who are far less comfortable with the warm and messy qualities of human interaction than with the digital precision of symbolic logic. Plenty of well-rounded technological experts are available. So how best can we meet the moral imperative to find them—to insist that those two qualities of humanity and subject matter are not washed aside in our search for this third area of technological competence?

- How can we overcome the dominance of the visual? The electronic classroom will be capable of highly visual activity. Let's discount the obvious ethical problems—the kinds of dishonesties made possible by today's computer imaging techniques, in which a few drags of the mouse can produce an apparently authentic photograph of, say, President Clinton with his arm around Saddam Hussein—and focus only on the conceptual problems of teaching in a strongly visual environment. There is much to be said for a visually stimulating classroom, in which students fasten on ideas through a grasp of their symbols. There is also much to worry about here as spatial relationships replace linear, sequential logic as the means of instruction. If the visual dominates, will reading fade? More seriously, if the acts of the mind required by reading are not developed, will imagination also atrophy? If students are never called upon to construct mentally ·the appearance of the world they are discussing, will they become increasingly reliant on the image-makers to do it for them—and less able to create a life of the mind for themselves? Is there a moral requirement to preserve, in the face of visual pressures, a verbal environment?

- How can we assure that humans, not machines, are still perceived as the instructors? Ernest L. Boyer, president of the Carnegie Foundation for the Advancement of Teaching, tells the story of visiting a classroom of very young and very disadvantaged children when researching his book on pre-school education in the 1980s.[1] There he found a child sitting in front of a computer screen with tears streaming down his cheeks. The screen was flashing an excited message—"Terrific job, Johnny, you got it right!"—or words to that effect. When Boyer asked him why he was crying, the boy replied, "It's the first time anybody ever told me I did something right." When the first "anybody" in that boy's life is in fact a soulless computer, the lesson ought to come home to us all: Love itself is the crying need. Is it ethical to replace genuine human caring with a mechanical pseudo-response that, however much it met that boy's need, tells us volumes about what's been lacking in the years before he met that machine?

These are, to be sure, important ethical issues. But they pale in significance before the other range of issues—those that involve not the ethics of teaching but the teaching of ethics. The question here can be stated baldly: How can we teach ethics in an electronic classroom?

The question starts with a prior one: *Why* should we teach ethics in an electronic age? The answer, I think, is equally bald: Because we will not survive the 21st century with the ethics of the 20th century. Some years ago, when I visited Chernobyl in the company of two engineers who had been called in shortly after the 1986 explosion to help clean up the mess, that lesson came home to me. What caused that explosion was not technology. It was, as Soviet documents later made clear, the deliberate and willful overriding of six separate computer-driven alarm systems by the control-room operators. Each alarm warned that the experiment being carried on that April night, involving a shut-down of Reactor Number Four, was terribly dangerous and should be aborted at once. Instead, the operators shut down the alarms and kept going—until the roof blew off in a meltdown and explosion that still holds the record for the largest industrial accident in the history of the world.

What went wrong here? One answer surely must be that conscience simply failed. It seems apparent that, before a single alarm could be overridden, there must have been an ethical override—that the nuclear meltdown must have been preceded by a moral meltdown. In fact, that moral meltdown took place in a context that involved two other factors: the intelligence of the operators and scale of the system. Clearly, those operators were smart and well-educated in the relevant technologies: Jobs at Chernobyl were plum jobs in the old Soviet system, going to some of the best-qualified minds in the nation. Add to that the scale of the system here: Chernobyl was no local coal-fired power plant, but a system capable of raining nuclear fallout so broadly that it was detected in every country in the world that had the capacity to measure it.

What if those three parameters of knowledge, ethics, and scale had been different? Suppose you had smart unethical operators working in a small-scale system. There would have been little damage. Suppose you had *dumb* unethical operators: Even working in a large system, they would not have known how to manipulate the controls to shut down the alarms. Finally, suppose you had smart, *ethical* operators in a large system: Nothing would have happened. Yet notice the points at which change can occur. We cannot alter the scale of the 21st century's technological systems: from global fiber-optics networks to multinational weather manipulating systems, they will only grow larger. That leaves us with two ways to change this equation: we can save ourselves by making people dumber, or by making them more ethical. And since there is not (nor should there be) any impetus to do the former, we have no choice but to do the latter. For if, as Chernobyl suggests, our technology can now leverage single unethical decisions into world-shaking consequences, the most dangerous course for humanity is to continue to produce very smart and very unethical individuals. The teaching of ethics is no longer (if it ever was) a luxury: it is absolutely essential to our survival. That is particularly true for the electronic classroom, which partakes of the very trend—the growth and complexity of technology—that created the conditions for ethical leverage in the first place.

How, then, can ethics be taught in the electronics classroom? Such classrooms present at least three avenues that should be particularly welcomed by ethics instructors: .

Research. Even the simple step of tying students to databases providing wire-service copy of international news provides a wealth of information for ethical analysis. An instructor making a simple observation—for example, that 1993 seems to be the year in which governments are trying to reconstruct themselves after having been shattered by ethical considerations—can then turn his students loose to find out to what extent that's true in Japan, France, Italy, Brazil, and various other nations. Assembling the data, students are then positioned to engage in intriguing discussions on such topics as whether ethics figures more prominently now than in the past, whether there is any such thing as a global ethical standard, and whether ethics actually matters in the "real" world of hard-ball politics.

Case studies. A great deal of ethics teaching is done through case studies. Various electronic media lend themselves well to case presentations, from a single computer disk containing multiple verbal records of cases (which can then be indexed and searched for congruent examples), through video cassette or video disk re-creations of ethical dilemmas by actors, and on to highly complex multibranching simulations that create new dilemmas with each decision made by the student.

Expert systems. The analysis of case studies, however, does not guarantee their resolution. Resolving tough dilemmas requires decision-making rules of the sort discussed down through the ages by moral philosophers. These include:

- Utilitarian principles, commonly known as the precept that requires you to act so as to produce the greatest good for the greatest number
- The Kantian principle of the categorical imperative, in which you are asked to act upon that precept that you would like to see made into such a universal law that everyone else would do what you are just about to do
- The Golden Rule, which calls upon us to do to others what we would like them to do to us, and which stands as a centerpiece of all of the world's great religions

Students could greatly benefit by having access to the systematic analyses of "experts" who have been called upon to think through ethical dilemmas from these (and other) perspectives.

None of this will make much difference, however, unless the instructor makes a conscious effort to establish an ethical climate for the electronic classroom. And that requires ethical instructors—individuals who understand that ethics is largely, as British jurist Lord Moulton once described it, "obedience to the unenforceable."[2] For the electronic classroom builds—or at least ought to build—measures of independence and opportunities for individual learning that go far beyond the lockstep atmosphere of so many classrooms of the past. As that lockstep breaks up, so do the possibilities for externally imposed discipline. If instructors feel they must police the electronic classroom, they have already lost the ethical battle: these arenas, precisely *because* they reward individual initiative and permit individual pacing, will be very difficult to monitor. Only if the instructors themselves understand that ethics requires obedience to the immensely powerful but ultimately unenforceable canons of a moral community—and work hard to convey that understanding to the students—will these classrooms work.

For all its glitz and gadgetry, then, the classroom of the future will depend on a fundamental set of core values embodied within and programmed by the instructor. On that crucial point, it will either resemble the successful classroom of the past, or it will help create a far more smartly unethical world—and a far more dangerous one—than we have ever known.

Notes

1. Personal conversation with the author, October 1985.

2. John Fletcher Moulton, "Law and Manners," *The Atlantic Monthly*, vol. 134, no. 1: July 1924, pp. 1-5.

The Future of Electronic Education

Robert A. Dierker

Robert Dierker was, at this writing, Senior Advisor for Multimedia Activities at the Library of Congress, Washington, D.C.

The Perspective

Turn the clock back five centuries. Now, picture yourself trying to predict the impact of the printing press on the process of education. Or, imagine what might have been the thoughts of those speculating about the impact on education of the development of methods for producing paper in bulk, or of mass producing writing implements. Doing so, one might be tempted to dwell on the technology itself. But over time, these technological advances, revolutionary in their time, simply have been absorbed, and now are taken for granted. They are each just one more link in the chain. . .one more tool available to educators. Is that what fate has in mind for the impact of the electronic, digital technologies on education?[1] Perhaps. But between now and then, the consequences of these technologies will be staggering.

Before we look into the crystal ball, a sense of perspective is essential. The extent to which the educational process will be altered by technology undoubtedly will reflect the impact of the technology on society as a whole. Is there a way to quantify that potential impact? The best attempt to do so that I have seen to date is that of Vinod Chachra,[2] amplifying an idea outlined by William McKeefrey. McKeefrey said that the impact of a given technology is capable of being quantified by determining the extent to which that technology multiplies human capabilities to accomplish the same task. In other words, according to Chachra, a car going 60 miles per hour represents only a 15 times more efficient[3] way to travel than unaided human transportation, i.e., walking at four miles per hour. Jet travel, at 600 mph, is only 150 times more efficient than walking. Two tenfold multipliers, the plow and chemical fertilizer, combined to usher in the agricultural revolution. The steam engine was a 1,000-fold multiplier, and brought the industrial revolution. According to Chachra, human history has experi-

228

enced a million multiplier only three times. The first was in communications. Initially by wire, and then by wireless, we became able to communicate a million times faster than previous technology allowed. The second million multiplier is nuclear technology, the full impact of which is still unknown. The third, Chachra posits, is computers. "With the convergence of computer and communications technologies, we will for the first time have a millionfold multiplication of a million multiplier."[4] Chachra calmly notes that if a 100-fold multiplier brings about the agricultural revolution, and a 1,000-fold multiplication causes the industrial revolution, the implications of a millionfold multiplication of a million multiplier are "very difficult to predict." That understatement is certainly true enough! Yet it is not at all hard to see, even without the ability to describe the magnitude with precision, that we are in the midst of a momentous step in the evolution of the intellectual growth capabilities of mankind. The storage and transmission capacities of technology seem almost limitless, with a consequence that the entirety of recorded history—the memory of mankind—may be efficiently, effectively, and conveniently available at a moment's notice. The implications may be difficult to quantify, but it is beyond serious dispute that there will be an extreme and dramatic impact upon the process of learning and education.

This point is worth making, because there are otherwise intelligent or articulate individuals who don't get it, or who even flatly disagree with the inevitability of the proposition. *Los Angeles Times* columnist Michael Schrage wrote, for example, that "Computers are irrelevant to the quality of education."[5] He believes that "Any school board that would import computer technology without insisting on explicit guarantees for improved student performance richly deserves to be impeached, voted out of office, or sued for malpractice."[6] Finally, Schrage notes that "If we really cared about a successful school system—which we clearly do not—we would forbid computers in the schools. . . ."[7] Those unable to distinguish between a solution and a tool will have difficulty assessing the likely impact of digital technology on the educational process. On the other hand, an appreciation for the power of the tool; an awareness of things made possible that were previously impossible; and the knowledge of activities that can be performed with far greater efficiency, in a fraction of the time previously required, will allow those with fertile minds to anticipate some of the attributes of the educational environment of the future.

Visualizing the Future

The learning process is in for change in big ways. The context will be different. The form will be different. The style will be different. The skills demanded to teach will be different. And the skills needed to learn will be different. For better or worse, like it or not, the revolution has begun. As stated earlier, we may not be capable currently of measuring or fully comprehending the dimensions of the revolution, i.e., the question of "how big," but the *if* and *when* has already been decided.

Context

The context of the learning experience will differ in the following ways. The currently existing line between formal education and other learning experiences will become blurred. The duration of the learning experience will be extended. The relative opportunities between learning at school and learning at home will shift. To illustrate, a description of the process today, compared to tomorrow, will help.

Today, for the most part, the education of children is an experience yielded by parents to outsiders. Certainly some parents are more involved in the education of their children than others, but, in the final analysis, teachers provide the bulk of the education. That is because they are trained and have the skills to do so; they have the subject matter knowledge to do so; and they have unique access to the resources needed to do so, primarily in the form of books. The value and importance of the training and skill is indisputable and a constant. However, the other two elements in the equation, i.e., the subject matter expertise, and the access to resources, are changing. Greater quantities of information are becoming available in electronic formats going into the home. The rate of growth in the number of homes with personal computers equipped with CD-ROM drives is soaring,[8] and the CD-ROMs each contain small libraries of information. . .complete sets of encyclopedias, hundreds of literary works including the complete works of Shakespeare, atlases, dictionaries, and almanacs. Complete courses, such as high school chemistry and language courses, are available. Equally explosive is the growth rate for online access to even greater quantities of information stored in mainframes, available to any personal computer owner with a modem, through America Online, CompuServe, other database services, and via the Internet.[9] The Library of Congress itself is striving to make as many of its resources available electronically to as many users as it can, as fast as it can.[10] Over 26 million bibliographic records are already available to Internet users, as are the contents of its recent major exhibitions.[11] By the turn of the century, Gregory Rawlins believes bookstores will work this way:

> [They] may become just wall-sized display screens electronically displaying an array of titles, with pictures. Each title may be in its own book-sized rectangle of the display. Customers could use their electronic pens to wand the appropriate titles and have it automatically delivered to their portable or home computer and their credit card automatically charged.[12]

Concurrently, as this massive quantity of information becomes available in the home, the importance of the school as a locus for resources will diminish. The balance between the need for educators to be subject matter experts and additionally "knowledge navigators" (described under Skills section) is likely to shift.

As each home becomes a library, the prospect for almost instant gratification of the familiar and natural curiosities of children emerges.[13] The inevitable "why is the sky blue" type of questions are not put off for the trip to the library that likely never takes place, or finessed by the "ask your teacher tomorrow" replies. Instead they are answered with the push of a button, essentially, by the child or parent, starting at any age, and ending at any age.

Form

Information delivery is technology-driven. The only reason that books haven't had a sound component capability and a moving image capability, for example, is because the technology to allow those things to happen did not exist. Not everybody that reads a book in which the author describes a stormy ocean night, with the fog horn of a ship sounding in the distance, would like to hear that ocean and fog horn, and see that ship gliding across the same page that now is occupied instead by a still photograph or illustration. But enough others would like exactly that, that we can surmise that it would have been done by now if it could have been. Some will say that such advances will hamper the imagination and the development of the mind's eye; others will say that they will stimulate the same. Some will be distracted by hearing the author tell his or her tale, while others will be captivated, as the differences between television, the movies, and books become technologically meaningless. For those who believe that a multimedia, multisensory, or multiple sensory presentation of material provides a more cohesive, digestible, and superior learning experience,[14] good news is here. Pocket devices with full-motion video and high-quality sound accompanying the delivery of text may have been utter fantasy as recently as a decade ago, but will be the format of the basic textbook beginning around the year 2000. In the meanwhile, conventional print publications with CD-ROM disks full of images, sound, and additional layers of information conveniently tucked in the sleeve, such as Rick Smolan's incredible *From Alice To Ocean*,[15] will serve as the transitional technology format for delivering educational material.

Style

Some educators simply lecture, while others engage students in dialogue or other activities. Participation intensifies the learning experience. Digital technology gives new dimensions to interactivity of at least two kinds. Between individuals, be they a couple or many students, or between student(s) and teacher(s), the opportunity for 24 hour dialogue through online communications presents an entire new world of opportunity. At any hour of day or night, computer users can communicate in real time with other individuals who self-select to discuss a given subject. America Online users are familiar with the experience of watching students who have never met one another[16] help each other with homework assignments from opposite ends of the country via electronic "chat rooms." Dr. James H. Billington, Librarian of Congress, and Dr. Rudolph Pikhoia, Soviet Archivist, conducted an online seminar for those interested in discussing the documents revealed in the exhibit of secret documents from the former Soviet Union.[17] With instant, multiparty communication so much more convenient and manageable, grouping students by level of competence and interest, without regard to location within a state, city, or school district, is a simple proposition.[18]

The second referenced kind of interactivity is that which takes place between the individual and the computer, now functioning as the book. "Imagine a physics book where an apparently alive Galileo, Newton, or Einstein propounds their various theories then guides you through developments and consequences, letting you ask questions or suggest alternatives. As technology improves, you will be able to change Galileo, Newton, or Einstein to whomever you wish: perhaps a favorite aunt, a teacher, Bugs Bunny, or Walter Cronkite."[19]

Because the increased interactivity will involve multiple media, multisensory materials, in a context wherein the experience may be taking place at the convenience of the student, aided by the power and efficiency of a computer, an impressive compounding impact is inevitable. The satisfaction of a simple curiosity involving the elephant would result in instant access to an encyclopedia, newspapers, still photos, documentary films, movies, and songs in which an elephant appears. If still not satisfied, the curious student will instantly query a potentially unlimited audience about when was the last time any of them saw a pink elephant. Undoubtedly a variety of responses would be forthcoming. The learning will have taken place in a virtual classroom.

Skills

Dr. Bernard J. Luskin, a highly regarded former college president and founding president of Phillips Interactive Media of America,[20] was asked what the development of interactive technology such as Phillips CD-I technology meant to educators. "It means that the teacher now has a device to help him or her teach better so that the learner can learn better. It is as simple as that," said Dr. Luskin.[21] It is, indeed, that simple on the one hand. On the other, educators and students unquestionably are going to have access to quantities and kinds of material not previously available. The skills needed will be those associated with helping students not just learn, but to learn how to learn. Teachers may continue to need specific knowledge about a given field or discipline, but in addition educators are likely to need more knowledge and ability about how to cull through an almost infinite quantity of interactive, multimedia material about the topic.[22] The role of educator is likely to involve added emphasis on teaching students to use critical thinking skills. It is likely to involve teaching students to differentiate between primary and secondary source materials. It may involve additional emphasis on teaching students research methodology. Drawing an analogy from our unsuccessful record as a society in teaching children to make qualitative judgments about television programming, or to differentiate between form and substance, it may involve additional emphasis on teaching critical viewing skills.[23]

It follows without needing explanation that the skills needed by students will change. Rote memory, and progressing by mere repetition of teacher-presented facts are apt to be insufficient. Students will be able to learn only after they first have learned how to learn, and the proper use of technology as a tool will facilitate that experience. There is every reason to believe that the development of these new skills will be beneficial to education. "Introducing technology into the learning environment has been shown to make learning more student-centered, to encourage co-operative learning, and to stimulate increased teacher student interaction."[24]

Conclusion

The way that we educate—by sending children off to a central location, grouped by age, to be instructed by a single individual—did not originate with Adam & Eve. Most likely it evolved as a way to manage (maximize) human and physical resources, primarily consisting of teachers and the various forms of the printed word. This method, with only slight refinements possible, was a necessity. It is no longer. The benefits of live human interactivity may have been a compelling reason to maintain the method, and may still be, but that consideration will have to be self-justifying, rather than being perhaps just a fortunate by-product of a teaching method taking place during times in history during which there were no alternative methods. Alternatives now exist. Choices and tools abound. Developments flowing from the use of digital technology in the communications field, and the power of the computer, have combined to result in an opportunity to change the basic nature of the educational experience. The availability and power of those tools, coupled with the desirable aspects of inescapable changes in the context, form, and style of learning, will result in an inevitable and profound evolution in the process of education. In essence, the process must be rethought from start to finish, not because of the alleged failures of the past, as is so often claimed, but because of major, consequential opportunities that now exist but that were only fantasy a few years ago, let alone when our present educational model was initiated.

Notes

1. Audiovisual equipment, including television and other electronic devices, long have been available in the formal education setting. The introduction of digital electronic technology is what is new.

2. Chachra is the President of VTLS, Inc. His observations were made at the 1991 Library Director's Multimedia Conference in Pembroke, Va.

3. The word efficiency here is meant in the same sense that McKeefrey thought of the multipliers of human capability. Strictly speaking, efficiency could mean more or less.

4. *Information Technologies and Libraries*, March 1992.

5. *The Washington Post*, February 7, 1993.

6. Id.

7. Id. Congressman Edward J. Markey also reminded those present at a March 31, 1993, luncheon speech that "Sometimes, even people familiar with the technology are not yet ready for what is to come." He went on to report that Mordaunt Hall, the picture editor of the *New York Times*, gave a speech in 1928 in which the several reasons for opposition to adding sound to motion pictures were defended. For example, "Chaplin's work needs no sound to attract an audience. . .To him the idea of [talking pictures] is tantamount to an abomination. He believes that the eyes can tell of love far more effectively than hearing 'I love you.'"

8. Approximately 7 million CD-ROM (multimedia capable) devices were sold between 1990 and 1994. Sales are projected to reach 22 million by 1996.

9. The highly prestigious Fielding Institute offers a doctorate degree in clinical psychology using the "external degree" model. It consists of a competency-based distance learning program that takes place, in part, on the Fielding Electronic Network (FEN). Electronic correspondence, discussions, and seminars are integral components. Drs. Ronald A. Gianetti, Kjell Rudestam, and N.R. Goldberg observe in an assessment of that program, "The External Degree Model in Clinical Psychology: Fact and Fallacies," that "Educators in the United States are generally unfamiliar with the external degree format. . .yet there are entire universities throughout the world that are based on this model. . . ." In Press: W.T. Forbes et al. (eds.). Training in Professional Psychology: Approaching Year 2000. Washington, D.C., American Psychology Association.

10. Money and copyright considerations are the primary obstacles—technology is not.

11. In 1991, the Library made history by unveiling the first-ever simultaneously presented conventional exhibition, accompanied by an electronic exhibition of the same materials. The electronic exhibition was instantly accessible around the world, and consisted, ironically, of previously secret documents from the former

Soviet Archives. Many more "visitors" enjoyed the exhibition from their home, office, or classroom than were able to visit in person.

12. The New Publishing: Technology's Impact on the Publishing Industry over the Next Decade. Gregory J.E. Rawlins. Technical Report No 340. Computer Science Dept., Indiana University. November 1991.

13. The optimal learning environment exists when curiosity is gratified and that gratification stimulates further curiosity.

14. That "An electronic book can be more accurate, more powerful, more flexible, more informative, more usable, more timely, more sophisticated, and more adaptable to its user than any number of paper books," is a well-stated observation by Mr. Rawlins in which I fully concur.

15. From Alice To Ocean: Alone Across the Outback. Photographed by Rick Smolan, With Excerpts from Robyn Davidson's Tracks. Viking, Penguin Books, and Against All Odds Productions, 1992.

16. The anonymity may facilitate rather than impair candid exchange in some instances, because, among other reasons, the fear of embarrassment for appearing ignorant is reduced or eliminated.

17. See footnote 11.

18. That every student will sit at a workstation, equipped with a computer that is networked to systems nationwide if not worldwide, rather than at a desk, is only a question of time and money, not technology. Probably the only unknown is whether the student will be at home or in a classroom, and whether the teacher will be live or electronic. For those repulsed by the notion of electronic teaching, recall that at the college level, lectures via closed-circuit television are nothing new, and they lack the benefit of two-way communication, i.e., interactivity.

19. Gregory J. E. Rawlins, Id at p.21.

20. Phillips is a leading manufacturer of CD-I players and software, including educational software.

21. *Journal of Instruction Delivery Systems*, Winter, 1993.

22. By contrast, school libraries typically now have very little material in media forms other than print, yet a good documentary film on a specific topic, or a recorded lecture by a renowned authority, could easily have far more practical educational utility than the sum total of those print sources.

23. Educational multimedia publications are every bit as capable of being produced using manipulative emotional production techniques for pedagogical purposes as television programs and certain movies are for commercial purposes.

24. A Conclusion of the *Report On The Effectiveness of Technology In Schools 1990-1992*, Conducted by Interactive Educational Systems Design, Commissioned by Software Publishers Association, Copyright 1993. Giannetti and Rudestam also report in their study of Fielding computer-based, distance learning program that "We have some preliminary evidence that the educational climate of the Institute fosters adult ego development while pursuing a doctoral education." (See Footnote 9.)

Index

Access, 16, 25
Ability tests, 139
Academic programs, 167
Agents, 100
Ahab, 3, 11
Annenberg/CPB Projects, ix
Appeal, 211
AT & T, 186, 215
AT & T Audiographic Teletraining
    Network, 188
Audio teletraining, 187
Audiographics, 187
Automaton, 68

Ball State University, 21
Beacon Expert Systems, Inc., 71
BESTNET, 183
BESTNET International, 195
Bilingual videotapes, 197
Binational English and Spanish
    Telecommunications Network
    (BESTNET), 183
Biology, 63
Bitnet, 178, 183
Boyd v. Deaver, 76
British Open University, 183
Buddy System, 9

CAI, 109
California State University, 130,
    180
Campus of the Future, 22
Case studies, 226
CBI, 148, 208
CBMI, 119
CD-I, 45, 232
CD-ROM, 92

Centro de Ensenanza Tecnica y
    Superior, 195
Chalkboards, 139
Challenge, x
Checklist, 220
Chemistry, 109
Clinical practice supervision, 158
Collaborative research, 180
Compact Disc-Interactive (CD-I),
    45, 232
Compensation, 222
Comprehension, 211
Computer Assisted Instruction
    (CAI), 109
Computer conference, 184, 201
Computer conferencing, 181, 198
Computer-based education, 94
Computer-based instruction (CBI)
    148, 208
Computer-Based Music
    Instruction (CBMI), 119
Computer-mediated communica-
    tion, 198
Computer-mediated courses, 183
Computer-mediated distance
    education, 149
Conscience, 225
Construction, 30
Context (of learning), 230
Corporate distance education, 186

Decision Systems Group, 94
Design, 30
Design document, 209
Design issues, 39
DeSyGNER, 97
Distance degree-level education,
    104

Distance education, 148, 192, 195
Distance learning, 181, 184, 234

E-mail, 148, 173
Edison Project, 4
Education Network of Maine, 14, 165
Electronic book, 235
Electronic classroom, 3, 30, 192, 215, 218
Electronic education, 228
Electronic Forum, 17
Electronic music classroom, 122
Electronic School District, 152
Entities, 98
Environmental design, 39
Ethical override, 225
Ethics, 222
Evaluation, 207
Examinations, 138
Expert systems, 226
External degree, 234

Faculty support, 158
Film Analysis, 133
Form (of learning), 231
Formative evaluation, 205, 207
Future, 22, 228

Global ethical standard, 226
Golden Rule, 226

Hackers, 223
Harvard University, 53, 73, 95
Harvard Law Videodisc Project, 73
Health care, 156
Horizontal technology environment, 94
Human-technology interface issues, 43
Humanity, 223
Hypertext, 71

ICW, 142
Implementation formative evaluation, 211
Indiana University Purdue University Indianapolis (IUPUI), vi, 3, 30, 63, 84, 119, 156, 173
Information Age, x
Information-rich maps, 65
Institute for Defense Analyses, 138
Institute for Global Ethics, 222
Instituto Tecnologico de Mexicali (ITM), 195
Instructor-technology interface, 157
Integrative technology environment, 94
Interactive capacity, 71
Interactive courseware (ICW), 142
Interactive television system, 168
Interactive videodisk, 208
Interactivity, 231, 235
Intercontinental team-teaching, 174
Interface issues, 43
International computer networking, 199
International distance education, 197
Internet, 147, 183, 230
Interpersonal interaction, 192
Intertidal zone, 63
Ishmael, 3, 13
ITM, 195
IUPUI, ix, 3, 30, 63, 84, 119, 156, 173

Jones, Loretta, 110

Kantian principle, 226
Knowledge navigators, 231
Kuhn, T. S., 217

Laboratory simulation, 112
Law, 71, 208
Learning, 10, 22, 59, 71, 84, 156,
    205, 216
Learning outcomes, 159
Lecture hall, 123
Library of Congress, 228
Literary analysis, 173
Litigation Strategies, 209

Maricopa Community College, 17,
    183
Many-to-many learning, 198
MathCAD, 114
McKeachie, W.J., 22
Media Aesthetics, 133
Medicine, 94
Melville, Herman, 3
Mentor, 10
MEU, 16
Military, 138
Mind Extension University
    (MEU), 16
Modules, 8
Moral meltdown, 225
Multiplier, 229
Music, 119
Music classroom, 121
Music studio, 121

Navigable scene, 65
Needs Assessment, 37, 207
Negotiator Pro, 79
Networked learning, 181, 198
Networking, 147
Northern Virginia Community
    College, 169
Nursing, 156

One-to-many learning, 198
Open University, 103
Optimal learning environment,
    235

Papert, Seymour, 15
Paradigm, 217
Paradigm shift, 217
Paths (guided database tours), 59
Pathways (multiple choices in
    videodisk simulations), 77
Pedagogy, 21, 196
Perception data, 212
Performance data, 212
Performance-Content Matrix, 190
Perseus, 53
Physics, 84
Physics: Cinema Classics, 85
Planning, 217
PLATO, 139
Portability, 142
Portable technologies, 32
Practice room, 121
Preproduction formative
    evaluation, 209
Privacy, 222
Problem-based learning, 95
Product development, 206
Production formative evaluation,
    210
Productivity, 25
Purdue University, 147
Pythagoras, 9

Quality, 16
QuickTime, 89

Reception site management, 158
Research, 225
Rio Salado Community College,
    169

Science laboratory, 103
Selective fidelity, 140
Simulations, 63, 208
Skills (of teaching), 232
Smith, Stanley, 110
Social learning, 217

Socialization, 161
Spatial relationships, 224
Standards, 142
Student response systems, 186
Student services, 165
Student support services, 160
Student-faculty interface, 160
Student-technology interface, 159
Style (of learning), 231
Symbolic processors, 114

TAG, 44
Teaching, 26, 222
Teaching of ethics, 222
Technology, 14, 30, 138, 205, 215
Technology Access Governor,
   (TAG) 44
Technology Design, 41
Technology-technology interface
   issues, 45
Teleconferencing, 157, 187
Telecourses, 156
Teletraining, 187
TENET, 9
Time travel, 140
Traditional classroom, 149
Training, 219

University of Idaho, 109

University of Illinois, 119
University of Maine at Augusta,
   165
User friendliness, 211

Vax Notes, 199
Verbal environment, 224
Vertical technology environment,
   94
Video teletraining, 187
Video-based technologies, 156
Virtual, 196
Virtual classroom, 148, 181
Virtual learning environment, 195
Virtual Learning Systems, Inc.,
   195
Virtual society, 196
Virtual space, xi
Visual analysis, 130
Visual environment, 223
Vygotskian theory, 216

Western Washington University,
   205
Workload, 158
Worldware, xiii

Zone of Proximal Development,
   216